EUROPEAN BUSINESS CULTURES

— ◆◆◆ —

Edited by
Robert Crane

An imprint of **PEARSON EDUCATION**

Harlow, England · London · New York · Reading, Massachusetts · San Francisco · Toronto · Don Mills, Ontario · Sydney
Tokyo · Singapore · Hong Kong · Seoul · Taipei · Cape Town · Madrid · Mexico City · Amsterdam · Munich · Paris · Milan

Pearson Education Limited
Edinburgh Gate
Harlow
Essex CM20 2JE
England

and Associated Companies around the world

Visit us on the World Wide Web at:
www.pearson-ema.com

First published 2000

ISBN 0 135 74559 4

British Library Cataloguing-in-Publication Data
A catalogue record for this book can be obtained from the British Library.

Library of Congress Cataloging-in-Publication Data
A catalog record for this book can be obtained from the Library of Congress.

10 9 8 7 6 5 4 3 2 1
04 03 02 01 00

Typeset by 3
Printed and bound in Great Britain by Henry Ling Ltd at the Dorset Press,
Dorchester, Dorset.

Contents

Contents

EUROPEAN BUSINESS CULTURES

◆ ◆ ◆

PEARSON EDUCATION

We work with leading authors to develop the
strongest educational materials in business and finance,
bringing cutting-edge thinking and best learning
practice to a global market.

Under a range of well-known imprints, including
Financial Times Prentice Hall, we craft high quality
print and electronic publications which help
readers to understand and apply their content,
whether studying or at work.

To find out more about the complete range of our
publishing please visit us on the World Wide Web at:
www.pearsoned-ema.com

Foreword

Robert Moran
AGSIM: American Graduate School of International Management

The emergence of a global economy has brought with it challenges for global organizations, global managers, and students preparing to work in today's global marketplace. The fact of a global economy is disputed by few; how to succeed is debated by many. "In today's economy, you are either global or you are gone," said one executive. Other global executives have wholeheartedly agreed. Their companies and organizations are facing the challenge of identifying a strategy and the appropriate organizational structure to succeed in the global marketplace. They are seeking ways to sell the "vision" to all their employees in order to gain support for the necessary changes. By collaboratively joining in the globalization effort, management and employees are synergistically attempting to create organizations that can respond to a flourish in a global economy through the creative training and development of their people and systems.

Change is becoming a way of life and stability is no longer the norm. Few, if any, accurately predicted the important changes in eastern Europe during the past decade. The rapid move toward democracy and a market economy has startled seasoned observers. With the flow of financial transactions, information, and technology exchanges increasing, the relevance of national boundaries is being challenged. In Europe as well, the concept of national sovereignty is being questioned and the emergence of a Euromanager is being advanced.

This new breed of manager is aggressive and better educated. Their country is France, Spain, Italy, or Germany, but their business world is Europe, North America, Asia, the Middle East, or Africa. To succeed, these European managers must have *greater knowledge* and *greater skills* than their predecessors. Skills such as possessing a global mindset are becoming more important. Ethnocentrism is learned – global-mindedness can replace this attitude, but the unlearning and relearning takes time.

In the early 1990s, from *Fortune* magazine's list of the largest 500 industrial corporations, about 25 percent lost money, total sales rose only 3.5 percent (equal to inflation), and the number of employees dropped. Most of the economies in Europe are facing major challenges as they ready themselves for the great leap forward into economic unity.

Within and outside Europe, Euromanagers are working and negotiating with their global counterparts regularly. One European executive stated the challenge this way: "I can't think of any situation in my 25 years of international experience when international business was made easier because people from more than one country were participating." Today's European global managers must understand the many beliefs and values that underlie their own country's business and management practices, avoid cultural mistakes, and understand the organizational and national culture of others.

Many years ago in *Les Pensées*, the French philosopher and mathematician Pascal wrote, "There are truths on this side of the Pyrenees which are falsehoods on the other." This quotation expresses well the reason why all persons working in a global economy must understand deeply their global competitors and partners. Robert Crane has selected authors to assist us with this difficult task. Underlying all behavior are historical, economic, and philosophical underpinnings, which the authors of this book unfold for the serious reader. The authors answer the question: "What do I have to know about each country of Europe in order to understand the perspective of the persons I will work with from that country?"

I invite the reader to begin ... and to learn from the insights and perspectives provided by this book.

Editor's Preface

Robert Crane

J.L. Kellogg Graduate School of Management, Northwestern University, Evanston, Illinois, USA; Institut de Gestion Sociale, Paris, France

The world is changing. In many ways, it is returning to an earlier, more complex time when cultures, languages, religions, and history were of key importance.

The fall of the Berlin Wall in 1989 marked the end not only of the Soviet empire – and indeed of the Soviet Union itself – but also of a bipolar, ideologically defined world. On the other hand, the event was not the end point of history, as some predicted at the time. It was the reawakening of cultural forces and identities formerly submerged by the ideological divisions of the Cold War. Underlying cultural identities quickly reasserted themselves in the break-up of both the Soviet Union and Yugoslavia. Given the extreme cultural, religious, and linguistic differences among the Soviet and Yugoslav republics, their dissolution had been predicted as early as the 1970s by close observers such as Hélène Carrère d'Encausse (*L'Empire Eclatée*).

In this global context, is there room for other large groupings of republics, like the European Union? If so, what role do west European cultural differences play in the cohesion of the EU and in the way business – and indeed life itself – is carried out in the EU? Clearly we the authors see the EU as a coherent whole with a long-term future. We see this coherence and stability as stemming from a shared (though often violent) history, a shared (though divided) Christian faith, and two shared (though multiple) language groups. We perceive Europe as a cultural unit from the Atlantic to a vague frontier that winds somewhere between the eastern-most limits of the former Austro-Hungarian Empire and the Urals. Thus, we have included in our study a central European state (Hungary), a nation divided between the Austro-Hungarian (i.e. west European) and east European spheres of influence, Ukraine, and a country that has long culturally and geographically straddled Europe and Asia, Russia.

Unlike other continents, the Old Continent juxtaposes many cultures on a small land mass. In an age in which technology and the force of history draw the peoples of Europe – and indeed of the world – ever closer, the differences in mindset become critical to the mutual understanding on which cooperation is based. Once again, cultural differences have become the backdrop of war in central Europe.

Currently two apparently contradictory movements are afoot in Europe, one centrifugal and the other centripetal. The centrifugal movement is clearly illustrated by the disintegration of the former nations of Yugoslavia and the Soviet Union. The centripetal movement is illustrated by the gradual building of the European Union. Is Europe both uniting and disintegrating at the same time? Are eastern and central Europe coming undone, while western Europe is becoming a single force, a fortress? In the longer run, is pan-European unity a pipe dream or the logical outgrowth of the EU?

The rationale

Just as Europe is strewn with the physical vestiges of lost civilizations, it is also encumbered by the intellectual and cultural debris of lost cultures. The ebb and flow of peoples with their thoughts and beliefs has left its mark upon the collective European mind.

This relatively small land mass has a thick overlay of history and blood that makes a labyrinth of the relations among the peoples and nations that compose it. The goal of this book is to look into the collective soul of certain nations in their relations with the others and with the European Union.

Where does one find the essence of a nation's soul? In its literature? In its myths and traditions? In the fairy tales it tells its children? Or is it rather in the social and political movements that shape the nation's destiny in the modern world? Or again in the history behind these movements? What explains a people's perception of other groups? Beyond being Greek or barbarian, for example, what factors account for the long-term feelings of enmity ("Perfidious Albion") or of kinship (France and Poland) among nations and peoples? What are the effects of this cumulation on business and management across these cultures?

The thesis of this collective work is that the cultural relations among peoples and within a single people are suggested by all of the factors above, and that the underlying character can be unearthed only by the use of many intellectual tools. Furthermore, our hypotheses are that the shifts in the forces that sway world power relationships are once again beginning to favor Europe as opposed to North America or Asia, and that these shifts, while undermining the unity of certain polymorphous nation-states (the former Soviet Union, Yugoslavia, Czechoslovakia, Belgium?), favor the long-term association, if not unification, of these peoples in a pan-European entity that may well be the European Union.

Our task is fourfold:

♦ To seek the cultural soul of the nations examined and their relations with the EU on both a visceral and politico-economic level.
♦ To see how this national character fits with or fosters the nation's adhesion to European unity and strengthens or weakens the continent as a whole.
♦ On a regional – or tribal – level, to imagine how the EU might serve as a common home for the regions, and particularly for those which do not integrate readily into a national framework.
♦ To indicate the implications of these social and cultural factors for business in, across and between the countries examined.

Thus, this book is designed for those who wish to work in or study Europe and who do not have the time to learn the history and language of the country in which they are

EUROPE AFTER THE CONGRESS OF VIENNA (1815)

Source: Delouche, F. (1993) *Illustrated History of Europe*, London: Weidenfeld & Nicholson

Political maps of Europe change, cultural maps do not: The balance of power established in 1815 lasted a century, but finally fell as political power could no longer contain cultural ambitions.

THE EMERGENCE OF LANGUAGE BARRIERS

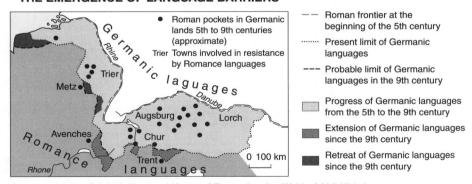

Source: Delouche, F. (1993) *Illustrated History of Europe*, London: Weidenfeld & Nicholson

Language and cultural borders change little over centuries: Once languages and cultures formed, their borders varied little.

interested. The book deduces, from a concise history of the countries treated, guidelines to the ways of thinking which will help the student or businessperson better understand the cultural background of his or her interlocutor's actions, and perhaps even anticipate them. This book does not deal with international etiquette, nor does it treat the "how to" of cross-cultural negotiations. It is intended rather as a broad introduction to the mindsets of selected European nations through the filter of their national histories.

The approach

To achieve this goal, we have selected certain key member nations of the EU for particular examination.

Germany is the economic locomotive of the continent. Due in part to its new-found unity, Germany is a nation torn between its European Union loyalties and its natural sphere of influence in central Europe. Moreover, Germany is now shedding the political reticence it has shown since World War II to pursue an aggressive diplomatic role. The latter development has many implications for:

France is the continent's conscience and, until recently, leader in diplomacy thanks to its special relationship with Germany. With the latter's current move to an increasingly active political presence, France can only wonder what role it can now play on the European scene. Moreover, France and Germany were two initiators of the postwar movement toward European integration. As a consequence, these two nations were and remain the crux of EU development.

The *United Kingdom* is the peripheral power whose interests do not readily correspond to those of the other member nations. In fact, the UK's traditions are antithetical to EU membership. Yet, guided primarily by economic – but also by political – factors, the UK has discovered its place within the EU concert.

Interestingly, these three nations are also major representatives of three of the main cultural groups in western Europe (cf. Geert Hofstede, *Culture's Consequences*): the Germanic powers, the French-speaking countries, and the Anglo-Saxon nations. The fourth of Hofstede's categories is the Nordic countries, which are treated through the example of *Sweden*. The Latin countries are represented by *Spain*, a relatively recent and initially dynamic member of the EU.

Switzerland is a former member of the European Free Trade Association (EFTA). It is the exception to all rules and the probable bellwether to European construction. What does the Swiss refusal to join the European Union bode for the future of Europe, and for the future role of Switzerland on the European stage?

As is readily seen, even the integration of this thoroughly western nation, with a standard of living quite comparable to, if not higher than, that of the EU, is problematic. How much more problematic will be the integration of the central and eastern European nations to which Germany is the natural cultural bridge? The logical first step east in our imaginary progression of EU development is the never-assimilated eastern half of the former Austro-Hungarian Empire, *Hungary* itself.

Rooted in the traditions of the Magyars, and often battered between the twin invaders of the Germanic Christian west and the Islamic Ottoman Empire, Hungary is a proud,

THE GREAT INVASIONS OF THE 5TH CENTURY

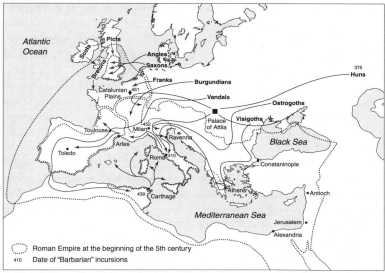

Source: Delouche, F. (1993) *Illustrated History of Europe*, London: Weidenfeld & Nicholson

New peoples invade and remain: The seeds were sown for cultural stability when invaders became sedentary.

THE ROMAN EMPIRE IN THE 2ND CENTURY – ITALY AND THE PROVINCES

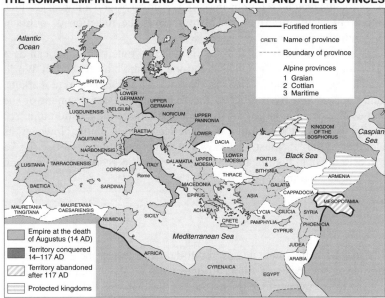

Source: Delouche, F. (1993) *Illustrated History of Europe*, London: Weidenfeld & Nicholson

The imprint of the Roman Empire still marks Europe: The former empire's imprint remains in the division of Europe north and south, Catholic and Protestant, Common Law and Legal Code.

independent nation that has learned to thread its way between the colossi to the west and to the east. In recent years, it has continued to quietly play this role between the eastern and western blocs. In fact, Hungary has played the part so well that the country has reached a remarkably high standard of living for a member of the former communist bloc.

In *The Rise and Fall of the Great Powers* (1988), the historian Paul Kennedy wrote of the military capabilities of the former USSR: "the end result is impressive ... it undoubtedly gives the USSR a range of military capabilities which only the rival American superpower possesses. This is not a twentieth-century Potemkin village, ready to collapse at the first serious testing." The author points out the difficulties facing the USSR in 1988, "without, however, jumping to the opposite conclusion that the Soviet Union is therefore unlikely to 'survive' for very long."

Obviously, even for an eminent historian in the context of a work surveying Russian and other European historical evolution across five centuries, this nation and its peoples remain full of surprises. Just as obviously, no general survey, particularly in such a recent field as cross-cultural relations, can predict precise events with accuracy. Nonetheless, we look at *Ukraine* and *Russia*, two of the new nations carved from the body of the former Soviet Union, through a cultural filter. We draw conclusions for their futures, including possible relations with the EU, based on the long-term character of the former Soviet peoples.

Naturally, the increasing economic power and unity of Europe cannot be viewed with equanimity by other major world powers, and in particular by the dominant world power during most of the twentieth century, the *United States*. America's relations with Europe have always been ambiguous due to the very origins of the nation. Inextricably linked to the Old Continent by its history and culture, the New World for generations rejected what it perceived to be a continent riven by religious intolerance, poverty, and autocracy. Thus, isolationism is a recurrent theme in American history, as is the rejection of political involvement with a continent over-prone to making war.

On the other hand, a "United States of Europe" is quite as much an American as a European dream. The support lent by the US to a Europe in rubble at the end of World War II sprang as much from altruistic motives as from a desire to create new markets. Later, the systematic support lent by the US to the founding and development of the European Communities also came in large part from the wish to see the creation of a free and independent Europe somewhat resembling the American federal union. However, as the leading power on earth, the US must also view the sometimes helter-skelter rise of Europe as a threat in economic and political terms, even while it perceives Europe – and more particularly the UK and Germany – as its closest allies.

The vision

To deal with what is an inherently vague and as yet ill-defined subject, the cross-cultural relations of Europe, we use a series of filters to detect the elusive cultural factors in European life. All of the following approaches are used in the chapters, individual authors varying the dosing and order.

First, the historical background of each nation is examined. What are the tribal origins of the people? What were the governments over time? Is there a democratic, monarchical, or autocratic tradition? What is the faith of the people? What is its strength? Are several faiths juxtaposed? Do they coexist peacefully? Is there a tradition of free trade and individual initiative, or is central control of economic affairs the historical bias? What are the values of the country? In Hofstede's terms, are they more masculine and aggressive, or more feminine and nurturing? What are the nation's dreams?

Second, what are the national attitudes toward the EU? The thesis of this book is that the ever-shifting balance of world power is again shifting toward Europe. The authors' consensus – with many shadings and variations – is that a gradually uniting Europe is gathering its economic and political, but also its moral and spiritual, strength.

The authors believe that this New Europe is slowly reassuming the major role it once played upon the world stage, and that this movement continues despite such setbacks as the so-called Eurosclerosis of the mid-1980s or the Danish initial refusal of the Maastricht Treaty, or again European non-intervention in the war in former Yugoslavia.

However, the national attitude toward this entity-in-the-making varies considerably from one nation to another within the EU and even more widely outside the Union's borders. Thus, where Denmark initially refused the tighter EU links proposed by the Maastricht Treaty, France (barely) accepted them. Each country perceives the EU in a different light for historical and cultural as well as economic reasons.

Third, a look is taken at the national stake in the European Union. Naturally this "stake" is perceived in large part through the national attitude discussed above, but our authors also examine the economic implications of EU membership in both financial and emotional terms. French farmers have benefited over the years from the Common Agricultural Policy (CAP). Yet the attitude of these farmers has clearly changed as the very success of the CAP has produced vast surpluses of foodstuffs that the EU is now seeking to reduce. The book deals with both the economic reality of EU membership and the present national perception of the benefits of that membership.

Fourth, as was mentioned earlier, Europe is a continent of regions not always corresponding to national borders. The ethnic strife in the former Yugoslavia and the former Soviet Union is proof of this fact. The regions include such entities as Brittany and Corsica in France, and Wales and Scotland in the UK. A part of the European Union's role is to gather these regions, often drawn from the tribes of antiquity, into its supranational structure. How do these regions fit into their national context, or do they not? What is the benefit of the EU to these regions? How is the EU perceived by the region's leaders?

Fifth, for both regions and the nations concerned, what hope does the EU represent for the people? Is their goal only enhanced prosperity? Does the nation hope to play a renewed global political role from an EU base? Does a people hope to avoid being trampled again by the boots of passing armies?

Sixth, the book considers the business impact of the EU, present and future, on the nation. How do business people see the present climate inside and outside the EU? What are their predictions for the future in both cases? What is the present reality of the "common" market?

What then is our goal in describing "cross-cultural Europe"? We want to sound the depths of feeling of Europeans for each other and for the emerging European Union. We want to reveal the half-submerged basis of the ways people think and feel in the so-called New Europe. We want to lay the groundwork for others to define and predict which way

EUROPE IN JULY 1999

New political borders reflect cultural divides: Cultural groups united as one nation under communism have resurfaced as separate states (e.g. the former USSR, Yugoslavia, Czechoslovakia).

Europe will develop in the future. We want to define how Europe is perceived by those outside the EU and speculate on how these perceptions impinge on the evolution of Europe's relations with the world. It is an ambitious task, but one whose time has come. We hope we have advanced it.

About the contributors

The authors are a group of men and women, drawn from academia, business, and public administration, who share a passion for Europe and its cultural dimensions. All of us like to work in the interstices between history, language, and religion, and to examine the practical impact of these influences on business and politics. All of us have our personal viewpoints and prejudices on the cultural issues we treat. There has been no attempt on the editor's part to mute these viewpoints. On the other hand, he has sometimes commented on them in the editor's introduction to each chapter.

Steve Anderson (Chapter 13, Japan) is an expert on Japanese political affairs who speaks fluent Japanese. He is based in Washington, DC. He is Commercial Officer in the International Trade Administration of the US Department of Commerce.

Alexander Bergmann (Chapter 6, Switzerland) is currently Dean of HEC (Hautes Etudes Commerciales), the business school of the University of Lausanne, Switzerland. Previously, he was professor at IMD in Lausanne. Of German origin and nationality, Dean Bergmann is widely published on Switzerland, his country of adoption, and its management style.

Robert Crane (volume editor) has always been interested in comparative civilizations, initially pursuing this interest through national literatures and later through management styles. Currently Associate Director of Executive Programs at the J.L. Kellogg Graduate School of Management at Northwestern University near Chicago, he has headed business schools in France and Hungary and has directed international affairs for management institutions in Europe and the association of business schools in the United States, AACSB.

Senior Advisor, Finance Policy at the US Department of Commerce since February 1994, **Dr Finel-Honigman** (Chapter 11, US) has advised, lectured, and written on EU and emerging markets, financial policy and issues, management training and technical assistance initiatives, as well as international relations and French intellectual and cultural history. She is also Adjunct Professor, Johns Hopkins University of Continuing Studies.

Prabhu Guptara (Chapter 12, India) is Indian by birth, upbringing, and education, though his continual travels made it impossible for him to continue on the limitations of an Indian passport. He has lived in Scotland for three years and in England for sixteen, and now lives in Switzerland where he is Group Director, Organizational Learning and Transformation, for the Union Bank of Switzerland, based at Wolfsberg, the UBS Centre for Executive Development. He is also non-executive Chairman of ADVANCE: Management Training Ltd (UK), which he co-founded; and he continues as Visiting Professor at various universities and business schools round the world. Widely known as a speaker and writer, he is included in Debrett's *People of Today* and in *Who's Who in the World*.

Rehan ul-Haq (Chapter 4, UK) is a Lecturer in Strategic Management at the Birmingham Business School of the University of Birmingham (UK). He holds undergraduate and graduate degrees from the University of Exeter and Henley Management College/Brunel University. Previously, he was a faculty member at Loughborough Business School (UK), as well as lending banker in the corporate, international, business finance, and treasury areas. He is currently an External Tutor at Henley Management College. His interests are in strategic alliances in the European banking sector, long-range development issues in Pakistan, and strategic management and management learning.

Formerly Senior Lecturer in International Marketing at the Manchester School of Management, University of Manchester Institute of Science and Technology, **Dr Nigel H. Holden** (Chapter 8, Russia) is Professor of Cross Cultural Management at the Copenhagen Business School (Denmark). He obtained his MA from the School of Slavonic and East European Studies, University of London (1981) and his PhD from Manchester Business School (1986). He has considerable experience of management training as an educator and researcher in Russia and Poland, specializing in problems of transfer of western management know-how. In December 1996, he was co-director of a program devoted to these issues sponsored by the Russian National Training Foundation.

Albert Hovius (Chapter 5, The Netherlands) is Course Leader for the MSc in International Business at the International Business School Hanzehogeschool in Groningen, the Netherlands. Following his Master's Degree in Economics, he studied American history, and international finance and accounting at Lewis and Clark College and the University of South Carolina in the US. Mr Hovius taught economics and business administration at the secondary level in the Netherlands for 20 years before joining the Hanzehogeschool. He has had particular experience in central and eastern Europe.

Robert Kovach (Chapter 10, Hungary) is Human Resource Manager for Pepsi Cola bottling in Warsaw, Poland. Previously, he was a tutor in Organizational Behavior at Ashridge Management College in Hertfordshire, UK. He holds a BA in psychology from Butler University (US) and an MA in industrial-organizational psychology from Radford University (US), and he is a PhD candidate in industrial–organizational psychology at Wayne State University (US). From 1991 to 1996 he was an assistant professor in Organizational Behavior at the International Management Center in Budapest, Hungary.

Robert T. Moran (Foreword) is an Organizational and Management Consultant with specialities in Cross-Cultural Training, Organizational Development, and International Human Resource Management. As an international consultant, his experience extends to a variety of organizations and institutions. He has designed and conducted seminars for Aramco, Arthur Andersen & Co., AT&T, General Motors, Honeywell, Intel, Bayer, Exxon, Volvo Truck Corporation, and Singapore Airlines among many others.

At present, he is Professor of International Studies at the American Graduate School of International Management. This institution is recognized as the foremost business school in the US for the training of international managers. He is the author or co-author of 13 books, many of them translated into several languages. His most recent book, *Managing Cultural Differences*, has been selected for use in over 100 colleges or universities.

Christer Nedstrom (Chapter 7, Sweden) has an academic education from Harvard Business School, IMI, and a number of management institutions. He served some 20 years within the Volvo group of companies in various positions, such as Vice President Public Affairs at the Group HQ and Vice President European Communities Affairs in the Volvo Car Corporation. He has been a Visiting Professor at the Johnson and Wales University, Providence, US, lecturing in "International Business from a European Perspective" and "the European Community Program." Christer Nedstrom is at present Director of the Stockholm European Liaison Office in Brussels. He is also the owner of a consultant company dealing with strategic analysis and business development from a European perspective and communication strategies.

Robert M. Orr, Jr (Chapter 13, Japan) is Vice President and Director of Government Relations for Nippon Motorola, Ltd. He holds a PhD in Political Science from the University of Tokyo and has lived in Japan since 1983. In addition to a business career, Dr Orr was a US government official and a university professor.

Michel Péron (Chapter 2, France) holds a Chair in economic history at the Sorbonne in Paris. He is a prolific and well-known author on economic topics. He is also mayor of St André la Côte (Rhône).

Collin Randlesome (Chapter 1, Germany) is Senior Lecturer in European Management at the Cranfield School of Management in Bedfordshire, UK. Before he joined Cranfield, Collin spent seven years in mainland Europe, lecturing at the universities of Erlangen-Nuremberg and Basle, prior to joining the English Institute in Zurich as Deputy Manager. He is the author of the Germany section in *The Making of Managers*, a report on management education, training, and development in the USA, West Germany, France, Japan, and the UK; co-author of a standard work on British and American institutions; English language editor of a book on model business letters in German and English; and editor of and main contributor to *Business Cultures in Europe*. Collin is also the author of a book entitled *The Business Culture in Germany*, published in May 1994.

Pavlo Sheremeta (Chapter 9, Ukraine) is Assistant Director of the International Management Institute in Kiev, Ukraine. Formerly, he was area director for the Soros Foundation in Budapest, Hungary.

Luis Torras (Chapter 3, Spain) is Director of Executive Programs at EADA, one of the most prestigious executive education institutions in Spain, located in Barcelona. In addition to his administrative and teaching roles, Luis is also widely published in both English and Spanish on management topics.

János Vecsenyi (Chapter 10, Hungary) is the Director of Training and Human Resources Programs at Budapest Bank, a GE Capital Corporation Company, in Hungary. From 1989 to 1997 he was a professor in Strategy and Entrepreneurship at the International Management Center, in Budapest, Hungary. He holds BA and MA degrees in mechanical engineering and industrial engineering from Budapest Technical University and a PhD in management at Budapest University of Economics and the Hungarian Academy of Sciences.

Acknowledgments

We are grateful to the following for permission to reproduce copyright material:

Appendix tables and graphs reproduced from http://www.eurunion.org/ with the kind permission of the Delegation of the European Commission to the United States; maps on pages xi and xiii reproduced with the kind permission of Hachette Livre.

Whilst every effort has been made to trace the owners of copyright material, in a few cases this has proved impossible and we take this opportunity to offer our apologies to any copyright holders whose rights we may have unwittingly infringed.

PART I

◆◆◆

The European Union

Editor's introduction: Germany

Germany sits astride Europe like a wall. Where the UK floats and bobs in the Atlantic sometimes closer to the USA and sometimes closer to Europe – but never really a part of either – Germany is unmoved and unmovable from its strategic position in central Europe. The former barrier to Roman expansion beyond the Rhine is now often perceived as a cultural barrier between eastern and western Europe. Whether recognizing the new nations of Slovenia and Croatia or buttressing the European Union's will to create its new currency, Germany is both master and gatekeeper.

How could it be otherwise? Created only in 1870, the force of this new nation's will is such that, despite shattering defeats in two successive world wars, it is the economic colossus of Europe and one of the major economic powers of the world. On the other hand, how comforting it is for the other European nations to know that this irresistible force is harnessed to the task of building Europe. Or is it?

Collin Randlesome examines the sources and manifestations of Germany's remarkable economic strength, as well as the nation's apparently steel links to the European Union. He leaves us with several topics of further reflection.

- As the horrors of World War II recede from the German collective memory, the nation is becoming more politically assertive. What are the implications of this unfettered German leadership for the European Union? For France?
- Anchored in central Europe, Germany faces both East and West, but its traditional sphere of influence is central and eastern Europe. Will Germany seek to promote the rapid entry of central European nations into the European Union?

Germany

East–west comparison of pay and income

Income category	East–west ratio 1997
Basic negotiated pay	89.5
Monthly rate of pay	87.0
Hourly rate of pay	83.0
Actual earnings	77.0
Compensation per employee	74.0
Disposable income per household	72.0
Nominal per capita GDP	56.75

Sources: Deutsche Bundesbank; Institut der deutschen Wirtschaft, Cologne

Total hourly wage costs in manufacturing 1996

GDP 1997

Western Germany DM3219.7bn

Eastern Germany DM422.1bn

TOTAL DM3641.8bn

Sources: Federal Statistics Office; DIW Economic Research Institute

1

Germany and Europe

Collin Randlesome
Cranfield University, UK

Introduction

The Federal Republic of Germany is situated in the very centre of Europe. Since the end of World War II, the country's leading western politicians have also been at the very heart of all major European developments. Germany's former chancellor, Helmut Kohl, was the Continent's undisputed champion of further European integration, i.e. of monetary union, political union, and eastward expansion. It seems likely that Chancellor Gerhard Schröder will maintain this position. Despite periodic complaints in the country's press about Germany being the highest net contributor to the European budget, with claims that the Germans are in reality "Europayer" (instead of *Europäer* = Europeans), the people as a whole are overwhelmingly pro-European. Their roots in the centre of Europe and their history as a central European power provide an explanation.

The land and the people

Germany today occupies almost the same territory as attributed by Tacitus, between Rhine and Saale, and by subsequent Roman historians, between the North Sea and the Alps. Though various German tribes did, in the course of history, break through their present frontiers, they were always assimilated by the races they conquered. The main German tribes were the Frisians along the North Sea coast; the Low Saxons from the Zuider Zee to the eastern frontier of Mecklenburg and north of Thuringia to the Baltic; the Thuringians in Thuringia and Upper Saxony; the Alemanni in Württemberg, Baden, and Alsace; the Bavarians in Bavaria and Austria; and the Franconians from Nuremberg to Amsterdam. Indeed, as Bithell states so poignantly: "The very name of the hereditary foe, the French, recalls the kingdom of the West Franks; that is Germany west of the Rhine."

Today, the country has nine immediate neighbors: Denmark in the north; the Netherlands, Belgium, Luxembourg, and France in the west; Poland and the Czech Republic in the east; and Switzerland and Austria in the south. Germany's central location has assumed even more significance since reunification on October 3, 1990 and the accession to the European Union (EU) of Austria, Sweden, and Finland on January 1, 1995. The country has become, almost more than ever, a link not only between east and west, but also between Scandinavia and the Mediterranean. An integral element of both the EU and the North Atlantic Treaty Organization (NATO), Germany is viewed by many as the bridge to the countries of central and eastern Europe.

Germany has a population of about 80 million (including 5.7 million foreigners), the largest in the EU, and is one of the most densely populated countries in Europe, with 228 people per square kilometer. Only the Netherlands and Belgium have higher population densities.

A brief history

In the books of the nineteenth century, it was widely held that German history began in the year AD 9, when Arminius, a prince of a Germanic tribe, defeated three Roman legions in the Teutoburg Forest. Arminius was thus regarded as the first German national hero, and a massive statue to him was erected near Detmold.

Twentieth-century history books, however, adopt a different view and emphasize the fusing of the German nation as a gradual process which lasted hundreds of years. Indeed, the word "Deutsch" did not begin to be used until the eighth century and initially referred only to the language spoken in the eastern part of the Franconian empire. This era, which reached its zenith under Karl der Grosse, or Charlemagne, who was crowned emperor by Pope Leo III in St Peter's in Rome on Christmas Day AD 800, embraced peoples speaking both Germanic and Romance dialects. According to Barraclough, Charlemagne's coronation marked the birth of western European civilization. He brought Christianity to the heathen Saxons. Elsewhere the earlier-established Christian bishoprics were strengthened and new ones instituted. Forests were cleared, roads and bridges built. Arts and letters flourished, and a school system of sorts was established.

However, after Charlemagne's death in 814, the empire soon disintegrated. On account of various squabbles over the Carolingian inheritance, a western and an eastern kingdom emerged, and the political frontier coincided approximately with the boundary between German and French speakers. Then the term "Deutsch" was extended from the language to its speakers and ultimately to the region where they lived, "Deutschland."

Only very slowly did the fusing of German-speaking tribes begin to take place. The transition from the east Franconian to the German "Reich" is normally dated from 911, when the Franconian duke Conrad I was elected king. Though his official title was Frankish King, later Roman King, from the eleventh century the name of the realm was changed to "Roman Empire"; from the thirteenth century it became "Holy Roman Empire"; and in the fifteenth century the words "of the German Nation" were added.

Thus the tradition of an electoral monarchy was gradually established, with the great nobles choosing the king. Moreover, dynastic right also applied, meaning that the new king had to be a blood relation of his predecessor. The medieval empire had no capital city to compare with London or Paris, with the German king ruling by moving his court from place to place. Nor were there any imperial taxes. The king sustained himself from the imperial estates which he administered in trust. Nor was his authority always recognized by the more powerful tribal dukes unless he was militarily strong or a successful forger of alliances. Built-in centrifugal forces thus prevented Germany from becoming a nation-state in the Middle Ages after the manner of England or France.

These disintegrative forces were arguably at their most powerful in the Treaty of Westphalia, which ended the Thirty Years War, in 1648. The treaty left more than 300 separate units of government in Germany. The power came to the princes as a result of the ruin of their subjects during the war and profoundly modified their relations with the empire. Thereafter, the princes were intent on the exploitation of their sovereign powers, and not even the most far-sighted of them had any vision of German unity. As Barraclough comments: "After 1648, the empire was a meaningless historical survival, Germany a geographical expression: the reality was embedded in the principalities, whose only ambition was to develop into sovereign monarchies."

This situation endured and even deteriorated over the next 200 years. At the beginning of the nineteenth century, there were some 2,000 territorial entities in German-speaking Europe, which enjoyed greater or lesser degrees of autonomy. They differed from one another so radically, in both size and importance, that a functioning system of mutual coexistence was practically impossible.

Eventually, Prussia emerged as the most powerful of the sovereign monarchies and the predominant economic power. Under Otto von Bismarck, Prussia's minister president, Austria was first obliged to relinquish its influence over Germany through its defeat in the Austro-Prussian War of 1866, thus permitting a confederation of the states to the north of the River Main, with Bismarck appointed federal chancellor. Second, France's resistance to German unity was broken in the Franco-Prussian War of 1870–1. Now the southern German principalities joined with the northern confederation to form the German Empire. King Wilhelm I of Prussia was proclaimed German emperor at Versailles on January 18, 1871; Bismarck imperial chancellor.

Thus, belatedly, Germany became a nation-state. German unity had, however, come about not by popular decision, or least of all by popular vote from below, but by treaties between princes from above. Prussia's dominance was stifling, and to many the new empire appeared like a Greater Prussia. Although Germany's gradual emergence as a modern industrial country strengthened the influence of a small, economically successful middle class, it was still the aristocrats who held sway and above all the army officer corps where they predominated.

A review of neither German militarism nor the mutual animosity between France and Germany, which arguably led to two world wars, need detain us here. Both phenomena have been sufficiently well documented elsewhere (see the select bibliography). What needs to be stressed is Germany's pivotal location in Europe – "das Reich der Mitte" ("The Empire of the Centre") – its belated arrival as a united country, and its infelicitous experiences as a nation-state.

The economic tradition

Germany was not only late to arrive as a united country; it was also a comparative late comer to the Industrial Revolution. Though the first railway line was built from

Nuremberg to Furth in 1835, it was not until after 1850 that the great coalfields of the Ruhr, which were under Prussian control, began to be exploited. They provided the basis for an iron and steel industry that challenged the long-established one in Bohemia.

The foundation for a social market tradition was laid shortly after unification. First, in 1871, Bismarck introduced an Employers' Liability Act applying to mines, quarries, and factories, with factory inspection being introduced in Prussia in 1874. Four years later, reacting to what he perceived as the threat of socialism in his authoritarian state, and two attempts on the emperor's life in 1878, Bismarck passed the Anti-Socialist Law. It gave the police draconian powers for the regulation of associations, public meetings, and the printing and circulation of books and newspapers. Socialist agitators were imprisoned, banished, or both. At the same time, Bismarck could not ignore the existence of certain social evils that contributed to the spread of socialism. In 1883 and 1889, he passed measures for the compulsory insurance of the working classes against sickness, accident, invalidity, and old age – the first such welfare state legislation anywhere in the world.

Second, from 1876 onwards the railways of Prussia and the other states were nationalized, and in 1879 the system of free trade was replaced by a customs tariff. This tariff was moderate at first, but gradually extended in both scope and severity. It proved to be the precursor of a general resurgence of protectionism throughout the Continent.

Another outstanding feature of today's economic system was established in the early years after German unification. In 1892, the Cartel Law was passed, which made commercial arrangements arrived at through a cartel as binding as those agreed to under a private contract. The result was that approximately 4,000 cartels were in operation by 1939, among them some of Europe's largest. I.G. Chemie, a massive chemicals cartel, was broken up by the western Allies after World War II and from it emerged BASF, Bayer, Hoechst and several medium-sized chemical companies. Though a Cartel Act aimed at preventing restraints on competition has been in force in the Federal Republic since 1957, those of a suspicious turn of mind still see vestiges of "cartels" in the large number of manufacturing companies in which private commercial banks in Germany maintain equity share holdings.

The economic system formally adopted by Germany since World War II is that of the social market economy. This system rejects both the old-style *laissez-faire* practiced in Germany before 1879 and government interventionism, which was prevalent in the empire from 1879 to 1918, in the Weimar Republic (1918–33) and under National Socialism (1933–45). It combines the free initiative of the individual with the principles of social progress. Indeed, Germany's Basic Law, which guarantees the freedom of private enterprise and the right to possess private property, stipulates that these basic rights be exercised for the public good. No less a personage than Konrad Adenauer, the first postwar federal chancellor, provided a significant definition of social market economy, which he called "a renunciation of planning and the direction of production, labour or sales, but within a comprehensive economic policy which also embraces social measures to ensure the welfare of the population as a whole, including provision for the needy."

Economic performance and business values

The western part of the Federal Republic of Germany has made a remarkable recovery from the devastation of World War II. In the 1950s and 1960s, this recovery was often hailed as an "economic miracle." However, Ludwig Erhard, the economics minister in the first four postwar cabinets, rejected the term. What Germany had achieved was not a miracle, he said, "merely the result of honest endeavor on the part of a whole nation who were given the opportunity and freedom to make the best of human initiative, freedom and energy."

Between 1960 and 1991, gross domestic product (GDP) increased by more than two and a half times in the western federal states. In 1985 prices, this is equal to a rise from DM860 billion to DM2,207 billion. Since 1975, Germany has participated in the world economic summit meetings of the seven leading western industrial countries (the G7) as of right. In terms of overall economic performance it is the fourth largest, and with regard to trade it holds second position, in the world.

The internal economic challenge for the recently reunited country is to bring conditions in eastern Germany up to the standards of the west. In the east, the transition from a command economy to a social market economy has been extremely painful. Literally millions of jobs were lost there after reunification in 1990, as outmoded and inefficient factories were either closed down or drastically rationalized. Despite the success of the Treuhandanstalt (Government Trust Agency) in privatizing some 14,000 former state-owned enterprises from 1990 to 1994, a stubborn rump of some 1,500 companies still remain unsold, accounting for some 20 percent of eastern German employment. If these enterprises were closed overnight, unemployment in eastern Germany would rise to a socially unacceptable 37 percent. Clearly then, in a social market economy, the ailing companies have to be subsidized, and at a cost of some DM170 billion per annum to the mostly west German taxpayers. Eastern Germany has also been in receipt of moneys from the EU's structural fund.

To raise standards in the east and to continue to enjoy prosperity in the west, German business people will adhere to the beliefs, attitudes, and values that have been such outstanding features of their national culture.

Conservatism

German business practitioners are on the whole resistant to change. They do not easily fall prey to economic or management fads and fancies, which, in their eyes at least, bedevil Anglo-American business practices. They believe that within their system they have discovered a winning formula, and they are unwilling to tamper with it.

While postindustrial societies in the UK and in the US have changed over the years into mainly service-dominated economies, Germany has resisted this change. In the UK, only 23 percent of GDP is accounted for by manufacturing; in the US, even less – 19 percent. The figure for Germany is some 38 percent.

Long-termism

German companies are in business in order to stay in business: they are not in business to disburse disproportionate dividends to voracious shareholders. Since the Big Three private commercial banks (the Deutsche, Dresdner, and Commerzbank) are major equity-holders in manufacturing companies, such businesses are not shareholder-driven in the Anglo-American sense. Moreover, the banks prefer to regard themselves as stakeholders rather than shareholders.

Long-termism is a value espoused not only by large German companies, but also by the *Mittelstand* (medium-sized and small, mostly manufacturing, companies) – the backbone of the German economy. If companies of all sizes are in business to stay in business, then over the medium and long term they can invest in new plant and equipment, train their apprentices, and develop their managers to a degree denied to profit-driven competitors.

It comes as no surprise that ten German companies figure regularly among Europe's top 25 as measured by turnover, but not a single one is among the 25 most profitable.

Environmentalism

A business value that has recently been espoused by German companies is environmentalism. The growing influence of Die Grünen (the Green Party), who have become the third force in German politics, in addition to resistance among the population at large to anything that might harm the physical environment, has obliged German companies, at least in the west, to become more environmentally responsible in all their activities. Moreover, many of them have made a virtue out of necessity by turning their research efforts toward products for the protection of the environment. Some have become world leaders in the design and manufacture of such products. Eastern Germany was given a ten-year moratorium, dating from 1990, to bring its environmental standards up to those pertaining in the west.

Attitudes to Europe in the past

Since the end of World War II, Germans in the west have been among the keenest of any peoples to become involved in European initiatives of all hues. This pro-European focus has been useful internally to ease the transition from dictatorship to democracy by aligning with other western democracies. Externally, it has been a means of proving to its partners that Germany's legacy of militarism as a nation-state has been well and truly overcome. Though the latter consideration has often cast Germany in the role of political pygmy but economic giant, the country's politicians were content to play the part over so many years. Latterly, however, and at the latest since reunification, Germany has been anxious to take the lead in matters European.

Germany's European credentials are impeccable: it has never adopted a policy of "the empty chair," as France did under Charles de Gaulle in 1965; it has never shilly-shallied about entry or uttered streams of Euro-invective, as the UK has done. What is more,

Germany has footed the Euro-bill since the outset. Although it has been the major bene-ficiary of liberalized trade in Europe, Germany has adopted a twin-track approach to Europe. It has been at the center of European institutional developments since the very beginning; at the same time, it has pursued a policy of overt friendship toward the former arch-enemy – France.

In 1952, together with France, Italy, Belgium, the Netherlands, and Luxembourg, Germany formed the European Coal and Steel Community (ECSC). This represented a major breakthrough in the process of reconciliation with France. Thus France was able to sign up to the Germany Treaty of 1954, in which the three western powers declared their common goal to be a reunited Germany which had a democratic constitution and was inte-grated within the European community of nations.

In 1957, together with the same partners, Germany established the European Economic Community (EEC) and the European Atomic Energy Community (Euratom) by signing the Treaty of Rome. Though this treaty was regarded by skeptics as a mere trade-off between the interests of German manufacturing industry and French agriculture, it did cement the alliance between Adenauer and de Gaulle.

In 1963, the Elysée Treaty strengthened the friendship between France and Germany still further. Then, in 1967, Germany was instrumental in merging the ECSC, Euratom, and the EEC to form the European Community (EC), and in the following year a customs union was established among its six member states.

In 1973, Germany lent its support to the accession to the EC of the UK, Denmark, and Ireland. It did so not entirely out of altruistic motives, reasoning that in a community of nine, instead of the original six, it would better escape the domination of France in European affairs. The same thinking lay behind Germany's acquiescence to the accession to the EC of Greece in 1981; Portugal and Spain in 1986; and Austria, Sweden, and Finland in 1995.

In 1979, Germany not only became a founder member of the European Monetary System (EMS), but also provided, in the Deutschmark (DM), the anchor currency in the Exchange Rate Mechanism (ERM). Throughout periodic ERM crises within the EMS, the independence of the Deutsche Bundesbank, the German central bank, has come to the aid of its politicians. Bound not only by abiding folk-memories of bouts of hyperinflation in 1923 and 1946–7, but also by the Act of 1957 that established it, the Bundesbank is required to pursue policies that safeguard the German currency. Thus it felt unable to assist, by lowering German interest rates, in both the sterling and lira crisis of 1992 and the French franc crisis of 1993. It adhered instead to the dictum that "stability begins at home." In 1994, Germany was rewarded for its financial stewardship of the EMS by the choice of Frankfurt-am-Main as the location for the European Monetary Institute (EMI), the forerunner of the European Central Bank (ECB). One-third of the staff are German.

In 1987, Germany was happy to adopt the Single European Act (SEA), which envis-aged the creation of a single market guaranteeing freedom of movement for people, goods, services, and capital within Europe by the beginning of 1993. In the meantime, German trade had grown to such an extent that 78 percent of its exports were destined for Europe, most of them to European partners in the EC. A more liberalized European marketplace meant an opportunity to sell even more goods "Made in Germany."

By late 1990, however, Germany had been reunited, and its leading politicians, especially Chancellor Helmut Kohl, were no longer satisfied with a mere free trade area in Europe. Together with François Mitterrand, president of France, and Jacques Delors, president of the European Commission at the time, Kohl became one of the main champions of European monetary and political union by signing in full the Maastricht Treaty of 1993.

Attitudes to the future of Europe

The death of Mitterrand and the departure of Delors from the Commission left Kohl in a powerful position in Europe. Though initial doubts about Jacques Chirac's "Europeanness" were largely dispelled, neither he nor Jacques Santer, the next president of the Commission, could match Kohl for seniority. He was Europe's longest-serving head of government, celebrating some 15 years in office, as Germany's longest-serving chancellor since Bismarck. Indeed, he was often referred to as "Bismarck in a cardigan," and like Bismarck he was also the Unity Chancellor of Germany. His ambition was to unite Europe – an ambition likely to be continued after Chancellor Gerhard Schröder's election in late 1998.

Kohl's vision for Europe was spelt out in *The Times* of December 7, 1994: "The unification of our country has not altered the European orientation of our policies. German unity and European unification – as Konrad Adenauer himself once said – are two sides of the same coin. One thing is certain as far as we Germans are concerned: there is no alternative to European integration."

This vision is encapsulated in a three-stage unification program: economic and monetary union (EMU) as already foreseen in the Maastricht Treaty; political union through the 1996–7 Intergovernmental Conference (IGC); and widening to include countries from central and eastern Europe.

However, Kohl faced isolated pockets of resistance to all three stages of his plan both at home and abroad. On November 5, 1995, Theo Waigel, Kohl's finance minister, told the lower house of the federal parliament that countries sharing a single European currency should aim for public sector deficits averaging 1 percent of GDP, well below the 3 percent ceiling set by the Maastricht Treaty as one of the EMU convergence criteria. This speech immediately provoked the wrath of the opposition Social Democratic Party (SPD). Ex-chancellor Helmut Schmidt criticized Waigel for "assuming imperial airs" in Europe, and Gerhard Schröder, the then SPD premier of Lower Saxony, accused the government of rushing blindly into monetary union.

Resistance within Germany to monetary union is not confined to certain opposition politicians. It has been led among the academics by Renate Ohr, professor of economics at Stuttgart University. She claims that a single currency is unable to enforce political integration in Europe, as is evidenced by similar such failures in the past.

Ordinary Germans also harbor doubts. According to opinion polls, nearly two-thirds of them were unwilling to swap their beloved Deutschmark for the euro, which under the Maastricht Treaty happened on January 1, 1999. Some even moved their money into Swiss francs. Indeed, in August 1995, a cooperative bank in Grafenberg Forchheim, a small town in southern Germany, set up special savings accounts to enable depositors to convert Deutschmark savings into Swiss francs without penalty.

A second integral part of Kohl's vision for Europe was its shape. Here the model that he favored was one closely based on the constitutional structures of Germany itself. The Federal Republic consists of 16 states. These are not mere provinces, but have been endowed with their own powers. Each has a constitution that must be consistent with the republican, democratic, and social principles embodied in the Basic Law.

Translated into the European dimension, Kohl's concept of Europe involved not only a single currency masterminded from Frankfurt-am-Main, but also an administrative base in Brussels, and greater power for the European Parliament probably located permanently in Strasbourg. Quite unashamedly, therefore, Kohl looked forward to a federal Europe – a Europe of the regions.

This model clashes in particular with the UK's vision for Europe as cherished by the Conservative Party under the former prime minister John Major (see also Chapter 4). Fearing a loss of sovereignty, their preferred concept harked back to that of the Gaullist "L'Europe des patries." But Germany could not embrace such a model, as it runs contrary to the lessons of German history, as was shown earlier.

To counter British opposition to a federal Europe, Roman Herzog, the president of the Federal Republic, made two speeches in 1996, recalling the words spoken by Winston Churchill in Zurich in 1946: "What is this sovereign remedy? . . . We must build a kind of United States of Europe." In both speeches, Herzog then went on to support Kohl's vision of a united, federal Europe on the German/American model. Neither speech was widely reported in the UK. Indeed, Germany's best hope of overcoming British resistance to both a single currency, from which the UK secured an opt-out in the Maastricht Treaty, and a federal Europe may rest with Tony Blair and the Labour Party after their winning the 1997 general election.

The third element in the German vision for Europe is its widening to the east. Germany is the one member of the EU that is equally committed to both deepening and widening. In a keynote paper entitled "Reflections on European Policy," published by Kohl's Christian Democrat (CDU) group in the lower house in September 1994, the rationale was clearly spelt out: "The only solution which will prevent a return to the unstable pre-war system, with Germany once again caught between East and West, is to integrate Germany's central and eastern European neighbours into the [west] European post-war system, and to establish a wide-ranging partnership between this system and Russia." The paper continues:

> Germany has a fundamental interest both in widening the EU to the east, and in strengthening it through deepening. Indeed, deepening is a precondition of widening. Without such further internal strengthening, the Union would be unable to meet the enormous challenge of eastward expansion. It might fall apart and once again become no more than a loose grouping of states unable to guarantee stability.

This is Germany's nightmare scenario – a weakening of western institutions, possibly including NATO, which have underpinned security and stability since 1945 at a time when central and eastern Europe are themselves under enormous strain.

Conclusion

Located at the very heart of Europe, Germany cannot remain detached from the problems that currently beset the Continent. The problems, towards the end of the millennium, are jobs and competitiveness; peace and stability in Europe; and overcoming the divide between rich and poor that threatens to engulf western Europe in a new wave of migration from both south and east.

Germany contends that none of these problems can be resolved by the traditional nation-state; all of them require transnational solutions, and preferably within the framework of a united, federal, and eastwardly expanded Europe.

Thus the former chancellor Helmut Kohl argued passionately to the lower house in 1996: "If there is no momentum for continued integration, this will not only lead to a standstill but also to retrogression. Nationalism has brought great suffering to our continent." The same audience was even warned by Wolfgang Schauble, the leader of Kohl's parliamentary party, that "Without European unification, the war in the Balkans will not be the last war in Europe."

The Unity Chancellor voiced similar opinions.

Bibliography

Ambrosius, G. (1984) *Der Staat als Unternehmer*, Gottingen: Vandenhoeck and Ruprecht.

Barraclough, G. (1957) *The Origins of Modern Germany*, Oxford: Basil Blackwell.

Bithell, J. (1959) *Germany: A Companion to German Studies*, London: Methuen.

Dobrinsky, R. and Landesmann, M. (eds) (1995) *Transforming Economies and European Integration*, Aldershot: Edward Elgar.

Eschenburg, T. *et al.* (1970) *The Road to Dictatorship*, London: Oswald Wolff.

Issing, O. (1993) *Unabhängigkeit der Notenbank und Geldwertstabilität*, Stuttgart: Franz SteinerVerlag.

Kloss, G. (1989) *West Germany: An Introduction*, Basingstoke: Macmillan.

Kohn, H. (1960) *The Mind of Germany: The Education of a Nation*, London: Macmillan.

Mau, H. and Krausnick, H. (1959) *German History 1933–45*, London: Oswald Wolff.

Randlesome, C. (1994) *The Business Culture in Germany*, Oxford: Butterworth-Heinemann.

Smyser, W.R. (1992) *The Economy of United Germany: Colossus at the Crossroads*, Boston, MA: C. Hurst.

Tacitus, translated by Mattingly, H. (1948) *On Britain and Germany*, London: Penguin.

Taylor, A.J.P. (1964) *The Origins of the Second World War*, London: Penguin.

Watson, A. (1992) *The Germans: Who Are They Now?*, London: Thames Methuen.

Welfens, P.J.J. (ed.) (1996) *European Monetary Integration: EMS Developments and International Post-Maastricht Perspectives*, Berlin: Springer-Verlag.

Wistrich, E. (1993) *The United States of Europe*, London: Routledge.

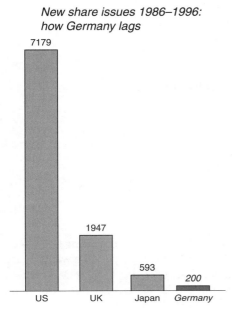

New share issues 1986–1996: how Germany lags

US 7179
UK 1947
Japan 593
Germany *200*

Sources: Deutsches Aktieninstitutit, International Bourse Federation

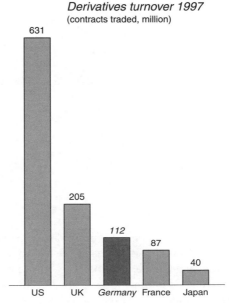

Derivatives turnover 1997
(contracts traded, million)

US 631
UK 205
Germany *112*
France 87
Japan 40

Source: Deutsche Börse, national exchanges

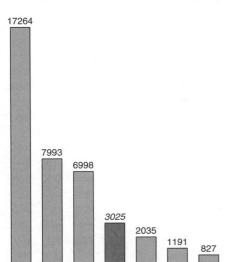

Bond market: Germany leads in Europe (DM bn)
Nominal value of domestic bonds at end-September 1997

US 17264
11 Emu countries 7993
Japan 6998
Germany *3025*
Italy 2035
France 1191
UK 827

Source: Bundesbank

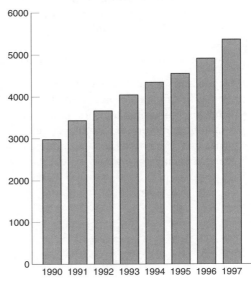

Total financial assets
(private German households, DM bn)

1990 1991 1992 1993 1994 1995 1996 1997

Source: Bundesbank

Editor's introduction: France

France has a visceral interest in seeing the European Union succeed. Having been occupied by Germany in three successive wars (1870, 1913, and 1940), France wants peace. Harnessing Germany to the EU seems to guarantee that peace and to provide a platform for French diplomacy on both the European and world stages. On the other hand, France's influence within the EU is clearly on the wane.

For France, the EU is not merely a club of neighboring countries linked in a trading association. Despite its sensitivity to issues of national pride and sovereignty, France clearly desires close ties among EU member states – the Gaullist vision of a European confederation and a centralizing bureaucracy notwithstanding. Indeed, the current structure of the EU bears the clear imprint of the Cartesian spirit of France.

Thus, the French attitude toward the EU is ambiguous. France insists on its prerogatives – notably in Africa – yet also presses for ever-closer union among EU member nations. However, the emphasis in France is clearly on the latter factor rather than the former.

Given this background, what are the issues for France which merit further study?

- France and Germany: As Germany sheds its reticence to act politically in the future, what role can France play in the Paris–Berlin axis and in Europe generally?
- What are the implications for agriculture in France of the potential EU membership of a major agricultural nation like Poland?
- What can France continue to bring to the EU as the membership increases and as France's relative economic weight declines?

France

Area: 549,090 sq km

Languages: French. Regionally – Provençal, Alsatian, Basque, Breton, Catalan, Occitan

Currency: Franc (FFr)

Population: 58.6m (July 1 1997 est.)

Main cities and population: (1995)

Paris (capital)	9,319,000
Lyons	1,262,000
Marseilles	1,230,000
Lille	959,000
Bordeaux	696,000

Constitution

National government

A clear separation of executive and legislative power exists. Constitutionally, the focus of executive power is the Council of Ministers, which is actively overseen by the president. The prime minister is appointed; according to the constitution he hands over his resignation to the president but in practice prime ministers have been dismissed by their president. Ministers are appointed and dismissed similarly but on the prime minister's suggestion, and they do not have to be members of parliament

National legislature

Bicameral. Senate of 319 members indirectly elected by local councils for a period of nine years, one-third retiring every three years. National assembly of 577 members directly elected from individual constituencies by a two-ballot system for a period of five years, but may be dissolved by the president

Main political parties and federations

Parti socialiste (PS); Rassemblement pour la République (RPR); Union pour la démocratie française (UDF)-Alliance, which includes Force démocrate (FD) and Démocratie libérale (DL), formerly the Parti républicain (PR); Parti communisté français (PCF); Parti radical socialiste (PRS); Mouvement des citoyens (MDC); Verts; Front national (FN)

Economic summary	1998 (forecast)	1999 (forecast)
Total GDP ($bn)	1,427	1,569
Real GDP growth (annual % change)	2.7	2.2
GDP per head ($)	24,200	26,600
Inflation (annual % change in CPI)	0.9	0.8
Wage rates, average (annual % change)	2.3	2.5
Industrial production (annual % change)	5.3	2.8
Unemployment rate (% of workforce)	11.8	11.2
Money supply, M3 (annual % change)	4.8	4.6
Three-month interest rates (%, annual average)	3.52	3.20
Budget balance (% of GDP)	−3.1	−3.1
Government debt (% of GDP)	59.5	59.7
Current account balance ($bn)	41.9	44.5
Exports ($bn)	389.0	429.0
Imports ($bn)	341	372
Trade balance ($bn)	28.7	34.6

Main trading partners (share of total trade to world 1997)

EXPORTS

BLEU*	Italy	UK	Germany	EU
8.1%	9.3%	10.1%	15.9%	62.9%

8.0%	9.8%	8.3%	16.6%	61.0%

IMPORTS

* Belgium–Luxembourg Economic Union

2

---◆◆◆---

France in Europe

Michel Péron
La Sorbonne, Paris, France

Voltaire observed that the Europe of the seventeenth century formed "a kind of grand republic, divided among several states," whose differences he clearly perceived. Montesquieu in *De l'Esprit des Lois* discerned "a genius for freedom which renders each part difficult to subjugate." In this time of European union, these remarks remain surprisingly pertinent. The concept of a "state" or "nation," which some feel is outdated, remains strong nonetheless in the supposedly ultra free-market UK. As regards the will to subjugate the current members of the European Union to a given central authority, it remains only wishful thinking. Europeans do not easily accept that which is "imposed by Brussels," as the standard phrase would have it. They indulge in behavior dictated by mood, impulse, and the political factors of the moment, refusing in particular to surrender their personal dispositions to react to external influences: that is, to surrender their idiosyncrasies.

It is in this sense that there exists, and will continue to exist, a French specificity within the European Union. Its historical bases cannot be questioned. The position of France on such-and-such an issue is often only the expression of permanent factors in France. It is indispensable to seek these constituent factors if one genuinely wishes to understand what underpins the French conception of the future of the EU – the EU *à la française*, of course. Indeed, it is quite false to pretend, as did *The Economist* (November 23, 1991), "that the frenchness is going out of a France that has pledged itself to europeanness."

Some historical benchmarks

The history of one of the world's oldest countries cannot be summed up in a few lines. France acquired its cohesion and its name between the fifth and the fifteenth centuries, when a veritable national consciousness formed in this nation, which was one of the most populous of Europe (18 million inhabitants, as opposed to 4 million in England). Confronted by the isolation of the Provinces, the Royalty gradually built an administrative mechanism to combat these fiefs. The celebration of the christening of Clovis (AD 496) marked a first halt to divisions and anarchy. Acceding to the throne in 987, the

18

Capetians put an end to economic and social disorganization. Historians already perceive in Hughes Capet and his immediate successors a clear penchant for administration and a lifestyle stamped with bourgeois respectability. Such was the arrival of the "national monarchy." The unity of France – already threatened several times – is henceforth assured. The king is the guarantor of the nation and personifies France.

Philippe-Auguste, king from 1180 to 1223, inaugurated the centralizing tradition of the Royalty by basing his policy on a corps of civil servants – the bailiffs and senechals whom he put into place. To more firmly establish royal authority, his successors carried out investigations into the administration of the bailiffs and senechals, from a desire to see justice done, but also to reduce their influence. The administrative structure thus established facilitated matters when, having fallen under English domination in 1415 and following a renewal of national feeling symbolized by Joan of Arc, it became necessary to rebuild the administration, finances, and army – that is to say, the state itself. This French national feeling is regularly confirmed in periods of war. It is at the beginning of the fourteenth century that the expression "Nation of France" was used for the first time.

However, it is uncontestably Louis XIV and his minister, Colbert (1619–83) who form the reference for the French conception of the state. Centralization, regulation, intervention by the state, economic planning, protectionism, and monopolies are the key terms which characterize the mercantilist economic system known as "Colbertism." For Colbert, state intervention in economic life should take place within a rigorous definition of an economic policy, through the creation of public companies, through public financing of private firms, and through direct orders from industry by the state. Such a strategy has several very modern aspects. Colbertism is often cited by the foreign press today when criticizing the functioning of France or its overstaffed administration. This explains why the French middle class quickly chose to live from tenured administrative positions rather than face the risks of industrial or business life.

Following the French Revolution, when the first conception of a united Europe appeared in the form of "sister republics," Napoleon launched a new reorganization that was administrative (creation of prefects and sub-prefects), legal (the Civil Code), and financial (the Bank of France). State intervention went a step further in 1803 with the creation of consultative chambers to make known the needs of and means for improving manufacturing, and in 1807 with the writing of a commercial code.

Closer to our time, General de Gaulle further reinforced the centralizing tendency by creating the Ecole nationale d'administration (ENA) to train the senior civil servants of the French government (Conseil d'Etat, Cour des Comptes, Inspection des Finances, Prefects ...). Mr Jacques Chirac is the first president of the French Republic to have studied only at ENA. However, countless ministers are alumni of the institution. Forty of the 200 largest French firms are directed by graduates of ENA (*énarques*). France is not prepared to give up the network of *grandes écoles* (exclusive professional schools) that train the nation's elite. The ministerial cabinets are likewise in the majority staffed by technocrats who spring from the administration, to which they return with each change in political majority, if not each change of minister.

The first French economic plan after World War II dates from 1947. France recently embarked on the eleventh such plan. However, as early as the seventeenth century, the

Council of Commerce – created in 1664 – brought together royal civil servants and representatives of 18 manufacturing cities to launch an inquest and draw a graph of the economic resources of the different provinces. General de Gaulle, Leon Blum, or Jean Monnet did the same by instituting these instruments for the rational development of national potential, the plans. The latter meet the French psychological need for centralization: that is, for organization from Paris. It can be argued that the issue is not state intervention, but flexible frameworks allowing for freedom of choice and program coordination. Yet the interventionist arsenal subsists in the form of fiscal encouragements, specific credits, public orders, etc. without taking European Union regulations into any great account. The French cannot help noticing the impact of government initiative on economic activity. The government absorbs some 55 percent of GDP.

A new political awareness concerning Europe

It quickly became apparent for the French government that if relaunching the national economy were the priority, and if structural changes were found indispensable to meet the post-World War II context, then it became imperative not to repeat the error of the post-World War I era: that is, the political isolation of Germany. All the foreign policy efforts of France must thenceforth aim at close cooperation with the rapidly rebuilding Germany so as to ward off any new attack by the hereditary enemy. Such an objective could be attained only by supporting the new European strategy of encouraging the economic integration of Germany into Europe. This integration would obviously have as a corollary a reduction in economic sovereignty, as implied by the heightened interdependence among European nations, as well as a desirable international division of labor.

Konrad Adenauer and Charles de Gaulle built the Paris–Bonn axis, whose fundamental importance, since the first treaty of cooperation in 1963, has always been cited as soon as a break-up of the EU has threatened. The Franco-German couple, through hell and high water, have ensured the stability of the institutions and defused crisis situations within the EU during the various phases of its development.

The ancient traditions of the French economy could not avoid being questioned by the competitive European free-market mentality. The finalization of the common external tariff, for example, signified deep cuts in the protectionist system of the French economy. Protectionary tariffs were radically reduced initially before being virtually eliminated. In this sense, it is correct to say that France turned its back on a long-standing system in its relations with other nations. But it is not at all certain that France has abandoned all recourse to subsidies or other types of aid – even if they are forbidden by Brussels – in the industrial sector as well as in agriculture. Firms recently privatized or *privatisable* have not been left on their own by the government and have been refloated financially by more or less disguised public funds before being offered on the Paris stock market (La Bourse). It is obvious that the French government cannot allow companies in difficulty to go under. The bankruptcy of the Crédit Lyonnais would have catastrophic repercussions for the banking sector in general.

The sensitive part played by agriculture in the French economy

Another historical factor that remains essential to an understanding of the French attitude within the EU was highlighted by the "mad cow" epidemic: France reacted quickly, since its long agricultural history is not finished and since agriculture and its problems remain a sensitive field, mined with conflict. The Physiocratic school of thought in the eighteenth century, which perceived in agriculture the essential source of wealth, was exclusively limited to France. Adam Smith should not have mocked the *General Maxims of the Economic Government of an Agricultural Kingdom* proposed by Quesnay. Today's France is certainly not an "agricultural republic," but the French are acutely aware of the importance of this sector of the economy – the first to bear the brunt of the creation of the EU. Let us note, moreover, that the Physiocrats coined the expression *laissez-faire* and that they were the first to give the main lines of a policy to "liberalize" economic life: that is, to make it more market sensitive. Many farmers continue to believe that, faced with "sterile classes," only the peasantry is truly productive. One might say: "Poor peasants, poor president."

Furthermore, General de Gaulle wanted to make of the Common Agricultural Policy (CAP) a model to establish an industrial common market. He was aware of the backward nature of French agriculture and did not hesitate to place the blame for the French lag in agricultural modernization on the protection long given to the French peasantry and the many high subsidies it received. The CAP was ultimately accepted thanks to bartering between France and its partners: the financial support of the member states to modernize French agriculture being given in exchange for increased opening of France's borders. The renewal of agricultural activity could take place only in the framework of the European single market, France and the Europe of Six possessing some 34 million hectares of arable land out of the EU's total of 73 million.

However, the impending enlargement of the 15 member state EU to central Europe can have only grave repercussions on French agriculture, and also on the industrial sector, where fully one-quarter of all French firms are directly or indirectly in agribusiness. Certainly, the agricultural production of eastern Europe will require heavy investment to become cost-effective, but the countries of central and eastern Europe (CEE) have enormous potential growth in productivity. Their soil is no less fertile than that of western Europe – the arable land in Poland is particularly rich. Moreover, the relatively inexpensive labor in the CEE can have negative consequences on the agricultural standard of living that the CAP was designed to maintain and protect.

New solutions must be found, and French agriculture must reinforce its presence on export markets. Agriculture has become the object of major maneuvering by France as regards the General Agreement on Tariffs and Trade (GATT). But is this new orientation realistic in view of the constant fall in agricultural prices worldwide? Can France long maintain its place as the world's second largest exporter of agricultural products, given the attacks to which it is subjected? It must be admitted that each time Europe is virulently criticized by the US in agricultural matters, American retaliatory measures seem to aim particularly at France.

France and its policy of regionalization

Speaking of France during a discourse pronounced in Lyon in 1969, General de Gaulle clearly indicated the new parameters of the problem: "the multisecular effort of centralization, long necessary to realize and maintain its [i.e. France's] unity despite the divergences of the provinces which were successively attached to it is no longer necessary. On the contrary, it is regional activities which appear to be the impetus of tomorrow's economic power." However, the French, consulted by referendum, rejected regionalization, which led to de Gaulle's resignation as president of the Republic. General de Gaulle had understood the consequences of regionalization long before the voters.

The penchant of France for centralized state economic planning and its interventionist industrial strategy (officially termed "indicative" rather than interventionist) is in violent contradiction to the conceptions of the other EU member states, where the attitude is more nearly to oppose central authority – an opposition that is reflected in the concept of a "Europe of Regions." The latter tends to correct the contradiction inherent between the concept of a "Europe of Nations" and that of union. The only solution for France, having lost the battle of its habit of concentrated powers, was to admit – or to pretend – that a phase of decentralization had now become necessary. This phase is represented by the establishment of a new layer of local administration: that is, the region. Let us note in passing that France was the only country in Europe or the world to possess a local structure in three layers: département, canton, and commune.

The regions were thought to be capable of developing peripheral powers that could influence the central government. However, the establishment of regional prefects in 1964 clearly indicates that, from the beginning, the French government was not willing to give free rein to the Regional Councils. In fact, these prefects today hold other posts that bring them close to the seat of power in Paris – several of them hold or have held major ministerial portfolios. Prior to the decision to elect the Regional Council by universal suffrage, the prefect of the region coordinated the tasks delegated to him or her by the central government: the prefect's decision-making powers had precise limits, those of implementing state policy. Since becoming an elected official, the prefect has certainly become the strong man of the region. However, he remains the man of the public powers as long as the presidential and national majorities coincide.

The stress placed on maintaining regional languages is intended to promote tongues long fallen into disuse. Their reactivation – often symbolic – in no way threatens central authority, except in the case of Corsica. The problems of Flemish in Belgium or of Catalan in Spain show the differences that exist in the Europe of Regions.

The emergence of the region in France was very gradual. The administrative organization resulting from the French Revolution in 1789 had no place for the region. The attempts made during the Third Republic (1852–71) all failed. It was only increasingly difficult problems of national development that pushed the governments of the Fifth Republic (1958–) to examine the territorial reorganization encouraged by the Treaty of Rome in 1957, which included regionalization. Efforts at administrative deconcentration were made, but it is generally agreed that the only reality is geographical, not political. The real goal of these initiatives was to paper over the cracks in an antiquated state centralization. The relocation of ENA to Strasbourg is typical in this regard.

The tenth plan, entitled *France, Europe* (the very title and its comma are pregnant with meaning), devotes one section to regionalization, which is considered vital in order to be aligned with France's neighbors in Europe and to more equitably distribute economic growth. The goal was to permanently put to rest the definition of France given in 1947 in a work entitled *Paris and the French Desert*. The desert has receded, but it has certainly not disappeared. France remains a great nation of small towns confronted by the *Länder* of Germany and by the city-states of Italy, which these two countries inherited from their histories, either ancient or more modern.

One can only agree with Jean-Jacques and Marie Dayries when they suggest that "the administrative regions were spawned by a dual imperative, economic and technical, and not by a political will to recognize a regional identity." Of course, the regional executive branch hopes to gain further autonomy and reduce its links to central authority. The latter, however, does not always look kindly upon the regions' opening representative offices in Brussels, or – worse yet – the regions' going outside the national borders to establish cooperative structures with their equivalents abroad. Such is the case, for example, for the Rhône-Alps region, the second most important economic region of France. Rhône-Alps has established permanent relations with Lombardy, Catalonia, and Baden-Württemberg, with which Rhône-Alps forms (a bit pompously perhaps) the four economic engines of Europe. By this very fact, Rhône-Alps usurps one of the prerogatives of the central government: foreign policy.

The developmental model is the same for the whole nation, making regional specificities secondary. The latter are taken into consideration only if doing so does not increase production costs, since the phenomenon of the globalization of markets scarcely facilitates the task of those who wish to establish an autonomous regional economic network. Moreover, the relatively low participation rate in regional elections in France proves that the French attach only secondary importance to regional bodies. Here again, the French testify to their attachment to the state, to the national integrity to which regionalization could give a lethal blow. If, despite everything, France has followed the movement initiated by the majority of EU member nations, which have granted their regions decentralized status, it is nonetheless true that France, in the words of the former president, Valéry Giscard d'Estaing, "is not rich enough to be the only country in the world to have four levels of administration, communal, departmental, regional, and national" (speech given in Dijon in 1975). Twenty-two regions is simply too high a number to hope to reduce developmental inequality. Furthermore, giving them political power would amount to diluting the responsibilities of the central authority, which is not the goal of this institutional reform.

The attitude of France toward Europe: a maze of contradictions

France was present at the creation of the European Coal and Steel Community (ECSC), whose unofficial objective was to counter any German thought of rebuilding a strong steel industry by using the resources of the Saar valley. The strategy decided upon was to place the whole of French and West German production under a "High Authority" of strongly supranational persuasion. According to Robert Schumann, the unification of steel pro-

duction should render any Franco-German war materially impossible. The ECSC constituted the first phase of a process of integration and of constructive cooperation.
Luxembourg, Italy, Belgium, and the Netherlands declared themselves favorable to the
coal–steel pool, with only brief hesitation by the Netherlands over loss of sovereignty. In
this instance, France accepted the creation of a supranational structure – a strange development in light of the nation's history – for the organization of economic development
programs, as it accepted the outbreak of the first open conflict with the UK.

France wished to continue its policy of anchoring West Germany in the western camp.
This policy could be followed through a generalized common market supported by the
other members of the ECSC. However, the goal of the other members at the time was to
create a free trade zone – an idea opposed to the strongly protectionist tradition of French
industrialists, who did not feel prepared to face fresh competition. In the end, France convinced its partners, obtaining their support for an organized common market rather than a
free trade zone. Six years after the creation of the ECSC, the same partners signed the
Treaty of Rome (1957) founding the European Economic Community and a separate
treaty creating the European Community for Atomic Energy (Euratom). The latter treaty
made no provision for the inspection of military installations and left France the possibility of developing atomic arms with the ultimate approval of Germany. We have already
emphasized the importance of the Common Agricultural Policy for a France with 30 percent of its population living from agriculture. Let it suffice to repeat the political importance of this sector, given its determinant weight during elections. The CAP represented
the first common policy that de Gaulle was able to impose by obtaining concessions from
Adenauer.

However, de Gaulle did not abandon his concept of a Europe of Nations, within which
the sovereignty of each member country would be safeguarded and at the same time the
cohesion of Europe would be affirmed. He spoke only of a confederation, insisting on
independence from the US as fundamental. This viewpoint became an ongoing determinant of successive French governments, and is current more than ever today.

The French atomic force or *force de frappe,* established in 1960, was constantly developed and modernized until 1996 – to the great discontent of many of France's partners.
This force represented a means of preserving not only French political independence, but
also that of Europe *vis-à-vis* the US. Let us not forget that France had also distanced itself
from NATO and from American leadership in matters of defense. However, France's
partners did not share the position adopted by de Gaulle toward Washington – a position
resulting in reinforced cooperation with Germany. Germany remained Atlanticist despite
everything (Paris Treaty of 1963), since it could not bring about a political Europe of six
nations. The creation of Eurocorps, a joint Franco-German military force, in 1991 continues in this direction. Eurocorps represents the commitment to assemble 40,000 men, of
whom 7,000 were designated following an understanding between the former chancellor,
Helmut Kohl, and the ex-president, François Mitterrand.

The Gaullist vision of Europe was a confederation, whereas the Community seemed to
lean toward supranational solutions. The move to majority voting on many issues was
symbolic of this evolution. Taking the pretext of institutional reforms which he judged
unacceptable (the extension of the European Commission's powers, among others), in
1965 de Gaulle suspended France's participation in the Council – the famous empty chair

policy. The crisis was resolved by compromise, as none of the members wished to risk the break-up of the Community. The departure of General de Gaulle in 1969 marked a sea change in French policy toward the UK, which remained attached to the idea of the supremacy of the nation-state. The Europe of Six became the Europe of Nine on January 1, 1973. Successive enlargements of the Community posed problems particularly for France. Spanish and Portuguese membership entailed conflicts for France in the wine industry, in the fishing industry (concerning the definition of fishing zones), and with regard to products of the south of France in general.

France faced by the new European reality following German reunification

No one can deny that France – pushed by François Mitterrand and to a certain degree unwillingly – facilitated German reunification, which could not have taken place without French approval. This new Franco-German *entente* should allow their joint project of a union – no longer merely economic, but unquestionably political – to advance. France did not expect an uneventful reunification and believed that East Germany would represent a considerable burden for the Federal Republic of Germany. As a result, France believed that the German chancellor would no longer be in such a favorable negotiating position.

The Treaty of Maastricht, its revision, and the many discussions of the "convergence criteria" for monetary union led France to hitch itself even more tightly to the German locomotive. As a result, the major macroeconomic indicators testify to a certain similarity between the two countries.

Together, France and Germany traveled a long road, strewn with compromises, before realizing the imperative nature of monetary union as an unavoidable preliminary to any political union. From the beginning, France's partners did not share General de Gaulle's vision of a european, non-American, Europe, which he wanted to be independent. Even Germany, which saw immediate advantages in an all-powerful dollar, remained attached to the Atlantic alliance. Membership of the Atlantic alliance implied a certain submission to the American currency and its fluctuations. Thus, the NATO member nations became tributaries of American policy. De Gaulle was never able to convince his partners to keep their distance from the greenback. However, in his attitude, one can discern the outline of a monetary system that would no longer be based on any national currency.

The idea of monetary union had to wait until The Hague summit of December 1969, when it was first broached under the influence of France. Once again, this was a decisive moment as the Franco-German couple laid the groundwork for monetary union with the creation of the ECU as a common accounting unit. The Treaty of Maastricht defined precisely the why and wherefore of the union. However, as Alain Prate wrote in *La France en Europe*: "The institutional leap which monetary union implied rekindled the debate in France between proponents of an integrated Europe and those of an unfettered France." If France struggled to meet the conditions set by the Treaty of Maastricht and placed its bet after 1983 on the "strong franc," it was above all because it did not want a monetary bloc whose pivot would be the German mark. France nevertheless intended, by respecting the deadlines set, to play the card of monetary union – a decisive step on the path to a political Europe, whose infallible supporter France was and still remains.

French diplomacy as a counterweight to German influence

The enlargement of the European Union to the east will considerably increase the German sphere of influence, going beyond that of *Mittel Europa*. When Spain and Portugal entered the Community, France understood that it too could have a certain weight as regards the countries of southern Europe, and that it could utilize its diplomatic expertise, recognized since the beginnings of European construction. As a common saying has it: "Any country adopts the politics of its geography." However, the cohesion of the Mediterranean countries has often been breached in the recent past. French diplomacy has chosen to favor *rapprochement* by smoothing divergences among interests or, better still, by participating in common objectives, such as the battle against terrorism.

Furthermore, the recent integration of Sweden and Finland struck a great blow to the delicate balance between the countries of northern and those of southern Europe. The center of gravity is shifting toward Germany. Hence, it is all the more urgent for France to reinforce its cooperation not only with Italy and Spain, but also with Portugal, Greece, and other countries of the Mediterranean world that are waiting at the door of the EU, such as Turkey and Morocco. This strategy may also be a means to regain the ground recently lost to the resolutely anti-protectionist member states.

Nonetheless, there is no question of relegating the privileged Franco-German relations to a lower plane. After all, France occupies a particularly exceptional position in the Europe of Fifteen, since it is both a country of the north and a country of the south. Thus, French diplomacy can intervene in both geographical zones. France can thus counterbalance German influence in the countries within Berlin's orbit. The alliance between France and Germany will then emerge strengthened, since both nations can influence the development of the EU in roughly equal proportions. However, the real issue should be their respective economic roles. Politically, France intends to maintain its preponderant role, even if this implies moving closer to a free-trading UK, as was the case during the Bosnian crisis, which saw Jacques Chirac and the former British prime minister, John Major, coordinate their viewpoints on the conception of Europe. France hopes in this way to keep Germany in the background. When the question of offering Germany a seat on the Security Council of the United Nations arose, France did not deem the dominant economic position of Germany sufficient reason to offer it a seat, France's fear always being to see the hereditary enemy affirm its importance on the world scene outside the European Union. But France also rejects the idea of a Europe transformed by successive enlargements into a free trade zone under Anglo-Saxon sociocultural domination.

This is why France, without wanting to oppose the enlargement of Europe, wishes first to "deepen" the EU, so as to develop a veritable European identity within a reinforced institutional framework. Unification, which is a process of ongoing negotiations, must not threaten the structure already built.

What are the implications for French business?

French entrepreneurs saw their salvation in the construction of Europe. On the other hand, the general French public has always adopted a more reserved attitude, sometimes bordering on indifference – not to mention the hostile reactions when the economic indicators are flashing red. Like their European partners, French company heads are sensitive to the additional costs of a "non-Europe." Not wanting a return to the protectionist past, they believe in the virtues of competition. They do not fear opening French public markets to all member nations. In a time of crisis, French entrepreneurs find themselves on an equal footing with foreign firms and accept the motivating challenge of this face-off. The unshackling and deregulating of certain economic sectors makes possible reforms in the field of financial charges. The unions, in a situation of Europewide unemployment, tend to adopt a less confrontational stance. The research and innovation that must be supported so as not to fall behind one's neighbors entail an offensive strategy totally contrary to an attitude of withdrawal – even if President Jacques Chirac decries French entrepreneurial immobility.

Conclusion

France holds a clear place in history as a guarantor of its ideals. When France assumed the presidency of the Council of Europe from July 1 to December 31, 1989, Social Europe and the Europe of Citizens were priority issues. The relations of the Community with the outside world, at the same time, were not addressed solely from the economic perspective. The gesture made at that time toward the countries of central and eastern Europe reflected not only mercantile concerns, but also the will to supply urgent assistance for structural adjustment. In harmony with its ideal of justice, France participated, wiping the slate clean of its colonial past, in the signing of the Yaoundé accords, and later of the Lomé conventions. President Jacques Chirac recently declared, during a brief visit to Gabon, that the world must not be built without Africa. France should not be accused of neocolonialism by its European partners. Unlike others, it is not attempting to reduce its commitments.

France is not among the "virtuous nations" from the point of view of European construction, but neither is it among the class dunces. It has put its "centralizing know-how" at the service of Europe, at all institutional levels. The influence exercised by its high technocratic civil servants is today being combatted. However, there would be no structured economic Europe without a bureaucratic, centralized Europe *à la française*, which does not mean red tape, but rather rational organization. The president of the French Republic solemnly launched the "National Dialogue for Europe" in Strasbourg. This initiative signifies that France remains ready to inspire the debate on the importance of Europe.

Bibliography

Bitsch, M.-T. (1996) *Histoire de la construction européenne de 1945 à nos jours*, Paris: Editions Complexe.
Bremond, J. and G. (1985) L'économie française face aux défis mondiaux, Paris: Hatier.
Dayries, J.-J. and M. (1986) *La Régionalisation*, Paris: PUF.

Delors, J. (1988) *La France par l'Europe*, Paris: Grasset.

Garaud, M.-F. and Seguin, P. (1992) *De l'Europe en général et de la France en particulier*, Paris: le Pré aux Clercs.

Gerbet, P. (1983) *La Construction de l'Europe*, Paris: Imprimerie nationale.

Morin, E. (1987) *Penser l'Europe*, Paris: Gallimard.

Petit, M. *et al.* (1991) *L'Europe interculturelle: mythe ou réalité?*, Paris: Editions d'Organisation.

Poncet, J.-F. and Barbier, B. (1988) *Une stratégie pour la France: l'Europe*, Paris: Economica.

Prate, A. (1995) *La France en Europe*, Paris: Economica.

Weber, E. (1971) *A Modern History of Europe*, New York: W.W. Norton.

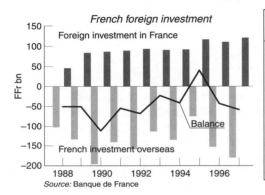

Source: Banque de France

	Exports (%)	Foreign direct investment (%)
US	6.0	20.1
Netherlands	4.6	13.0
UK	9.5	9.4
Belgium/Luxembourg	8.6	11.5
Germany	17.3	5.4
Spain	8.0	5.1
Italy	9.3	4.4
Switzerland	3.8	4.0
Brazil	0.5	2.5
Others	32.3	24.7

Editor's introduction: Spain

When standing before El Escorial, the dour but monumental palace near Madrid built by Philip II, the modern observer can only wonder, "what became of Spain after the seventeenth century?" Traveling a few short miles from El Escorial, the same person would find the sinister tomb of General Francisco Franco, gouged into the earth by the hands of prisoners of the Spanish Civil War. The stern Catholic authoritarianism of the two men is a continuous thread in the Spanish character.

The contrast is great with the liveliness of modern Spain and the buoyancy of the Spanish economy in the 1980s and 1990s. Spain has been readmitted to the fold, has again become a part of Europe. Spaniards are passionate Europeans. Thanks to Europe, Spain has once again found a place in the sun. The glories of global empire are part of the distant past, of course, but the shadows of religious and political persecution have also been erased.

As Luis Torras so aptly points out, Spain has undergone a renaissance. The transformation has been striking: from entrenched dictatorship to democracy, from economic backwater to economic dynamo, from pariah to southern pillar of the European Union. Certainly, however, many challenges remain – the Basque and Catalan independence movements being two obvious ones.

Given its new-found confidence and European identity, what are the issues that bear further investigation for Spain?

* Spain has clearly chosen a European identity. What are the implications for the country's relations with its former colonies in Latin America?
* Given its long occupation by the Moors, does Spain have a pivotal role to play *vis-à-vis* North Africa? If so, what role?
* What are the implications of the eastward expansion of the European Union for Spain politically? Economically?
* What are the implications of membership in the EU currency, the euro, for Spain?

29

Spain

Area: 504,880 sq km

Languages: Spanish (Castillian), Basque, Catalan and Galician

Currency: Peseta (Pta)

Population: 39.4m (mid-1998 official estimate)

Main cities and population: (1996)

Madrid (capital)	2,867,000
Barcelona	1,509,000
Valencia	747,000
Seville	697,000

Constitution

National government
Council of ministers headed by the president (prime minister), appointed by the king, but must win investiture vote in parliament

National legislature
Bicameral Cortes, Senate of 257 members, 208 directly elected and 49 appointed as regional representatives, but with little influence; Congress of Deputies of 350 members, elected from closed party lists in individual constituencies

State legislatures
17 autonomous community (regional) parliaments

Economic summary	1997	1998
Total GDP ($bn)	532.0	554.7
Real GDP growth (annual % change)	3.5	3.8
GDP per head ($'000)	13.5	14.1
Inflation (annual % change in CPI)	2.0	1.8
Average hourly earnings (annual % change)	2.9	2.6
Industrial production (annual % change)	6.9	5.4
Unemployment rate (% of workforce)	20.8	18.8
Money supply, M3 (annual % change)	4.5	8.2
Foreign exchange reserves ($bn)	68.4	55.3
Government balance (% of GDP)	−2.6	−1.8
Current account balance ($bn)	2.5	−1.1
Merchandise exports ($bn)	104.5	109.4
Merchandise imports ($bn)	−117.8	−129.4
Trade balance ($bn)	−13.3	−20.0
10-year bond yield (%, end period)	5.63	3.99
Three-month inter-bank rate (%, end period)	4.80	3.23

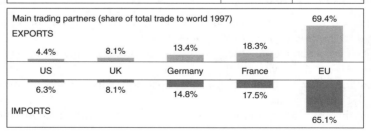

Main trading partners (share of total trade to world 1997)

EXPORTS

US	UK	Germany	France	EU
4.4%	8.1%	13.4%	18.3%	69.4%
6.3%	8.1%	14.8%	17.5%	65.1%

IMPORTS

Credit rating

Moody's *AA2*   Standard & Poors *AA+*   Fitch IBCA *AA*

Sources: Economist Intelligence Unit; Datastream/ICV

3

◆ ◆ ◆

Spain

Luis Torras

EADA (Escuela de Alta Dirección y Administración) Barcelona, Spain

Introduction

"The future treaty which you are discussing has no chance of being agreed on; if it was agreed on, it would have no chance of being applied. And if it was applied, it would be totally unacceptable to Britain."

Those were the final words uttered by the British representative at the Messina Conference that laid the foundations of the future European Union in November 1955. This state of mind reflects the mixed feelings that some European countries have about this long thought-about and sought-after project called Europe, and the frustration generated by the fact that the price one has to pay in order not to become an off-shore irrelevance is to give up part of one's national sovereignty.

The recurrent outbursts of Europhobia and insularity periodically haunting countries like the UK, Austria, and Sweden, not to mention Norway, are unknown in Spain. Even the dilemma between a Europe of nation-states or a federal Europe does not generate outbursts of passion, although some of the historic regions like Catalonia and the Basque Country would obviously favor the second choice. For a country that tried to impose its own view of Europe during the sixteenth century through sheer force – and having failed, initiated a long process of decadence that lasted for four centuries – being a full member of Europe is a rewarding feeling.

Ironically, Spain's attempts to impose a transnational state in Europe during the sixteenth century ignited in the rest of the Continent, and especially in France, its closest neighbor, the need to consolidate the nation-state and its institutions. It resulted in a centrally controlled civil administration and armed forces, a centrally controlled judiciary system, and finally a centrally controlled coinage and tax system to support financially all those new institutions.

The history of Europe has consisted of a steady search for a project with a common identity and civilization. From the days of the Roman Empire till the present, European history has been dotted with different projects. Charlemagne tried to give continuity to the Roman Empire; the Renaissance tried again through the development of the concept of the individual. And since the creation of the modern states, they have all tried to impose their own model of Europe.

31

After Spain in the sixteenth century, other nation-states followed suit. France in the seventeenth and nineteenth centuries, Germany twice in the twentieth, and the Soviet Union through Stalin's attempt during the late 1940s to create a Russian-ruled Europe – all tried to put into practice their own idea of a European superstate. After the tragic experience of 1939–45, Europe tried to develop a model of society based on an authentic spirit of peace and consensus, where ideas could circulate freely from nation to nation, and where, instead of being manipulated by totalitarian ideologies, its citizens could be brought up in a system defined by reason.

Nowadays, we are witnessing the implementation process of this collective effort to establish what it is hoped will be the definitive attempt to create a transnational state on the continent of Europe through consensus rather than force. This old project, which is in the process of becoming reality, should be able to compete with the main world economic powers, such as the US and Japan, and mostly should be able to prevent any other individual attempt to transcend the nation-state and replace it with a transnational superstate based on a model imposed by force.

Historical background

The history of Spain consists of a long series of ill-fated attempts to develop a modern nation-state out of a conglomerate of small kingdoms, separated by a rugged landscape that had kept them semi-isolated for centuries. From Ferdinand and Isabella's short days of glory (1474–1516) onwards, Spain's political leaders were never able to create a common goal; a common sense of mission that would have helped develop a unitarian concept of the nation-state. From the beginning, there was an official obsession to ignore the profound federal feelings that were generated by the historical, economic, and linguistic diversity of the Iberian peninsula.

What Spain had really started developing since the fall of the Roman Empire was a confederation of small independent kingdoms – Castilla, Aragon, Navarra, and Portugal – related through dynastic intermarriages, but quite often with very different political objectives. At the end of the fifteenth century, Ferdinand and Isabella began, with the enthusiastic help of the Catholic Church, the first attempt to unify the peninsula, and they tried to destroy its varied cultural and economic genetic code through forced conversion and subsequent expulsion of the two most entrepreneurial minorities: the Jews and the Muslims.

The conquest of America during the sixteenth century became a dual process of plundering natural resources and forcing conversion of the native souls to the Catholic faith. The precious minerals were shipped to Spain to finance the Spanish bid for mastery of Europe, instead of financing the development of the productive and commercial pillars of a modern state. Economic policies consolidated a traditional agrofeudal system and generated an industrial and technological dependence of the northern European nation-states. Some of the former kingdoms and principalities of Spain, such as Catalonia, were never given the chance to trade with the emerging colonial markets and to develop the resources of the New World.

The Counter-Reformation, initiated by Pope Paul III in 1543, largely in response to the

Protestant Reformation, generated a dogmatic atmosphere in Spain, which increased the need to control and unify the state. The development of the Spanish Inquisition was a consequence of this orthodox atmosphere and of the need to have an armed instrument to control any deviation from the dogma. The Catalan and Portuguese insurrections in the seventeenth century were a reaction against this oppressive political situation and the economic policies implemented by the central government. The intellectual predominance of France during this century and the installation of the French royal family, the Bourbons, on the Spanish throne in 1700, after the War of the Spanish Succession, ended the already slim hopes of a confederated model of state. But ironically, this new situation brought into Spain some of the fruits planted by the Age of Reason and its philosophers: Voltaire, Montesquieu, and Diderot.

The division installed by the new ideas between the supporters of the Old Regime (Conservadores) and its critics (Liberales) divided the country and sparked, with the addition of some collateral dynastic claims to the throne, a series of localized civil wars during the nineteenth century. The loss of the three remaining colonies, Cuba, Puerto Rico, and the Philippines, to the US in 1898 ended the century with a general feeling of despair about the future of the country, expressed in the writings of some of the most influential intellectuals of the time, the famous "Generación del 98."

The history of Spain during more than two-thirds of the twentieth century has been colored by a series of attempts and counter-attempts to recover the country's European identity and overcome the inferiority complex developed during 400 years of increasing isolation, backwardness, and dogmatism. The conflict between the supporters and opponents of rejoining mother Europe became an "official matter" when Napoleon Bonaparte – frustrated by the overwhelming military and political problems he encountered during his invasion of Spain, in what he had previously considered an easy task – furiously stated that Europe ended at the Pyrenees.

The first serious and pacific attempt to recover Spain's European identity occurred when the Spanish monarchy was democratically repudiated in the 1931 municipal elections, in which the Republican and Royalist candidates were trying to gain control of the local governments throughout Spain. After the victory of the Republican candidates in the majority of the urban areas, the king wisely decided to leave the country in order not to interfere with the will expressed by the majority of Spaniards to install a republican political system that would place Spain into the twentieth-century European political mainstream with a series of structural reforms, among them the long-sought status of autonomous regions for Catalonia and the Basque Country.

The sincere but often clumsily implemented efforts of the new republican regime were considered too far-fetched by a mixed opposition group of right-wing extremists, conservative parties, and a majority of members of the Catholic hierarchy and the armed forces. Their ill-conceived *coup d'état* of July 18, 1936, succeeded in a majority of the rural areas and small towns, but failed in most of the big cities and industrial areas, dividing the country into two opposing sides and igniting what is universally known as the Spanish Civil War. The fighting lasted almost three years, from July 1936 to April 1939, leaving the country devastated and divided, and inaugurated a period of autocratic rule by General Franco that lasted almost 40 years.

These four decades were different in many aspects. During the 1940s, Spain suffered complete political isolation and economic autarky. The Spanish government had rejected Hitler's invitation to enter World War II as an ally of Germany, but its sympathies towards the Nazi regime were nevertheless evident, and Spain sent several thousand volunteers to fight against the Soviet Union. After 1942, when it became evident that Germany was not going to win the war, the Spanish government began a slow and subtle process of separation that was ignored by the majority of western democracies. At the end of World War II, the western democracies decided to punish Spain for the support and sympathy it had shown toward Germany and Italy. France closed its borders with Spain, and in 1946, following a resolution by the United Nations, most of the foreign governments that had diplomatic relations with Spain recalled their ambassadors.

The 1950s brought a slow process of political recognition led by the US. This change in attitude by the western countries had to do mainly with the beginning of the Cold War and the geostrategic importance of Spain's geographical location at the main entrance to the Mediterranean Sea. The confirmation of this change of attitude toward Spain took place in 1955, when it was officially admitted into the United Nations.

The 1960s brought a period of strong economic development, ignited by the remittances of foreign currency sent home by the hundreds of thousands of Spanish emigrants working mainly in France, Germany, and Switzerland, and by the heavy influx of tourists from northern Europe, who had plenty of cash and free time as a consequence of the European economic recovery and the implementation of the welfare state. The economic recovery initiated in the late 1950s ushered in the development of two types of organization. The public sector invested heavily in shipbuilding, mining, iron and steelworks, public utilities, and the automotive sector, creating huge overstaffed organizations in what were considered strategic industrial sectors. The private sector invested mainly in small and medium-sized organizations, normally family owned, to satisfy, in most cases, a localized demand for products by a growing population. They generally continued supplying local markets and very seldom tried to conquer new markets. The growth of most of these small and medium-sized organizations was slowed down by their traditional negative attitude toward external financing – a very paternalistic leadership style that created a high level of conformity and dependency, and a lack of personal autonomy, maturity, and responsibility in most of their staff. These obstacles to growth were further compounded by a very poor road, railway, and public transport network, which prevented the development of all sorts of communications and increased the cost of transport of supplies and final products. This decade experienced, too, the timid efforts of the regime to offer a minimum amount of political rights to its citizens, in order to appease the activism of both students and workers, and to improve its international image.

The 1970s saw the decline of a very personalized and outdated political system that was trying by all means possible to perpetuate itself, and an economic slowdown initiated by the 1973 oil crisis. The political and economic crisis became more relevant as the country became aware of the physical and mental deterioration of the man who had been ruling the country since 1939, General Franco.

To summarize what we have been saying, we should underline the main features of Spain's political regime and business environment during these decades. Franco's regime featured three main characteristics: first, it was a product of the Civil War (1936–9), whose effects were still felt 40 years later; second, it was an effective agent of economic development; and third, it was not a totalitarian, but rather an authoritarian system of government, in which power was concentrated in the hands of the head of state, elections were indirect, restricted, and without true political pluralism, and regional and local autonomy did not exist at all. However, the rule of law did exist, and quite a few civil nonpolitical liberties were actually recognized.

The private business sector also featured three main characteristics: first, a very rigid framework of labor relations that limited the flexibility of the businesses and the adaptation of their capacity to the changes in the market; second, a network of small and medium-sized companies, with a very weak technological base, unable to generate the necessary economies of scale and scope to compete internationally; and third, a lack of internal financial resources needed to grow, and an inadequate debt structure that generated high financial costs.

With the death of Franco in November 1975, a series of important events took place one after the other, as Spain progressively integrated itself into the international and the European communities. Political democratization, the alternation in power of moderate right-wing and moderate socialist parties, and the modern concept of the monarchy, enacted by a new constitution and embodied by a very competent young king, gave Spain a new image and put an end to the previous one, which had been forged through centuries of incompetent monarchs and politicians.

The transition

What is nowadays known as the Spanish transition is the period between Franco's death in November 1975 and the approval of the new constitution in December 1978. The Spanish transition is relevant in political theory because, in the phenomenology of transition from autocracy to democracy, the Spanish case is the only one that combined a complete change of political institutions with the maintenance of the chain of legality. This process took place during the years 1976–8. Two different phases should be distinguished:

- The first phase runs from July 1976 to June 1977: that is, from the appointment of Adolfo Suarez as prime minister by the king, until the first elections of 1977. During this first transitional period, three main steps prepared the restoration of democracy: the amnesty of July 1976 erased many of the scars of the Civil War; all political parties were legalized; and the authoritarian constitution was amended in order to allow for full democratic elections and the drafting of a new constitution.
- The second phase covers the period from the first general elections, which produced a democratic Parliament, until the approval of the new constitution in December 1978. The adoption of the new constitution brought three fundamental elements to the Spanish political arena: the transformation of the authoritarian monarchy into a parliamentary monarchy; the recognition of fundamental rights and the formal establishment of the rule of law; and the implementation of wide regional autonomies.

The Spanish transition had 30 million protagonists, but among them there were a few who stood out:

♦ The true leader of the change was King Juan Carlos I. In July 1976, he appointed a new prime minister for the purpose of achieving a constitutional transition. Adolfo Suarez encouraged its work toward full reconciliation – through amnesty – and full democratization. He endorsed the constitutional task of the newly elected Parliament. He was, during and after the transition, the most effective defender and protector of democratization and democracy.

♦ The cabinet that was appointed in 1976 and remained in office until the next year was politically responsible for drafting and implementing the main legal steps that made the democratic elections of 1977 possible.

♦ After the 1977 elections, the political forces represented in Parliament were responsible for debating and endorsing the new constitution drafted by a seven-member committee that they had previously elected.

The most relevant aspect of the transition is that it was made without breaking with the previously established law. This formal continuity was politically relevant because it prevented any revolutionary leap. Franco's constitutional laws had their own provisions for amendment. Amendments to the Fundamental Laws required the approval of the oligarchic assembly and a popular referendum. All these requisites were fulfilled in 1976 to adopt the Law for Political Reform, which was formally a partial amendment of Franco's Fundamental Laws. In the framework of this new law, the democratic Parliament was elected in 1977 and the new constitution was drafted and approved.

At the same time, a process of social consensus took place at different levels. The political forces reached an agreement on several common goals and values (monarchy, democracy, free-market economy, human rights, regional autonomy). This political consensus was complemented by a simultaneous social consensus. Society wanted a peaceful transition through consensus, and the political agreement was a reflection of this social will.

The "Pactos de la Moncloa," an agreement among the government, the political forces and the social partners on key aspects of the economy, was the best example of this two-way relationship. The situation of the Spanish economy was in fact catastrophic, due in part to the international crisis of 1973 and to the lack of confidence exhibited by the international financial community regarding the Spanish situation.

This social consensus has become a fundamental new element in the history of Spain. The achievement of social consensus requires that the community feel that its own existence is not in danger. Never before, since Spain had become a nation-state in the fifteenth century, had this social consensus been achieved. Some thought that the coming of the Socialist Party to power in 1982 could take Spain back to a period of political turmoil and instability and break the economic liberalism developed by Adolfo Suarez and the Moncloa Pacts in 1977. Nothing of that sort happened because the Socialist government made an effort not to make the same mistakes that the French Socialists had made in 1981. The economic policies of the center-right were continued, guaranteeing a quiet evolution that allowed for impressive economic development. The rise to power of the Socialist Party in 1982 marked, for some commentators, the real end of the Spanish transition. The outcome of the elections of 1982 had a tremendous impact in Spain. A party, historically on the left of the political spectrum, had reached power through democratic elections, and for the first time in Spanish history, the will of the majority of voters had been accepted by the stakeholders that had for centuries ruled the country: the church, the armed forces, and the old aristocracy.

Economic and social changes

During the decade between the death of Franco in 1975 and the entrance into the Common Market in 1986, the country suffered the collapse of the traditional authority models of family, church, and state. In addition to these fundamental changes, Spain witnessed membership of the EEC, economic deregulation, and a wave of foreign investors eager to take advantage of a young and growing market. The social changes that took place affected the whole of society. The Spanish people emerged in the mid-1970s from the long period of Franco's autocratic rule with a tremendous amount of energy and a need to recover from the backward position that the old regime had imposed on them. Despite strong pressure from the Catholic hierarchy, Spanish society strongly favored the new governmental laws to legalize abortion and divorce, and the constitutional separation of church and state. The process of urbanization that took place during the 1960s had weakened the structure of the extended family by separating the different generations. Quite often the older generations remained in the rural areas, and the younger and more able moved to the urban areas. During the 1970s and mid-1980s this trend increased, and it was paralleled by the massive incorporation of women into the labor market, mostly to fill badly paid jobs within the growing service sector.

All these changes had a tremendous impact on the business environment that can be summarized as follows:

- The traditional barriers protecting the Spanish businesses from foreign competition were slowly dismantled. At the same time, a very lenient regulation system in issues such as quality, safety, and environmental protection became stricter, slowly incorporating a number of regulations in order to adapt itself to the pressing demands of consumers and to the regulations of the European Community, which Spain was to join in 1986.
- A traditionally very light tax system, which had incorporated a great amount of tolerance for fraud, became increasingly heavy in order to help finance the important investments in infrastructure and the development of the welfare system by the Socialists after 1982.
- The trade unions became very active, after decades of forced inactivity, and began to state their demands. During these years, their main objective was to increase their purchasing power, which had been eroded by high inflation rates.
- Competition became much stronger because of the increasing maturity of certain sectors, which reduced their growth rates, and because of increasing foreign competition resulting from the liberalization of the Spanish economy. Large salary increases and the weak peseta, which increased the costs of energy, raw materials, and the technology that Spain needed to become more competitive, added fuel to inflation, which reached a double-digit high.

Table 1   Evolution of foreign trade (billion pesetas)

Year	Total exports	Exports of energy products	Exports of non-energy products	Total imports	Imports of energy products	Imports of non-energy products	Trade balance
1967	84.7	4.9	79.7	211.8	26.1	185.7	−127.2
1968	111.2	9.6	101.6	246.5	37.9	208.6	−135.3
1969	133.0	8.6	124.4	296.3	37.1	259.2	−163.2
1970	167.1	9.2	157.9	332.3	43.9	288.4	−165.2
1971	205.6	8.8	196.8	347.4	56.8	290.6	−141.8
1972	245.2	8.9	236.6	437.6	62.9	374.7	−192.3
1973	302.7	14.2	288.5	561.5	72.8	488.8	−258.9
1974	408.0	27.6	380.4	888.7	224.9	663.8	−480.7
1975	440.3	14.5	425.8	932.2	240.1	692.1	−491.9
1976	583.4	21.7	561.7	1,169.4	341.0	828.4	−586.0
1977	775.3	28.7	746.6	1,350.5	382.3	968.2	−575.2
1978	1,001.6	25.2	976.4	1,430.9	405.7	1,025.2	−429.4
1979	1,221.2	23.3	1,198.0	1,704.0	514.2	1,189.8	−482.8
1980	1,462.2	57.2	1,405.1	2,424.2	932.0	1,492.2	−962.0
1981	1,888.4	99.1	1,789.3	2,970.4	1,259.6	1,710.8	−1,082.0
1982	2,233.9	160.0	2,073.9	3,476.1	1,377.3	2,098.8	−1,242.2
1983	2,833.3	252.4	2,590.8	4,175.4	1,672.5	2,502.9	−1,342.1
1984	3,730.8	335.3	3,395.5	4,629.0	1,742.7	2,886.2	−898.2
1985	4,104.1	384.0	3,720.1	5,073.2	1,809.3	3,264.0	−969.1
1986	3,800.2	239.7	3,560.5	4,890.8	931.8	3,959.0	−1,090.5
1987	4,195.6	249.9	3,945.7	6,029.8	979.9	5,050.0	−1,584.9
1988	4,659.5	210.9	4,448.6	6,989.4	789.9	6,199.5	−2,076.0
1989	5,134.5	244.6	4,889.9	8,396.4	990.0	7,406.3	−3,261.8
1990	5,630.6	272.5	5,358.0	8,898.4	1,051.4	7,847.0	−3,267.8
1991	6,064.7	184.6	5,880.1	9,636.9	1,046.7	8,590.1	−3,572.1
1992	6,657.6	194.3	6,463.3	10,204.8	1,017.4	9,187.3	−2,547.2
1993	7,754.6	219.8	7,534.8	10,131.0	1,101.4	9,029.6	−2,367.4
1994	9,796.3	207.1	9,589.2	12,348.7	1,158.0	11,190.7	−2,552.4
1995	11,423.1	186.8	11,236.3	14,318.3	1,187.7	13,1300.5	−2,895.2
1996*	1,955.0	53.0	1,902.0	2,366.0	235.0	2,130.0	−411.0

*January–February.
Source: Bank of Spain, *Customs Statistics*.

At the same time that the internationalization of the Spanish economy was taking place, a similar movement in the opposite direction was gaining importance. The reticence of the multinational companies to invest in Spain was being softened by the reassuring political changes taking place and by the confirmation of the future entry into the Common Market. The attractiveness of the Spanish market was evident. On the one hand, there was the possibility for non-European multinationals to establish a foothold in Europe through Spain. On the other hand, the host country still had a GNP far below the European average and a very large young segment of the population eager to increase their consumption

Table 2   Collections and payments for technical assistance and royalties (billion pesetas)

Year	Collections (A)	Payments (B)	A/B (%)
1975	2.9	17.3	16.8
1976	4.1	31.2	13.1
1977	4.5	28.7	15.7
1978	5.6	30.5	18.4
1979	7.6	34.7	21.9
1980	10.9	44.4	24.5
1981	16.7	52.4	31.9
1982	15.7	79.0	19.9
1983	18.3	88.3	20.7
1984	20.8	84.7	24.6
1985	24.5	104.0	23.6
1986	26.2	107.7	24.3
1987	21.3	114.3	18.6
1988	22.0	162.3	13.6
1989	35.5	192.7	18.4
1990	43.4	224.9	19.3
1991	69.1	240.6	28.7
1992	93.9	361.0	26.0

Source: Bank of Spain, *Statistics Bulletin.*

rates. The growth rate of the Spanish economy during the 1980s doubled that of Europe. This growth was necessary to make up for the delay accumulated over centuries, but it entailed a price to pay: the balance of trade deficit increased year after year, and inflation reached a high of 24.5 percent in 1977. Five years later, in 1982, it was 14.6 percent, and it has been decreasing ever since, though remaining a few points higher than Spain's main competitors. Unemployment rose to over 20 percent and has remained there. In 1996, unemployment in Spain (at 22.7 percent) doubled the European median.

The internationalization of the Spanish economy is best reflected in the spectacular increase in the exchange of goods and services with other countries, which has multiplied almost twenty-fold since 1976 (Table 1). This increase reflects the process of the Spanish economy's integration into the world economy. On the one hand, the agreements with the European Union and the General Agreement on Tariffs and Trade (GATT) required the dismantling of the country's protectionist barriers. On the other hand, the improvement of the international division of labor increased the general level of welfare by generating an easier access to cheaper and better products. This process of integration created the need to consider competition at an international level, which required technological innovation in order to remain competitive. This confirmed the traditional technological dependence of Spain on its northern neighbors (Table 2).

Although this dependence has decreased since 1975, when Spain's receipts for royalties and technical assistance covered 16.8 percent of the payments made for the same reasons, in 1992, the percentage was still a meager 26 percent. This dependence is a product of a traditionally autarkic economic system. In that context, external competition did not exist and internal competition was minimal. The technological gap generated over all these years will be difficult to overcome in a country where the attitude toward R & D was epitomized by the Spanish philosopher Miguel de Unamuno, when he expressed his disdain toward modernity by making the famous statement: '!Qué inventen ellos!' (Let them invent!).

Back to Europe

What the 1970s witnessed was the development of the interest of individuals and businesses in Europe. This interest had been thwarted during the Franco days by the nature of the regime, but it would nevertheless be false to state that the end of isolation began with the death of the autocratic ruler. Since the early 1970s when it became evident that the regime could not succeed itself, the move toward Europe became stronger, gaining momentum in 1977 with the consolidation of the political transition.

Two main developments consolidated the move toward Europe: first, the internationalization of the Spanish economy; and second, the configuration of a new state structure capable of integrating a plurality of nationalities while respecting their democracy.

The internationalization of the Spanish economy had generated an important reorientation of its economic activity and confirmed the soundness of the interest in the Old Continent. For historical reasons, Latin America had been Spain's main market until the loss of most of the colonies at the beginning of the nineteenth century. Europe had always been an important trading partner, but the relationships with the European countries have increased dramatically since Spain's entrance into the EEC, despite the fact that Spain is trying to restore its cultural presence and increase its political, diplomatic, and economic weight in the former colonies. This increase in Spain's presence in Latin America will continue to expand despite a number of obstacles related to the limited number of economic resources and institutions devoted to the task. But this political decision, aimed at increasing Spain's presence in the former colonies, cannot overshadow the fact that joining the EEC has forced Spain to choose its future partners and main political and economic priorities. Probably the best way to see where Spain's future lies is through the evolution of commercial relationships with its traditional partners. The exports to Latin American countries dropped from 12.7 percent of the total amount in 1965 to 2.3 percent in 1991. Since then they have been slowly increasing, reaching 4.6 percent in 1995. As far as the imports are concerned, the situation is quite similar. They fell from 8.6 percent of the total amount in 1965 to 2.8 percent in 1991, but since then they have increased only slightly, remaining in 1995 at 3.1 percent of the total (Table 3).

Spain's adherence to the EU has not only changed its trading relationship with Latin America. It has also affected its trading relationship with the US, which since the end of the Second World War had taken an important role in the Spanish economy through postwar credits, agricultural agreements, military bases installed in the 1950s and American multinationals. The evolution of Spain's trading relationship with the US is similar to its evolution with the Latin American countries. Although exports to the US have increased in absolute value, they decreased in percentage terms from 8.1 percent of the total amount

Table 3 Foreign trade structure by geographical area (% over the world total)

Years		EU	Non-EU	US	Japan	OECD	Developing countries					Ex-USSR Eastern Eur.	Rest of the world
							Total	OPEC	(A)	(B)	Other		
1987	Exports	65.8	34.2	8.1	1.1	79.8	15.4	4.5	3.0	1.0	6.9	1.6	3.3
	Imports	57.7	42.3	8.3	4.5	76.8	19.6	9.5	3.1	2.2	4.8	2.6	1.0
1988	Exports	67.6	32.4	7.9	1.2	81.5	14.9	4.5	2.6	1.4	6.5	1.3	2.3
	Imports	60.2	39.8	9.0	5.1	79.4	17.6	6.7	3.4	2.6	4.9	2.6	0.4
1989	Exports	68.8	31.2	7.5	1.2	82.5	13.1	3.9	2.7	1.2	5.2	1.5	2.9
	Imports	60.4	39.6	9.1	4.8	79.3	17.1	7.4	3.0	2.4	4.3	2.5	1.1
1990	Exports	71.5	28.5	5.9	1.1	83.3	12.1	3.4	2.5	1.1	5.0	1.2	3.4
	Imports	62.6	37.4	8.4	4.5	80.1	16.7	7.4	2.7	2.2	4.5	2.1	1.0
1991	Exports	74.6	25.4	4.9	1.0	84.7	12.4	3.6	2.3	1.5	5.0	1.4	1.5
	Imports	63.0	37.0	8.0	4.7	80.3	17.6	7.2	2.8	2.6	5.0	1.3	0.8
1992	Exports	73.1	26.9	4.8	0.9	83.7	13.3	3.7	2.9	1.4	5.3	1.2	1.8
	Imports	63.7	36.3	7.3	4.7	80.5	17.1	5.9	2.7	2.6	6.0	1.5	0.9
1993	Exports	69.0	31.0	4.8	0.9	80.3	16.3	4.1	3.8	2.0	6.3	1.6	1.8
	Imports	62.3	37.7	7.3	4.3	79.0	17.6	6.0	3.0	2.3	6.4	2.0	1.4
1994	Exports	70.6	29.4	4.9	1.3	81.9	15.1	3.2	4.0	2.3	5.5	1.7	1.4
	Imports	64.1	35.9	7.3	3.6	79.2	17.7	6.2	3.1	2.0	6.5	2.1	1.0
1995	Exports	72.3	27.6	4.1	1.4	81.9	15.0	3.1	4.6	2.0	5.3	1.7	1.5
	Imports	65.4	34.6	6.4	3.3	79.4	17.4	5.7	3.1	1.9	6.7	2.6	0.6
1996*	Exports	74.5	25.5	3.7	1.1	83.0	13.0	2.6	4.1	1.7	4.6	2.0	2.0
	Imports	64.5	35.5	7.4	2.9	79.2	17.6	6.1	2.9	1.7	7.0	2.5	0.7

*January–March.
A: Includes all the American continent with the exception of US, Canada (OECD), Venezuela and Ecuador (OPEC).
B: New industrialized countries: South Korea, Taiwan, Hong Kong, Singapore.
Source: *Foreign Trade Customs Statistics*.

Table 4   Distribution of direct investment of foreign capital in Spanish corporations according to their geographical origin (million pesetas)

	1980	1981	1982	1983	1984	1985	1986	1987	1988	1989	1990	1991	1992	1993
France	10,122	8,491	7,991	29,396	15,534	28,789	25,053	50,076	65,085	160,473	447,110	354,571	261,818	221,278
Bel. and Lux.	2,681	3,393	6,727	5,727	9,707	3,932	11,465	33,542	25,397	22,432	56,966	95,062	59,502	45,673
Low Countries	6,752	2,734	16,272	10,532	18,396	20,002	30,474	122,452	186,505	190,425	386,588	651,760	552,152	424,686
Germany	9,999	7,436	18,871	20,742	26,921	28,905	104,510	26,831	65,085	83,674	123,103	97,423	118,369	95,219
Italy	2,797	784	2,002	4,524	4,300	6,296	2,531	67,088	10,634	38,470	64,071	54,293	67,842	50,682
UK	2,734	17,410	10,292	10,791	20,638	18,238	27,981	45,420	111,392	142,701	151,117	214,000	109,575	130,821
Denmark	222	103	257	155	359	4,305	705	10,501	3,642	3,479	5,636	15,789	12,115	8,836
Norway	15	87	51	78	504	216	597	2,571	2,247	2,996	2,574	1,582	6,437	3,111
Sweden	528	237	1,875	1,163	2,464	4,001	4,058	10,597	10,148	33,619	9,682	20,335	10,364	21,609
Finland	334	537	636	79	504	613	524	2,894	823	4,159	8,001	4,525	231	2,738
Switzerland	14,153	7,875	35,374	14,402	25,509	21,657	21,116	60,950	52,093	90,798	85,010	79,658	49,231	75,662
Liech.	2,521	2,574	1,822	1,609	1,291	***	***	***	***	***	***	***	***	4,186
Subtotal	52,858	51,711	102,170	99,197	123,147	136,954	229,014	432,922	533,051	773,226	1,339,858	1,588,997	1,247,636	1,084,501
US	20,813	9,575	42,237	18,513	35,028	62,340	32,067	40,145	33,984	50,873	44,768	69,231	152,256	144,200
Canada	323	1,449	1,283	758	1,981	3,044	15,861	5,574	820	214	936	2,334	965	269
Subtotal	21,136	11,024	43,520	19,271	37,009	65,384	47,928	45,719	34,804	51,087	45,704	71,565	153,221	144,469
Japan	73	417	3,536	4,248	15,613	14,133	9,906	33,288	13,201	23,475	36,169	47,495	25,242	20,368
Mexico	52	25	23	144	111	3,574	772	2,137	727	1,152	2,331	4,242	165	4,590
Panama	277	253	1,139	3,508	31,077	6,109	7,313	10,533	9,945	13,235	18,119	10,448	13,503	8,790
Subtotal	329	278	1,162	3,652	31,188	9,683	8,085	12,690	10,672	14,386	20,450	14,690	13,668	13,380
Spain	6,774	11,953	20,357	19,297	33,032	39,572	85,954	187,009	197,240	343,739	321,333	471,267	396,686	263,830
Others	4,245	3,222	12,095	12,512	27,016	14,356	20,015	15,649	60,532	64,844	102,295	116,346	103,283	329,060
TOTAL	85,415	78,605	182,840	158,177	267,005	280,082	400,902	727,277	849,500	1,247,282	1,829,640	2,262,865	1,914,494	1,855,608

in 1987 to 4.1 percent in 1995. The imports of American products remained stable until 1990. Then they started decreasing slowly. In 1995, they represented 6.4 percent of the total amount of goods imported by Spain (Table 3).

The growing confidence of the international community in the changes that are taking place in Spain is reflected in the important level of foreign investment in the last 20 years. From 1980 to 1993, foreign direct investment in Spain multiplied more than 20 times from 85,415 million pesetas to 1,855,608 million pesetas (Table 4).

The information available shows too that the bulk of the investment comes from countries belonging to the European Union. In 1993, the total amount of foreign direct investment in Spain made by countries belonging to the EU was eight times the amount invested by the US, totalling 60 percent of the overall foreign investment in Spain.

One of the main tasks of Adolfo Suarez, when he was appointed prime minister by King Juan Carlos in the spring of 1976, was to give a new structure to a state that contained a plurality of cultures. These had survived under the unitarian political framework created by the Catholic Kings, and had been enthusiastically reinforced by the Franco regime. This diversity has historical, cultural, and linguistic roots. The inhabitants of Catalonia, Galicia, and the Basque Country speak a language in addition to, or instead of, Castilian, the language spoken in Castile and internationally known as Spanish. Quite often they see themselves not as Spaniards but as Catalans, Basques, or Gallegos. Their attitudes toward the rest of Spain, and particularly toward Castile and its capital, Madrid, are ambivalent. A lot of Catalans and Basques feel closer to Europe than to the rest of Spain.

The new 1978 constitution created 17 autonomous regions out of 50 provinces. Three of them, as we have seen, are *nacionalidades historicas*. The rest are in some cases rather artificial and in others mere creations, but the new situation seemed to have fulfilled a general feeling of autonomy. In a pluralistic Spain, European integration offers an attractive aspect. According to some political analysts, in the framework of a united Europe, the present-day states are going to lose weight in favor of the historical nationalities and regions. This will mean that the recurring problem of the amount of self-government allotted to these historical nationalities and regions in relation to the state will get on the right track. On the other hand, the protagonism left by the present structure may be taken over by new regional entities that may have nothing to do with the traditional historical, cultural, and linguistic parameters, but instead may relate to the new economic parameters drawn by the big American, European, and Japanese multinational corporations.

The consolidation of a pluralistic state and the internationalization, or rather the Europeanization, of the Spanish economy have helped normalize the relationship between the center and the periphery and, at the same time, have facilitated the approach to Europe. Having solved its problems, or at least having been given a political framework and the correspondent institutions to deal with them, Spain, as a community of nationalities, should theoretically be able to move closer to the rest of Europe at a steady and regular pace.

Conclusion

We fully agree with Howard Wiarda, when he affirms that Spain's entry into the European Union has not been just political and economic. It has been social, cultural, psychological, and particularly emotional. Spain has proudly joined the first division of nations and become, according to World Bank nomenclature, an "industrial market economy." It has taken Spaniards 400 years to overcome their inferiority complex and recover their European identity. And this, to the immense majority of Spaniards, is much more important than any other benefit they may obtain from their new status as members of the EU.

Let us recall that Spain's identity began falling apart in the sixteenth century when the Pyrenees became more than a physical barrier, through the prejudices, abuses, mismanagement, and lack of vision of a long cohort of intolerant and incompetent rulers. Since the day Luther questioned the religious monopoly of Rome – of which Spain was the main supporter – the country's relationship with Europe has been dotted with successive shows of love and hate. An increasingly ambivalent feeling has affected the traditional division between the two Spains: the reformist and the traditionalist. Faced with this situation, both sides have traditionally reacted with extremism and narrow-mindedness: the traditionalists rejecting all European values and trying to transform the Pyrenees into a totally insurmountable barrier; the reformists rejecting most values that had the slightest traditional Spanish component.

This lack of European identity haunted Spanish reformers for centuries. Finally, Spain has been able to develop the institutions it needs to become a fully fledged member of the EU. And most important of all, Spaniards have fully and wholeheartedly assumed their new European condition. As *The Economist* stated in its "Survey on Spain" of April 25, 1992, "the obsession of Spanish reformists has been to make up the lost ground with modernised Europe. If all goes well, by the end of the century it could be celebrating its fellowship among the EEC's elite." The immense majority of Spaniards would undoubtedly bet in favor of this statement.

Bibliography

Albi Ibanez, E. (ed.) (1992) *Europa y la competitividad de la economía española*, Barcelona: Ariel Economia.

Clark, P. and Haltzel, H. (eds) (1987) *Spain in the 1980s*, Cambridge, MA: Ballinger.

Garcia, F. and Gonzalez, J.M. (1994) *Breve historia de España*, Madrid: Alianza Editorial.

Graham, R. (1985) *Spain: Change of a Nation*, London: Michael Joseph.

Hooper, J. (1986) *The Spaniards: A Portrait of the New Spain*, London: Penguin.

Jackson, G. (1965) *The Spanish Republic and the Civil War (1931–1939)*, Princeton, NJ: Princeton University Press.

Mole, J. (1990) *Mind your Manners*, London: The Industrial Society Press.

Preston, P. (1986) *The Triumph of Democracy in Spain*, London: Methuen.

Renaud, A. (1992) *Le Marché espagnol*, Paris: Les Editions D'organisation.

Wistrich, E. (1993) *The United States of Europe*, London: Routledge.

Spain's recovery
GDP (annual % change)

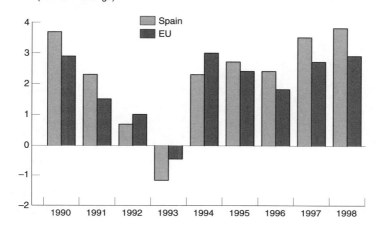

Source: Ministry of Economy and Finance

Unemployment rate

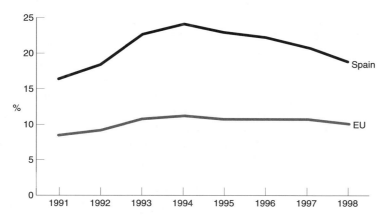

Source: Ministry of Economy and Finance

Editor's introduction: United Kingdom

"Storm in the Channel" shouted the English newspaper headline. "Continent cut off from Britain."

This hopefully fictitious anecdote illustrates the pride that is often perceived in continental Europe as the quintessence of the British mindset. However, perhaps the essential element of the headline is not so much arrogance as physical separation. Geographically distinct from the Atlantic promontory that is Europe, the British evolved differently from it. Unlike the US, the UK is too close to Europe to assume an isolationist posture toward it, and thus has been constrained to play a role on the European scene.

However, for most of its modern (i.e. post-seventeenth-century) history, Britain's role has been one of balancing opposing continental nations. Its goal has been some degree of political influence, certainly, but also and more importantly, the creation of economic advantage for the island kingdom. Henry Kissinger's *Diplomacy* (1994) clearly describes this long-standing British attitude toward Europe.

The UK's ability to play nations off against each other has declined with its military and political stature in Europe and the world. Still, the itch is there and the economic goals remain unchanged. Thus, the UK perceives the European Union as a vaster market, which to many Britons supersedes the Commonwealth and, indeed, the British Empire.

The grand visions for Europe that one finds in France of Charlemagne's reunited empire are received with a distance in London. In the British capital, Europe is perceived in terms of markets, not political power. For that very reason, the British – even under the Euro-friendly government of Prime Minister Tony Blair – seek no "ever closer union" with their European neighbors, preferring the good relations that (may) accompany free trade. It is this vision and this position that make the UK the odd man out in the European Union. From this fundamental observation stem several issues for further study:

- In the not-so-distant past, the UK was called an "American Trojan Horse" by some European observers. In light of the special relationship between the UK and the US, does the observation have any political or economic validity today?

- Given the key role played by the City of London in world finance, can the UK long remain aloof from the European currency, the euro?
- Given the antithesis between the British view of the European Union as primarily a grouping of nations to foster trade and the notion of political union found in Germany and France, will the UK remain a member state of the EU in the longer term?

United Kingdom

4

◆ ◆ ◆

United Kingdom:
A Pebble in the maelstrom?

Rehan ul-Haq
University of Birmingham, UK

Introduction

The very title of this book leads to the question of how a nation's culture may impact on the "strategy" it employs in its relationship with the outside world. It is my view that the cultural antecedents, however defined, of the UK have predisposed its people to develop an outwardly oriented stance while maintaining the UK's internal integrity. Furthermore, it is this stance coupled with expertise in certain areas, such as finance, which have led to the current profile of the UK. This chapter will examine this contention in greater depth.

Historical background

The UK has seen the continual movement of peoples, cultures, and aspirations throughout its turbulent history. What is now the UK has been subject to many such forces. Agricultural settlements started in Britain around 4000 BC, changing the nature of the population from hunter-gatherers to relatively settled peoples.

The disparate tribes were subject to continued overseas influences. The best known is probably the subjection of Britain by the Roman Empire from AD 43 onwards. This subjection excluded the Scottish, who were held back from incursions into Roman Britain by Hadrian's Wall. After the Roman period and starting from AD 449, the Angles, Saxons, and Jutes began the conquest of Britain. This ebb and flow of influences on Britain's psyche continued with raids, mounted by the Vikings, into parts of Britain; the unification of England under King Eadgar; the rule of England, Denmark, and Norway under Cnut the Great; and the Norman conquest of England. By 1453, England had lost most of its continental European possessions (see Stone and Barraclough, 1989).

Internally, a number of events drastically changed the nature of Britain and contributed to the culture and character of the UK as we now experience it. These included the following:

+ The transfer of the state religion from Catholicism, and allegiance to the Pope in the Vatican as the conduit to God, to Protestantism and its emphasis on the individual's direct access to God. Thus occurred the effective "nationalization" of the church in Britain.

+ The establishment of a constitutional monarchy in England and with it a substantial reduction in the arbitrary exercise of power by the monarch. The monarch exercised power at the behest, nominally if not in reality, of the people, with attendant checks and balances.

+ The Union of England and Scotland in 1707, thus enlarging Britain.

+ The Industrial Revolution, which generated substantial wealth for the *rentiers* or financiers, and the newly emerging industrialists, but did very little for the lot of working people. Indeed, many commentators have noted the exploitative nature of the relationship – the case of five-year-old children working in the textile mills of the north-west being an often-cited example. While one could presuppose that the growth of a new wealthy industrial class would have led to substantial changes in the quasi-feudalist nature of Britain, the industrialists in fact sent their children to the newly formed "public schools" (private fee-paying schools), where they internalized the education, values, and mores of the land-owning aristocracy.

+ This early industrialization led to Britain's reaching the "industry fully competitive" stage of national development prior to other trading partners, and an early adoption of a free trade ethos. (See the section 'Business culture' below.)

Britain also suffered a civil war from 1642 between the Royalists and the Parliamentarians. This war led to a victory for the Parliamentarians, whose leader, Oliver Cromwell, subsequently established a dictatorship. The long-term effect of this civil war was a further decline in the power of the monarchy and a concomitant increase in the power and prestige of Parliament. A belief in democracy as the best form of societal governance accompanied this movement. This deeply held view continues to the present. From the seventeenth century, England expanded into North America, Australia, and New Zealand. Expansion into Africa, Asia, the Middle East, and the Far East followed, turning England into a substantial colonial power.

While the empire thus established did increase the nominal value of trade, the net effect of this process of seeking and securing new and profitable markets was to increase the wealth of the financiers and industrialists with little benefit either to the British state or to the colonies.

The UK's expansionist history has had the effect of broadening the variety of external cultural influences on the British psyche. In addition, many of the early links, at least in terms of cultural exchange, have been maintained through the Commonwealth. The remaining agreements are paralleled by the current relationships between, for example, France and Francophone Africa, and Spain and Latin America.

This diverse and exotic history has predisposed the psyche of the British to be generally open and welcoming toward external influences and dialogue with different cultures, thereby generating a predisposition toward a diverse internal culture. Within this varied culture, a premium is placed on fundamental freedoms, a parliamentary democracy, and a sense of "fair play." Having said this, the last time the UK was invaded was hundreds of years ago. Hence the country has developed an "island" mentality, with secure and unchanging boundaries, within "middle England": that is, the UK as experienced by "the average Briton."

Given the disparate influences on the UK, including invasion and immigration (the Romans, Vikings, Saxons, Normans, Europeans, and most recently the Commonwealth), the differing English, Welsh, Scottish, and Northern Irish emphases, and the fact that a multicultural society has variations in its cultural homogeneity, is it possible to identify a specific "British culture"?

Cultural signposts

Bryson (1995), an American writer who lived in the UK for two decades, referred to the country as "this wondrous land where the relics of genius and enterprise confront you at every step, where every realm of human possibility has been probed and challenged and generally extended, where many of the greatest accomplishments of industry, commerce and the arts find a seat."

Tayeb (1993) identified and ranked 30 characteristics of "Englishness" as identified by a representative sample of 100 English respondents. The first ten characteristics, in order of ranking, were as follows:

1. Strong sense of responsibility.
2. Trustworthiness.
3. Ability to cope well with setbacks.
4. Desire to see things through.
5. Generally honest.
6. Displaying self-control.
7. Displaying self-confidence.
8. Generally independent.
9. Generally law abiding and able to cope well with new and uncertain situations.
10. Generally disciplined and friendly.

Hofstede (in *Culture's Consequences*, among other works), considered to be a leading commentator on national culture, analyzed Great Britain's national culture as being a low or small power distance society, where individuals had weak uncertainty avoidance tendencies, a highly individualist streak, and a masculine outlook. While Hofstede's analysis does provide some insights into the societal culture of Great Britain, it assumes that there is cultural homogeneity within the national boundaries. Nevertheless, Tayeb and Hofstede provide valuable insights into culture even though they address disparate aspects – "Englishness" and "Great Britain" respectively – rather than the United Kingdom.

Lawrence (1996), analyzing one area of the British psyche, suggests that British management tend to have the following characteristics:

♦ They are *generalists* – that is, good all-rounders.
♦ They are *mobile* – functionally mobile, with a focus on character, personality, and judgment.

- They are *leadership oriented* – the leader with charisma, character, and flair is the focus of loyalty, not the system.
- They are *informal* in their interactions – the intuitive, interpersonal, and judgmental are important.
- They develop *informal systems* – these operate in parallel to the formal systems.
- They favour *consensus-based decision-making processes.*
- They have *discretion bias* – that is, they value the right to decide in an area that has not been systematized.
- They are pragmatic – the supreme value is common sense.
- They seek to *manage compliance* – "the appeal to acceptability, social integration, expectation, political convenience and common sense are relatively strong."
- The use of *humor* is a national characteristic in business, professional, and social life.

Thus the profile of a British manager, suggested by the above analysis, is a generalist, versed in the arts of "getting things done," who is socially competent, has character, charisma, leadership, and good judgment, all supported by a sense of humor.

National attitudes toward Europe

The forerunners of the European Union were established as mechanisms to engender closer cooperation between the European nation-states in an attempt to preclude further wars in Europe. This initial aim developed into the broader aims of the European Union, as exemplified by Article 2 of the Treaty of Rome, signed on January 1, 1958:

> the Community [later "Union"] shall have as its task, by establishing a common market and progressively approximating the economic policies of the Member States, to promote throughout the Community a harmonious development of economic activities, a continuous and balanced expansion, an increase in stability, an accelerated rise in the standard of living and closer relations between the states belonging to it.

This common market – that is, a market involving the free internal movement of labor, goods, and capital – is a view of the world that the UK fully believes in, if it is in its national interests. Its historical antecedents date back, in the British psyche, to the early adoption of free trade policies based on Britain's early industrialization.

The view of the world where nation-states freely trade with each other and where one of the functions of government is to facilitate this free trade is a strongly held one in the UK. However, subjugating the government's responsibility for facilitating the national interest of the British people to some form of "federated" Europe is clearly becoming a less and less attractive option to some sectors of British society. The Euro-skeptic element in the Conservative government of John Major (1992–7) became more and more vocal, and the Conservative Party is still going through a period of soul searching to determine their stance with regard to further integration.

In May 1996, John Major was quoted in the *Sunday Telegraph* as saying, "Britain is a member of the EU for one simple reason; because it is in our national interest." The present Labour government's pro-European stance has nonetheless not fundamentally modified this position. This view is clearly portrayed in the UK's stance toward entering into the single currency: the UK has decided not to join the first group of member states in the new European currency, the euro, but to wait and see whether it is successful and how far it is consistent with the UK's economic interests. Tony Blair's government (1997 onwards), while embracing the notion of a federated Europe, still maintains this caution regarding the entry of the UK into a single European currency.

The model of the "United States of Europe" has been put forward to explain the possible future outcome of the centripetal process of the European Union: that is, the process of bringing independent nation-states into a collective and consistently acting group. However, while it is in the national interest of all the European nation-states to cooperate both to preclude another pan-European war and to encourage the trading and economic benefits of the EU, the British government believes that the targeted end result should not be some form of "United States of Europe," but rather that Europe should continue to enjoy cultural diversity while cooperating to secure the economic benefits of a "domestic" market of about 380 million people. In short, Europe should be a free trade zone, but not a centralized political – and currently undemocratic – super-bureaucracy, able to override the interests of elected national governments and their people.

A Europe of nation-states

From the British perspective, Europe has seen centuries of independent and highly successful nation-states, whose populations are fiercely proud of the diversity of their histories, cultures, and languages. This diversity has been further enhanced by each nation's being subject to changing national boundaries and political allegiances over time. Europe is fundamentally heterogeneous, and it is this historical heterogeneity and the lack of a need or desire to form a "new" superstate or culture that precludes the formation of a "United States of Europe." The UK, having not been subject to invasion during World War II, is still clearly philosophically in favor of retaining its independence. This is at the root of the UK's indecision and hesitation about its commitment to the European Union.

The UK is clearly of the view that political integration is undesirable, and it is a vocal critic of those who consider it possible. However, the question of the degree of real economic, and therefore political, independence that the UK possesses is an important and unanswered one. As a full member of the global financial, economic, and trading system, the UK is subject to massive external pressures that reduce the validity of the demand for political independence. Nevertheless the UK clearly believes that the EU's prime function is to focus on measures to facilitate economic growth rather than to achieve political integration.

For this reason, the concept of "subsidiarity" was strongly supported by the British in relation to the workings of the EU, and this principle is becoming accepted as a mechanism in the EU. Subsidiarity allows each decision to be taken at the lowest level that can make that particular decision (i.e. only those decision that require a pan-European agreement should be taken by the EU, the individual nation-states continuing to be the overriding political decision-makers in the individual states).

On the other hand, the internal workings of the UK have not generally followed the concept of subsidiarity as they have become increasingly centralized. For example, the government determines and imposes a "national curriculum" in children's education on to state-run establishments up to secondary school. The local authorities – that is, locally based government, run by locally elected councilors – have been drastically disempowered, and more and more functions transferred either to central government or to, for example, the individual school or hospital. Thus policy is no longer locally determined, but rather is determined by central government, with the individual school or hospital being made responsible for its implementation within centrally determined budgets. While the government supports subsidiarity in Europe, it has not supported it fully in the UK, although recent devolution of a degree of political power to Scotland and Wales may indicate a change in attitude.

National stake in Europe

The UK is committed to the economic benefits of the EU. In 1996, a British government publication entitled *Britain: The Preferred Location* stated that "Investors can be sure that the UK will remain at the heart of European economic development." However, this commitment to remain at the heart of Europe's economic development is tempered by an aversion to the perceived "bureaucratization" of Europe through the establishment of a political superstate. This negative perception of the EU stems from the belief that capitalists should be unfettered in the pursuit of profit and that a political superstate will increase the costs of business, but has been tempered by the more active role in Europe taken by the Labour government.

The UK's commitment to the EU, as an investment in the enlargement of the European free market, is shown by its position as a major net contributor to the EU. In addition, the UK has a higher commitment to pan-European cooperation on defense issues than some of its EU partners, and is clearly in favor of the widening rather than the deepening of the EU. Widening the EU, primarily through the inclusion of eastern European states, would lead to an enlargement of the European free market and to a decrease in the perceived political interference of the EU in UK national governance.

The UK's regions

The administrative regions for foreign investment in the UK include Scotland, Northern Ireland, the North-East, the North-West, Yorkshire and Humberside, Wales, the West Midlands, the East Midlands, East Anglia, Greater London, the South-East, and the South-West. These administrative regions overlay, especially in the case of Scotland and Wales, the county, district, and unitary authority subdivisions. Each of the regions has a responsibility to develop foreign direct investment, in competition with global, other European, and other British sites. With the exception of Scotland and Wales, these regions are perhaps regions only in the sense that they are used by the EU in administering grants and by the UK in attracting inward investment; they may not necessarily denote a political or cultural grouping.

It is probably true to state that a sense of cultural identity is found closer to the county or city level, or at the Scottish, Welsh, Northern Ireland, and English levels. Each county and city has a social and cultural history that has determined and continues to determine its business culture, strengths, and profile.

The West Midlands Development Agency (WMDA), to cite one regional example, actively markets the economic and social benefits of locating inward investment in its region through a program of proactive marketing. In 1994/5, WMDA dealt with about 400 inquiries leading to 99 inward visits and over £1.1 billion invested. Of this investment, £730 million was invested by North American companies and £340 million by European companies.

The regions of the UK have direct links with regions in Europe through twinning arrangements, but also, perhaps more importantly, through clusters of expertise (such as car manufacturing in the West Midlands) and investment links. In addition, the UK regions have, through the representation of the locally elected Member of the European Parliament (MEP), a direct, but limited, influence through the European Parliament on the Council of Ministers. The Council of Ministers, the body in which European decision-making power resides, is made up of the relevant ministers of the member national governments.

While central government is responsible for paying the national contribution to the EU budget, it is largely the regions that apply for and receive assistance from the EU for local infrastructure and regeneration projects. The North-West of England, for example, was due to receive about £120 million in European structural funds in 1997. This regionally based relationship with the EU is both a financial relationship and an opportunity for the regions to assert a degree of independence under a centralizing government. It is not, however, perceived as a vehicle – except by the Scottish Nationalists – for the break-up of the UK and the establishment of a "Europe of Regions" governed from Brussels.

Within the UK, the previous Conservative government increasingly centralized the direction of a variety of state activities and disempowered the local authorities. The current Labour government is considering changes in the electoral system to introduce forms of proportional representation, thereby allowing a greater tendency toward consensus rather than adversarial politics. It has also implemented devolution of power to the Scottish and Welsh regions through a Scottish Parliament and a Welsh Assembly. The issue of devolution is an attempt to meet the twin pressures of maintaining the territorial integrity of the UK while also allowing a degree of self-government in both Wales and Scotland, engendering a "federated" UK.

Thus the nature of the relationship between central government and the regions has changed substantially since the British general election in May 1997. The resultant changes may also lead to changes in the relationships between the British regions and the regions of mainland Europe. The Labour government is also discussing the creation of regional chambers, regional development agencies, and regional banks. If these projects occur, the nature of the relationship between central government, the British regions, and the regions of Europe would change dramatically.

Business culture

The UK and its regions have a tradition of being active members of the global economy. Historically, Britain's free trade bias was perceptible at least as early as the leadership of Sir Robert Walpole from 1721. List (1904) identified three stages of economic development in a nation-state:

1. Primarily agricultural.
2. Industry developing.
3. Industry fully competitive.

He argued that, at each stage, the attitude toward free trade was necessarily different. In the case of stages 1 and 3, a policy of free trade was the norm. In stage 2, when the indigenous manufacturing sectors were developing, the appropriate policy would be for the nation-state to protect its evolving industry. List argued that the British bias toward free trade stemmed from the fact that it had a comparatively early Industrial Revolution, which led it to stage 3 before its competitors, and which helped the country develop a focus on exporting its products to less developed countries. In other words, the policy of free trade was in the best economic interest of Britain. This approach was supported by the cultural bias toward adventure, domination, and the key value of profit generation among the ruling aristocrats and the industrialists.

Later, the British Empire, though certainly not a free trade zone, was one of the largest and most diverse internal free markets known, with a wide range of goods and services traded both internally and externally. Since the independence of its former colonies, the UK has retained cultural links through the Commonwealth, its membership in the G7, and the EU. It has also maintained an intermittently strong relationship with the US. These cultural links are also, to varied extents, paralleled by trade and other economic links.

The relative ambivalence of the UK to the EU has been based on the country's perception of its "three spheres of influence." The UK has traditionally considered that moving towards the third sphere, the EU, would damage its relationship with both the US and the former empire, now the Commonwealth. However, there is now a realization that, while the UK and the US share certain links, the focus of the US is on the whole European regional bloc, with Germany, as both geographically central and economically powerful, becoming more important. The UK is now questioning its role in the world as other countries have begun overtaking it in economic terms. One example is Italy in the 1980s.

This long-established involvement in trade in the international arena is nowhere more pronounced than in the UK's involvement in the financial services sector. The focus on this sector is an outgrowth both of the long-standing differentiation between living on investment income and being involved in "trade," and of the investment needs of the empire to finance its growth and development.

The financial sector

The London Stock Exchange provides equity finance for small companies through the Alternative Investment Market, and through the main stock exchange which lists over 460 foreign companies – more than any other stock exchange in the world – and provides equity and fixed-interest products. London's equity market, in terms of the share value of listed companies at the end of 1995, was larger than the German, Paris, Madrid, and Amsterdam stock exchanges combined. The Euromoney markets, the London International Financial Futures Exchange, the International Petroleum Exchange, the London Commodity Exchange, and the Baltic Futures Exchange are among the exchanges and markets present in London.

The London International Financial Futures Exchange (LIFFE) was set up in 1982 to provide, through the option and futures instruments traded, a mechanism to manage interest rates and other financial risks exposures. LIFFE is now the leading futures and options exchange in Europe, with 70 percent of the 200 member firms being owned overseas, and the second largest in the world after the Chicago Board of Trade. While the establishment of the European single currency will inevitably reduce the number of currencies in which LIFFE products are denominated, there is a perception that the value of trades between the major currency blocs (US dollar, Japanese yen, and the euro) will increase. LIFFE has prepared for this eventuality by allowing contracts that mature from early 1999 to be settled in euro or in the denominated currency. In addition, LIFFE is strengthening its international links through bilateral agreements with the Tokyo Stock Exchange, the Tokyo International Futures Exchange, and the Chicago Board of Trade.

These virtual financial and commodity markets or exchanges, coupled with the presence of a multitude of commercial and investment banks, insurance companies, fund managers, and lawyers and accountants with financial sector expertise, make the City of London cluster the undisputed center of commercial financial expertise in Europe. However, the position of London could change if it does not continue to provide the environment for such expertise and markets to flourish.

London has about 500 banks from 70 countries located in it. By comparison, Paris has 280 banks and Frankfurt has 250. London is one of the three financial centers (New York, London, and Tokyo) that constitute the heart of the global financial system. The size of the banking sector and its importance in the international arena are borne out by the figures for 1994, when 17 percent of worldwide bank lending was carried out in the UK, compared with 8 percent in Germany. This substantial expertise in finance is both a source of pride for the British as well as a source of concern in the degree of short-termism in the financial sector and its impact on the manufacturing sector.

Furthermore, the UK's free trade policies, coupled with the global trend toward consolidation and the pursuit of size in the banking sector, have led to the recent acquisition of British merchant banks by a number of non-British financial institutions. The acquisition of S.G. Warburg by Swiss Bank Corporation; of Barings by the Dutch bank, ING; of Smith New Court by Merrill Lynch; and of Kleinwort Benson by Germany's Dresdner Bank are the more recent examples. This process has important implications for the culture of the City of London. The City has, since its liberalization in the 1980s, rapidly developed an international and diverse culture. This cultural change is now also affecting the bastion of "Britishness," the British merchant bank.

The manufacturing sector

The free trade policies of the UK, the encouragement of inward investment, and the specter of a possible, though highly unlikely, "fortress Europe" have led to an increase of foreign investment into the UK. This inward investment has included substantive investments in the manufacturing sector. The acquisition of Rover by BMW led to some xenophobic reporting in the tabloid press, but the degree of xenophobia displayed was somewhat muted compared to that displayed when the Swiss company Nestlé acquired Rowntree Mackintosh during the 1980s.

Many investors have established manufacturing plants in the UK with a view to sourcing production for the European market, at least in part, from these plants. In total, by 1994, £131 billion had been invested in the UK by foreign firms. About half of the projects reviewed by the Invest in Britain Bureau were initiated by North American investors and a substantial amount of the remainder came from Far Eastern investors. The UK is perceived by potential investors as encouraging foreign investment, providing the appropriate degree of infrastructure and a relatively softly regulated environment. In addition, products manufactured in the UK count as European and are therefore not subject to the quotas imposed on non-EU countries by the EU.

The share of foreign enterprises in the total sales of British manufactured goods was 24.06 percent in 1984, while the share of foreign enterprises in the total employment of British manufacturing was 14.86 percent in the same year (Bailey *et al.*, 1994). These compare with 20.33 percent and 13.98 percent respectively in 1975. Foreign companies provide 18 percent of manufacturing jobs, and about 20 of the top 100 firms in the UK by manufacturing output are foreign owned. This increase in foreign firms' participation in the British economy is the fulfillment of a predetermined national strategy, but it also has the effect of opening up the manufacturing sector to the vagaries of international forces and global trends. Overall, the UK has attracted about 40 percent of American and Japanese investment into the EU. Some American firms, such as Heinz, Ford, and Hoover, have been in the UK for so long that they are often considered to be British.

The indigenous manufacturing sector has, with notable exceptions such as pharmaceuticals, suffered from the bias in the UK against long-term investment in the domestic arena by both entrepreneurs and capital providers. This deindustrialization was also prompted through British firms becoming transnationals and relocating activities in low-wage economies overseas. The movement toward a service-based economy is nowhere more discernible than in the south-east of England, where over three-quarters of the workforce are employed or involved in the service sector. Nevertheless in certain geographical areas, such as the West Midlands and Birmingham, a concentration of industrial and manufacturing capability is still clearly visible. In cultural terms, the historically first industrial economy has now de-emphasized indigenous heavy manufacturing, concentrating instead on services and providing a favorable climate for inward investment. Where indigenous manufacturing continues, it is in areas that require a high degree of intellectual input rather than manual labor.

The Formula 1 racing car design and production cluster is one of these areas. Most serious Formula 1 cars, such as Williams and McLaren, are designed and built in the UK. Ligier and Ferrari are exceptions, but even the Ferrari cars use a British chassis. In addition, Indycar teams such as Lola, Penske, and Reynard are also UK based, with Ilmoor providing engines for both Indycars and Formula 1 cars. The 600 firms that make up the British motor sports industry enjoy a collective annual turnover of £1,500 million and employ up to 30,000 highly qualified people (*Sunday Times*, July, 1996).

While the British economy generally has moved from manufacturing to services, and although investment in manufacturing has been low, there is a declared acceptance by government of the need to create a world-class manufacturing base in the UK. Nevertheless the creation of this manufacturing base, to replace the heavy and extractive industries, seems to be largely through the encouragement of inward investment by foreign firms rather than through investment in and encouragement of British firms.

The change from heavy industry to service, part-time, and specialist jobs has led to an increase in long-term unemploymemt and a growing underclass of people who do not have the skills to succeed in the changed economy. Unemployment and the devastation of shipbuilding, mining, and other heavy industries have distorted the foundations of British working-class culture and family life. Moreover, some 31 percent of government spending goes on social (welfare) payments, as against 16 percent on health and 12 percent on education.

Under a succession of Conservative governments, the UK saw itself as "Europe's competitive base" and changed its internal structure and culture to meet this objective by developing a deregulated, low-wage and increasingly low-skill, assembly operations-based manufacturing sector. This evolution was perceived as one that may well be good for shareholder profits, and which increases the power of management to hire and fire workers. However, it is considered to have fundamentally and negatively changed the nature of work from long-term and secure jobs with reciprocal loyalty between managers and workers, to a short-term contract-oriented culture, with increased personal financial uncertainty.

Professor Kumar Battacharyya, at the University of Warwick in the UK, was quoted as asserting that "Britain is becoming Europe's Pacific Rim. The industrial-relations framework, the cultural and linguistic environments, economic deregulation and political stability have changed the face of British manufacturing. Any manufacturer that wants to come to Britain can make a success quickly, because there are no negatives left here" (*Sunday Times*, October 13, 1996). This success has been bought at substantial human cost.

It is worth noting, however, that the Labour government's introduction of a minimum wage, together with its stated policy priorities of education, education, and education may indicate a reversal of the previous government's policy in this respect.

Privatization and "marketification"

The UK has been undergoing a process of rapid withdrawal of the state from economic activity through privatization. The recent British view has been that "market forces" and unbridled competition would of themselves lead to competitively priced, high-quality products and services. The appropriate products and services would be provided through the mechanism of supply and demand, where consumers of those products and services would continually make rational and fully informed choices between conflicting options.

This process has subjected all aspects of British life to its vagaries. While direct taxes have decreased, indirect taxes have increased, the gulf between the rich and the poor is ever widening, the poor and unemployed are disenfranchised, and their labor is bought and sold as a commodity. The marketification of the UK is perceived as a dehumanizing process for those who are not receiving its financial benefits. Furthermore, the costs of this process are borne by all citizens due to the ever-increasing social costs paid by taxpayers.

The philosophy of marketification has been followed through in the institutions of the UK. The remaining state entities, such as the National Health Service (NHS) and the government departments, have been changed in line with neoclassical market-based views of economic and business management. While there was some opposition to this process, the power of the Conservative government to impose its will, through the UK's parliamentary system, was high and continuous over a 17-year period, until its defeat by the Labour Party in 1997.

In the case of the NHS, a great internal market of health care consumers (general practitioners, acting as purchasing agents for their patients) and producers (the hospitals providing health care) was established. In the case of government departments, they were required to enter into a process of "competitive tendering," under which external private firms were asked to tender to carry out previously internal departmental functions. Many government functions have been formed into semi-autonomous "agencies," such as the Driver Vehicle Licensing Agency and the Highways Agency, whose functions are to carry out tasks using the managerial precepts and ethos of private sector companies without close public scrutiny.

Changes in the labor market have steadily increased the level of uncertainty and anxiety among the people of the UK, as in other countries, and have precluded many from making long-term decisions. This short-termism in employment prospects, coupled with increased commodification (labor being treated as a tradable commodity), has been a requirement of businesses that focus on the returns achieved per quarter, rather than on the long-term health and development of business and society.

As long ago as June 1986, Nigel Lawson decried the short-term pressure placed on institutional investors and the resultant tendency for them not to support long-term investment and research and development. The government has not taken any substantive action to deal with this issue. Again, it would prefer the market to rule.

The changes in the modern UK are not only economic. In the social sphere, the post-war welfare state, which was established to provide a reasonable standard of living, health care, education, etc. for all members of society, has gradually seen its scope and funding reduced, with a corresponding increase in the role of private welfare provision.

The nature of the contract between the citizen and the state has changed substantially, with the UK moving closer to the American model in which the corollary of increased rewards for enterprise is an increase in the disparity between rich and poor. As a result, the UK now has one of the largest gaps in the western world between these two groups.

There is an increasing backlash to this process. A growing debate, led by Will Hutton and Richard Hoggart among others, concerning the marketification of the UK and its damage to the quality and nature of British life recently took place nationally. Seventeen years of Conservative government have led to some economic gains but enormous social costs. Events such as the shooting and murder of a number of very young children at a school in the Scottish village of Dunblane, and the stabbing and murder of a school head-teacher when he tried to stop a pupil from being beaten up by a gang, have led to a consensus that the social changes in the UK are unacceptable. A campaign to outlaw the private ownership of handguns, initiated by the parents of the Dunblane children, caught the public mood and forced the government into banning the private ownership of all but the smallest-caliber handguns. The wife of the murdered headteacher appealed to the nation for a return to sound moral values. Her call led to the drafting up of a statement of national moral values, which is now to be taught to all children. The government, pressured by public indignation at the increasingly violent society in which they live, has announced a move to control the degree of sex, violence, and drug-related content in children's television programs, and to increase the strictness of film classification criteria, especially for video. These changes are symptomatic of two major ills in the UK:

♦ The impact of increased crime and self-centeredness, resulting from an increasingly fragmented and uncaring social attitude. This phenomenon is worsened by the break-up of communities, work patterns, employment opportunities, and family-based support networks.
♦ The lack of public regard for the institutions of the state. While the UK public institutions may have been considered to be relatively effective in earlier days, they are now perceived to have lost their way.

Members of Parliament are no longer held in the high public regard that they once enjoyed. Corruption allegations, the arrogance of the previous Conservative government, and an increase in MPs' pay by over 30 percent while other public sector employees, such as doctors and nurses, have seen increases below the rate of inflation, have damaged all MPs' credibility as representatives and leaders of the nation.

The House of Lords has provided a useful "second chamber" where intelligent debate and legislative review have taken place away from electoral pressures. However, a growing number of people are of the view that members of the Lords who are there only because of an inherited title should not retain their places. Reform of hereditary rights is now under way by the Government.

The Church of England is no longer regarded, by the vast majority of the British, as the guardian of national morals. Indeed, it was a private individual, as we have seen, who called for a debate on morality that led to the drafting of a statement of morals, which is now to be taught in all schools.

The monarchy, under the long and exemplary reign of the current queen, has guided and supported the people of the UK. The marital problems of some of the younger members of the royal family have damaged the prestige, perceived sobriety, and future of the monarchy.

The call for substantive reform of the major institutions of the state to meet the needs of the twenty-first century is gathering force.

Commodification of labor

Some national attitudes also hamper the British ability to obtain the best outcome from participation in and encouragement of competitive markets. Tayeb (1993) lists the following:

- Capital market short-termism.
- Less-than-favorable attitudes to business.
- Traditionalism and a reluctance to embrace new technology wholeheartedly.
- Antipathetic industrial relations.
- Ill-prepared school leavers and university graduates.

These attitudes have led to a capital market structure where institutional investors hold about 70 percent of the listed shares available on the London Stock Exchange, and therefore have great economic power.

Investors are rewarded through annual dividends and are informed by analysts' recommendations and relative share performance among other factors, leading companies to focus on the achievement of quarterly financial returns. This short-termism leads to the need for managers to be able to take on and dispose of the resources necessary to carry out their business on the basis of short-term fluctuations in demand for products. As we have seen, this has led to the increasing use of short-term contracts and casual or temporary labor, which has increased uncertainty in the stability, longevity, and quality of employment and income.

The endemic short-termism of markets and the commodification of labor impact on both the economic and social well-being of the people of the UK. This is currently a major issue that is being discussed at all levels (for a more detailed discussion, see Hutton, 1996).

The UK has, according to some commentators, sacrificed the ideas of social justice to the greedy search for individual economic gain, regardless of the consequences for the nation as a whole. Money is important to people in the UK and is increasing in importance due to the need for money to obtain good health care, education, safe housing, etc. It is clear that a return to the "cradle to grave" welfare state is not possible, yet many Britons feel that the pendulum has swung too far in the other direction.

Cultural ebb and flow

The UK is influenced by the cultural traditions of its group of Anglo-Saxon nations, its own particular history, and global events. In the post-Bretton Woods economy, during the global move toward the liberalization of capital markets, the UK was an early adopter of these ideas. Its adoption of market capitalism has made its financial sector a world leader, but it has also led to criticism about the lack of domestic focus and the support of domestic manufacturing industry. The City of London is appreciated more in the "Far East than in Northern Britain" (*Financial Times*, 1996). This early adoption of a worldwide stance accords with the individualism of the British noted by Hofstede.

The UK has alliances with its Anglo-Saxon group of nations, the Commonwealth, and now increasingly with mainland Europe. The world economy is no longer a place in which individual nation-states can continue to prosper in isolation, continuously buffeted by global trends and forces. The UK's strategy, based on and informed by its cultural antecedents, is to be an integral part of the global economy. However, the UK needs to be aware that global forces are leading to the increasing banding together of nation-states into regional groupings – NAFTA, ASEAN, the EU, etc. It needs to wholeheartedly involve itself in its region, the European Union, if it wishes to retain any chance of maintaining its position as one of the seven biggest world economies. This involvement poses as many challenges as it brings benefits, given the UK's distinctively individualistic culture and history.

The dichotomy between, on the one hand, remaining a small, though in some areas (e.g. the financial sector) very important pebble, buffeted by global economic, commercial, and political tides; or, on the other hand, allying itself with the boulder of the European Union, is the crucial issue for the UK's future and is hotly debated.

The general election held on May 1, 1997, led to the election, with an overwhelming majority, of the new Labour government led by Mr Tony Blair. The prime minister will have to decide the UK's future response to these issues.

Acknowledgments

The author wishes to acknowledge the very useful observations made on an earlier draft of this chapter by Professor Peter Lawrence (Loughborough University Business School) and David Bailey (Birmingham Business School, University of Birmingham), both in the UK.

Bibliography

Bailey, D., Harte, G. and Sugden, R. (1994) *Making Transnationals Accountable: A Significant Step for Britain*, London: Routledge.

Bryson, B. (1995) *Notes from a Small Island*, London: Doubleday.

Hamilton, R., Morison, I.C. and ul-Haq, R. (1996) "Towards a working definition of a 'strategic alliance,' " conference paper presented at the ESRC Fellows' Research Colloquium, University of Leeds, UK, March 25.

Hoggart, R. (1995) *The Way We Live Now*, London: Chatto & Windus.

Hutton, W. (1996) *The State We're In*, London: Vintage.

Lawrence, P. (1996) "Through the glass darkly: towards a characterisation of British management," in Glover, I. and Hughes, M. (eds), *The Professional Managerial Classes*, Aldershot: Avebury.

Lawrence, P. (1996) *Management in the USA*, London: Sage.

Lawrence, P. and ul-Haq, R. (1998) "Qualitative research into strategic alliances," *Qualitative Market Research: An Integrational Journal*, vol. 1, no.1, MCB University Press, UK, pp. 15–24.

List, F. (1904) *The National System of Political Economy*, London: Longman.

Morison, I.C. and ul-Haq, R. (1997) "Banking sector alliances – is there scope for increased cooperation?", OMIS Working Series, no. 972, Birmingham Business School, University of Birmingham, UK, September.

Savery, L., Mazzarol, T. and Dawkins, P. (1996) "The quality of British management: Asia Pacific perceptions," Warwick Business School Research Bureau, no. 228, March.

Stone, N. and Barraclough, G. (eds), (1989) *The Times Atlas of World History* (3rd edn), London: Times Books.

Tayeb, M. (1993) "English culture and business organisations", in Hickson, D.J. (ed.), *Management in Western Europe: Society, Culture and Organisation in Twelve Nations*, Berlin: De Gruyter.

Editor's introduction: the Netherlands

The Netherlands – literally, the "Low countries" – is in large part a land recovered from the sea. If, as Arnold Toynbee believed, civilization is a response to challenge, then the Netherlands is an ongoing response to a relentless challenge. Perhaps it is this constant struggle with the sea which explains both the solid ("stolid," some would say) character of the Dutch and their natural propensity for sea-faring and, thus, for trade.

However, there is a second challenge which the Dutch have met: the challenge of a small nation without natural defenses. The Dutch suffered a lengthy occupation by the Spanish and, more recently, invasion and brutal occupation by Germany. The Dutch emerged from this double crucible as hard-headed business people and strong democrats.

The Netherlands has also coalesced into a mini-Europe. The cultural distance from the Calvinist north to the Catholic south is considerable, even if the geographical distance is not. As a result, the Netherlands falls not too far from the center of Geert Hofstede's cultural maps. In a word, the Dutch can work – and trade – with anyone.

Is it this central cultural position which explains the Netherlands' consistent support for Europe? Or is it fear of yet another invasion? Or again the belief in federation and democracy? In any case, Dutch attachment to Europe is real and profound.

Issues meriting further discussion are as follows:

- Is the Netherlands a model for Europe, given its strong economy and its equally strong system of social protection?
- Virtually deprived of natural resources, the Netherlands has nonetheless succeeded economically. How do you explain this?
- What role do you see the Netherlands, as a small but open nation, playing within the European Union?

The Netherlands

Area: 41,526 sq km

Language: Dutch

Currency: Guilder (Fl)

Population: 15.7 million (Jan 1998)

Main cities and population: (Jan 1997)

Amsterdam (capital)	1,103,000
Rotterdam	1,079,000
The Hague (seat of govt)	697,000
Utrecht	551,000

5

♦ ♦ ♦

The Netherlands

Albert Hovius
IBS Groningen, Netherlands

Introduction

The Netherlands, also widely known as Holland, is the biggest of the smaller members of the European Union from the economic perspective. Its main port, Rotterdam, situated at the mouth of the River Rhine, is the world's leading one, and can be regarded as the gateway to Europe. The combination of a population of just over 15.3 million and the smallness of the area makes it the most densely populated country in Europe, with over 400 people per square kilometer.

Since the country has a multiparty system with three major political parties and quite a number of smaller ones, governments are always coalitions. In 1994, the outcome of the elections and political negotiations afterwards led to a coalition of the Dutch Labour Party and the Liberal Party, with the support of one of the smaller political parties. Thus, for the first time in the last 70 years, the Christian Democrats were in the opposition. This can be regarded as a novelty in Dutch politics and it may be a token of a culture change. Over the next two years, this government seriously began to redefine the welfare state by drastically pruning some of its very generous benefits. The combination of low inflation, a relatively high growth rate, one of the lowest unemployment rates, and a diminishing budget deficit makes the Netherlands one of the first countries in the European Union to qualify for participation in the European Monetary Union, the EMU.

Geography

In the north-west, the European continent gradually drops off to meet the North Sea. In the early history of this region of mainland Europe, the delta of three major rivers, the Rhine, the Meuse, and the Scheldt, was referred to as the "Low Countries." These flat, wet coastal plains, criss-crossed by the numerous ramifications of these rivers, were low in contrast to the hills and mountains of central and southern Europe. In the eastern and southern parts of the region, there are a few ranges of lower hills, pushed up as lateral moraines by the Saale glaciers in the Pleistocene era. This part of the country is now named the High Netherlands, in contrast to the Low Netherlands in the north and west.

The very cold Saale period, roughly between 200,000 and 180,000 years ago, disrupted the global water cycle. The seas fell to a much lower level than today, and the northern part of the Netherlands was completely covered by huge icecaps. The icecaps contained large boulders from as far away as Scandinavia. The boulders were later, around 3000 BC, used by the early settlers for their typical "megaliths" or graves. More than 50 of these very old graves can be found predominantly in the province of Drenthe, in the north of the country. Toward the end of the Pleistocene era, temperatures went up once more, and water stored for thousands of years in large expanses of snow and ice began to melt. The seas rose more than 50 meters over a period of some 10,000 years, and the North Sea basin filled up again to meet the boundaries of the High Netherlands. The Low Netherlands became a huge marsh, criss-crossed by rivers and their tributaries.

The ridge at Bretany broke down and Britain became an island around 7000 BC. This created a constant flow of water along the coastline of the Low Countries, throwing into the North Sea huge amounts of sand, which were carried down by the rivers Meuse, Rhine, and Scheldt. The sand banks eventually dried up and became important protective barriers against the sea. Behind these banks, lagoons developed, which gradually silted up and created a large area of marshland. Vegetation under wet and swampy circumstances eventually created a surface peat layer. In later centuries, large amounts of the peat were dug out, dried, and used for fuel. The dug-out areas filled up with water and became lakes, which enlarged themselves during heavy storms. In the course of the fifteenth, sixteenth, and seventeenth centuries, these lakes were drained gradually by usage of windmills, one of the national symbols of the country. The Amsterdam (Schiphol) Airport is located on the bottom of one of these former lakes, the "Haarlemmermeer."

Around 50 BC, when the Romans were expanding their empire to the north, they found the Low Countries thinly populated by Frisian tribes in the west and north, by Saxons in the eastern parts, by Franconians in the southern regions, and by Bataves, perhaps a Celtic tribe, between the rivers Rhine and Meuse. The Romans were quite surprised that people could actually survive in such a hostile environment. Pliny, the Roman historian, wrote: "There, every day and night at twelve-hourly intervals, the sea invades the land with immense waves over a vast area, so that in the eternal struggle people do not know whether the ground belongs to the earth or to the sea." In his *Annals*, Publius Cornelius Tacitus mentioned the "Frisii," among other Germanic tribes, as the inhabitants of the coast of the Low Countries. Only the name of the Frisians remains.

In the north of the country, where the incoming and outgoing tides had deposited a thick layer of clay, the inhabitants built low mounds to protect themselves from the sea. The old word for such a mound ("weird" or "werd") can still be recognized in many of the placenames of the small communities (e.g. Dorkwerd and Leeuwarden). In the western parts of the country, the early settlers were regularly confronted with changes in the courses of the rivers. In their attempts to tame the slowly flowing but massive rivers, dams and dikes were built. This activity is also still reflected in names of cities, such as Amsterdam (dam on the little River Amstel) and Rotterdam (dam on the River Rotte). Towards the end of the twelfth century, monks started the continuous process of land reclamation by building dikes around the slightly higher wetlands. Windmill technology, invented in the early thirteenth century and further developed into a pumping mechanism, made it possible to reclaim the marshlands in the western part of the country. The impression of the Netherlands that exists in the minds of many people from other countries is amply confirmed by the view that greets the eye of the traveler flying into Amsterdam Schiphol Airport. The country is flat, neatly divided into rectangular lots, green, and crossed by numerous small watercourses.

The Zuyder Sea, the large inland sea, has been subject to reclamation plans since as far back as the seventeenth century. At that time, a Dutch engineer and inventor, Hendrix Stevin, launched plans to reclaim the whole area. It would take more than 250 years and several plans before the Zuyder Sea was cut off from the North Sea by the Barrier Dam in 1932. After that, five polders could be created in the area formerly claimed by the sea, consisting of a total surface of roughly 225,000 hectares, surrounded by reserves of fresh water. Hence the saying: "God created the world, but the Dutch created Holland."

Until recently, the battle between the waters from seas and rivers and the people of the Netherlands has been a contest with varying fortunes. At intervals, disastrous floods brought to nought the human efforts, with high death tolls (e.g. the Saint Elizabeth's Flood of 1421 and, most recently, the February Flood of 1953, during which almost 2,000 people drowned). In order to prevent all possible future floods, the government launched a multi-billion-dollar project, "The Delta Project," entailing the further reinforcement of dikes and the closing of some dangerous openings to the sea. In this respect, many people know the story of the "Boy with his finger in the dike," who prevented disaster by stopping a leak with his finger. Curiously enough, the story is almost unknown in the country itself.

The fight against the waters required a well-organized and disciplined society. And from a very early stage in the country's history, a dense pattern of "water control boards," headed by a "dike count," covered the entire country. More than 40 percent of the country is below, or almost below, sea level and would be flooded should the dikes be removed. The country's lowest spot (more than 6 meters below sea level) is situated close to the city of Rotterdam.

History

For the Romans, the River Rhine effectively formed the northern border of the Roman Empire. Many times they attempted to subdue the population north of the Rhine, but they never really managed to gain complete control over the area. And the Frisians managed to maintain their relative independence after a revolt against the Romans in AD 28. Names given to certain areas still stress the relative importance of these tribes: the region north of Amsterdam is known as West Friesland and the north-west region of Germany is called Ost (East) Friesland. Nowadays one of the 12 provinces of the Netherlands is still called "Friesland," and the Frisian language is spoken by quite a high percentage of the local population. It is also recognized as the official language in the administration. The Frisian language is one of the languages in the Anglo-Frisian branch of the Germanic languages, and is closer to English than to Dutch or German. As of the early 1980s, it even became a compulsory language in secondary schools in that province. One very interesting aspect is that strong stereotypical traits are attributed to the Frisians, not only in the Netherlands, but in Germany too. They are supposed to be silent, reserved, and stubborn.

Toward the end of the third century, the Roman Empire started to weaken, due to internal problems and the devastating incursions by Germanic tribes from the north. Eventually, the Romans handed over the defense of the north to the Franconians, a tribe already settled in "Texandria," now known as Brabant. The establishment of later linguistic boundaries between the Germanic and Romance languages is heavily influenced by this migration of tribes. Eventually it was the Franconian Carolingian dynasty that managed to exercise a more stable form of control over the country. One of the rulers from this dynasty, Clovis I, expanded the territory in the south and the east. He founded a new kingdom, the Merovingian, and took the important step of conversion to Christianity.

In the eighth century, the Carolingians, who had grown powerful in the service of the Merovingians, ousted them and took over. The best-known representative of the Carolingians is Charlemagne. At the peak of his power, his realm stretched from the Low Countries in the north as far as the Pyrenees and far to the east of the River Rhine. He even forced the Frisians and the Saxons to officially adopt Christianity. He reorganized the administrative system by redividing the realm into smaller entities, governed by officers of the king. Eventually, he had himself crowned emperor by the Pope in Rome in AD 800, and tried to stop cultural decline by attracting scientists and artists from the Anglo-Saxon islands and from Italy.

Later, the realm was divided in three among his grandsons. This was the beginning of a gradual decline. Indeed, much of what had been achieved was lost. Only after AD 1000 did French kings and German emperors bring order to western Europe. Formally, the German emperor became the feudal lord to the Netherlands. The era between the tenth and the fourteenth centuries witnessed the transformation of regional states into provinces of a kingdom. The Low Countries were made up of 17 provinces in which the richer upper class in the cities, the burghers, gradually increased their political influence and power.

Through clever marriages, the Habsburger Maximilian of Austria managed to become the ruler of the main part of the Low Countries. His son Philip I married Joan of Aragon, daughter of the Spanish king. In 1519, after Joan and her father had died, Philip's son Charles V inherited Spain and its American colonies, the German Empire, and the "Lordship of the Netherlands," as it was now officially named for the first time. After the death of Charles V, the throne went to his son Philip II, an earnest man dedicated to maintaining the authority of both the monarchy and the Roman Catholic religion. He sent his sister Margaretha as a regent to the region, since he was too busy fighting the Turks at the borders of Austria. This, however, coincided with the emergence of Protestantism. The most northern parts of the country, in particular, were very much in favor of the new religion as they were opposed to the "Spanish" rulers. Over time, the citizens of the cities had developed a strong sense of independence and self-confidence.

The swarm of "heresies" coincided with an economic downturn in the provinces of Flanders and Brabant, two important contributors to tax collection. A drastic reorganization of the tax system, proposed by Philip II, proved to be unacceptable to the people. A group of "stadholders," led by William of Orange, tried to persuade Philip to change his tax plans, but they failed. The rising discontent about Philip's complete lack of understanding and the Iconoclastic Fury added more fuel to the latent fire. Philip replaced his sister by a new regent, the Duke of Alva, who was given the task of exterminating Protestantism and opposition.

Two of William of Orange's supporters, the counts of Egmond and Hoorn, were arrested and beheaded. This fact is traditionally regarded as the beginning of the Eighty Years War, which led eventually to the formation of the Netherlands. The 17 provinces first united in the revolt against the Spanish king, but failed to reach an agreement on religion and a form of government. Then the southern provinces made a separate Treaty of Arras with Philip, pledging their allegiance to him. The seven northern provinces signed the Treaty of Utrecht in 1581, declaring that they no longer recognized Philip II as their king. This resulted in the ultimate separation of the north from the south, both politically and religiously. Over a relatively short period of time, after the fall of Antwerp to Spanish troops, an exodus of tens of thousands, predominantly rich and powerful, people from the southern provinces started, adding substantial resources to the north. This combined with the growing importance in international trade of the provinces of Zeeland and Holland to create an unprecedented economic upswing, the beginning of the Golden Age.

Entrepreneurial merchants sent out fleets to discover new markets, and expeditions to open the way to south-east Asia. They set up a supply station in South Africa and joined efforts to form trading companies. Earnings were abundant and gave rise to an ever-increasing demand for beautiful dwellings, not only from individuals, but from local authorities too. These structures were decorated richly with paintings by the famous painters of the times – Rembrandt, Vermeer, Jan Steen, and Frans Hals. The two most important trading companies were the United East Indian Company (VOC), with a trade monopoly between the Cape of Good Hope and the Straits of Magellan, and the West Indian Company (WIC), once the administrator of New Amsterdam, or New York as it later became. In this period, the Netherlands laid the foundations for its later colonial power, in Asia (Indonesia), America (Surinam), and the Dutch Antilles. The government normally did not interfere with imports and exports, and the Dutch comparative advantages in trade and transportation made the country a firm advocate of the principle of free trade. Hugo de Groot or Grotius became renowned as a jurist and for his works on the freedom of the seas. Other well-known scientists were Christian Huygens (inventor of the pendulum clock), Jan Swammerdam, and the philosopher Spinoza. The downturn began in the early decades of the eighteenth century, due to the combination of complacency and lack of momentum – the price of being such a small country.

The republic's political decisions were made in joint meetings of representatives (Staten Generaal) from the seven provinces, of which Holland was the most powerful. A member of the House of Orange always had the position of stadholder or vice-regent, as appointed by the Staten Generaal. Toward the end of the eighteenth century, tensions between two groups, the Patriots and the Orangists, started to grow. The Orangists were in strong support of the stadholder, while the Patriots were touched by the ideals of the French Revolution. Eventually, the Patriots won and ousted the stadholder, who fled to England. In 1795 the French army overran the country and the Netherlands at first became a vassal state of the French Empire, before being finally annexed by Napoleon. The impact of the French occupation is reflected still in the organization of the country and in its legal system, based on the principle of the Law Code.

Gradually, the initial enthusiasm for the French tapered off. After Napoleon's defeat, the people were happy to see the French leave and invited the House of Orange to come back. The Congress of Vienna (1815) unified the northern and the southern Netherlands again, thus once more creating the Low Countries as an entity. William I, son of the last stadholder, became the first king of the constitutional monarchy; the first monarch from the House of Orange, of which the current queen Beatrix is the sixth generation. Due to the length of separation, the different religions, and economic development, the unification did not work out. In 1830 the southern provinces started to revolt. Thereafter, Belgium (the southern Netherlands) officially broke away from the Netherlands in 1839 and became a monarchy in its own right.

Culture

In Geert Hofstede's well-known cross-cultural studies, he distinguishes a number of characteristics typical for the members of a specific society or culture. The most important dimensions are: power distance, uncertainty avoidance, masculinity versus femininity, and individualism versus collectivism. The Dutch people show the following characteristics:

- A small power distance, tending toward an egalitarian society.
- Weak uncertainty avoidance, indicating an openness to new situations.
- Rather feminine, creating a caring society, with very individualistic members.

The combination of these cultural idiosyncrasies governs social relations and is incorporated into the way people do business. Seats in buses, trains, theatres, etc. will fill up in such a way that proximity is postponed as long as possible and people seldom speak to each other, unless acquainted. Individualism and a strong sense of privacy are thus expressed. The sons of Queen Beatrix lived normal lives as university students. As mentioned, it is an egalitarian society. So even members of the royal family are expected to behave like everyone else. Showing off is not acceptable. Thus, building expensive and impressive houses, or driving extravagant luxurious cars, to show how well one is doing, is not done. A popular Dutch saying states: "Act normal, that is crazy enough." The title of Simon Schama's work about the Dutch Golden Age, *The Embarrassment of Riches*, indicates exactly the Dutch feelings and attitudes toward wealth. They will deny, hide, and apologize for any wealth they may have, and talking about income is almost a complete taboo. You can ask almost any question, whether family related or not, but you should never bring up the issue of someone's income.

The average Dutch person lives according to a rather strict and, more often than not, self-imposed schedule. Certain activities happen at certain times of the day, and many Dutch people find it difficult to deviate from these schedules without advance warning. Some of these activities are regarded as extremely private family business, such as dinner. Between 6 and 8 p.m. one had better leave the Dutch undisturbed. Unlike people in some other cultures, the Dutch do not automatically invite visitors to stay for dinner; instead they will say, "Sorry, but we are having dinner now. Will you please excuse us?" or something similar.

Dutch society is a consensus society, which implies that confrontations are generally avoided and disputes are settled through instant meetings, in which everyone has his or her say. In 1992, working days lost due to strikes averaged only 15 days for 1,000 workers for the Netherlands, while Belgium lost 30 days and Germany 60. Dutch managers have developed a non-directive management style. (In a recent popular song among Dutch youth, it is explicitly said that "we do not take orders from any one.") As a foreigner, one has to brace for the directness and straightforwardness (some call it bluntness) of the Dutch. The openness of the Netherlands has led to constant exposure to foreigners and foreign customs, mores, values, and languages. In combination with the sense of privacy, this contact resulted in the proverbial liberal attitude of the population, which in turn has attracted persecuted people from other societies. For ages the Dutch have tried to find a way to combine the dogmatic moralism of Calvinism (the rigid religious code) with the easygoing practicality of the merchant. This effort has led to an attitude of almost supreme tolerance for deviating beliefs and behavior.

A good example is the Dutch national drug policy. Although all drugs are illegal in the Netherlands, Dutch authorities distinguish between "soft" and "hard" drugs. Marijuana, regarded as a soft drug, is tolerated for personal usage. The result is that so-called coffee shops, where small amounts of marijuana or hashish can be purchased, exist throughout the country. This kind of flexibility and tolerance accounts for the informal attitude of Dutch business people toward their business partners from other cultures.

On the other hand, traces of Calvinism can be found in the way that Dutch people perceive the world and their role in that world. They seem to know exactly what is right or wrong, and they are always prepared to tell everyone. The proverbial "Dutch uncle," who lectures the world on how to behave and how to act, is an excellent expression of how English-speaking nations perceive the Dutch. Another Dutch saying reflects the flexibility of the Dutch merchant's ideology: "You shall never be a thief of your own purse." Thus, one should be more flexible in business than in religious matters.

In contradiction to the Netherlands' liberal attitude and egalitarian philosophy, the active participation of Dutch women in the labor force has traditionally been one of the lowest in Europe. It has been suggested that Dutch "neutrality" in World War I did not force women to work in the factories as they did in other European countries. Although the participation rate of women has been catching up over the last decade and now ranks close to the European average, the increase is predominantly in the part-time sector and the lower wage brackets. Nevertheless, women are regarded as completely equal to men. While 25 years ago only 20 percent of Dutch students were women, today the gender split is even.

A startling aspect of Dutch society is its apparent lack of pride in its own culture and language in the eyes of a foreigner. Words are very easily borrowed from other languages, incorporated into the vernacular, and treated as if they were Dutch. Recently, the Minister of Education proposed to replace Dutch by English, the international language, in higher education. However, should a foreigner observe the overwhelming abundance of orange, the national color derived from the House of Orange, whenever a Dutch national team plays or when Dutch speed skaters are in competition, he would know that the lack of pride is, indeed, only apparent. The Dutch merely do not show how proud they are to be Dutch on a day-to-day basis.

Economic and commercial structure

The Netherlands economy is a market economy, with a high degree of security built into the system. Three parties are actively involved: the unions, the employers' associations, and the government. The Dutch attitude of avoiding conflicts and striving for consensus has resulted in low numbers of strikes and other work-related conflicts. The other side of the coin is the relatively inflexible labor market. The overall participation in the labor force (just under 50 percent) is one of the lowest in the EU.

After World War II, Dutch politicians decided to build up a social system providing care literally "from the cradle to the grave." This policy was strongly supported by the discovery of what was then the largest-known reserves of natural gas. The government's participation in the development of these reserves created a broad financial base for the implementation of the social system. The system entails generous benefits for the unemployed, disabled workers, and sick workers, and also early retirement schemes. Gradually, Dutch society began to realize that the system had been too generous and that some of the generosity had to be cut.

Recent government policies are a clear sign of this realization. The Labour (red) and Liberal (blue) government, labelled "Purple" on the Dutch political scene, started off with the slogan: "Work, Work, Work." It is strongly believed that a drastic lowering of social payments can effectively contribute to the creation of more employment. This policy is currently practiced in combination with drastic cuts in government expenditure. Dr Tietmeyer, chairman of the German Bundesbank, in a recent speech for journalists in Bonn, stated that the Netherlands is "the best student in the monetary class."

The most important economic sector in the Netherlands is the service sector, employing roughly 70 percent of the total workforce. Industry accounts for a little over 25 percent and the remaining 4.5 percent is in agriculture. High employment in the services underscores the important position of the country in trade and distribution. Rotterdam, with a well-developed hinterland in Germany (the industries of the Ruhr area), and Schiphol, the national airport, illustrate the country's epithet of being the "Gateway to Europe."

The Netherlands' historical role of trading nation has created an international attitude and atmosphere that is reflected in the relative emphasis given to language education. English is almost the second language. Before World War II, the Netherlands was very much focused on the European continent, predominantly on Germany. That situation has changed dramatically. After World War II, Dutch society gradually turned mentally away from Germany and, like many other European societies, became fascinated with the US. German, like French and English a compulsory language in secondary school, lost its position of equality with the other two languages. English is now taught in primary school, French from year 1 and German from year 2 in secondary school. Foreign programs on TV and in cinemas are subtitled. Thus, there is a wide exposure to American and British English. Although Germany is Holland's largest trading partner – Germany accounted for almost 30 percent of total exports and 25 percent of total imports in 1994 – Germany is not a country favored by the majority of the Dutch people.

The Netherlands were "late bloomers" in the Industrial Revolution. Only toward the end of the nineteenth century did the industrialization of chemical and electrical production gather momentum. However, the country hosts some major players in the world of electronics (Philips), oil and oil products (Royal Shell), food production and personal care products (Unilever), and chemicals (DSM and AKZO/Nobel). In terms of added value, the chemical sector is the leader in manufacturing.

Many internationally operating companies have located their headquarters in the

Netherlands – and not only because of its friendly tax environment. The country itself has an open international atmosphere, and in many places international education in English is offered. However, tax policies are indeed used by the Dutch government as a tool in the international competition for investors. Within the legal regulations, the regional tax officers have reasonable freedom of action to negotiate with companies.

In the country's peripheral areas (i.e. the north, the east, and the south), economic development lags behind that in the crowded, completely urbanized west, where 60 percent of the total population is concentrated. In an effort to tackle the underdevelopment and higher unemployment rates in the peripheral areas, the government created Regional Development Agencies. These agencies offer assistance and support to any companies wanting to start new business or expand current business. The support ranges from simple advice to the writing of complete business plans and to participation in the company's financial capital. All prospective investors, whether Dutch or foreign, can benefit from these regulations, since equal opportunity and equal treatment are basic philosophies in this country.

Economic past and future

From the early Middle Ages onwards, in the area that is now the Netherlands, a society gradually developed specializing in agriculture, trading, and fishing. The soil was very good for pasture, but not for grain production. So almost automatically, trading developed, exporting cheese and butter, and importing grain predominantly from the Baltic states. For all these transportation activities, vessels were needed. So shipbuilding became an important industry. Since the region did not produce enough wood for all the planks needed, wood had to be imported from Scandinavia. A special type of freight vessel, the "flute," was invented, with a very high freight to crew ratio. Almost naturally, the Dutch created a competitive advantage in the fields of trade and transport.

A special process to preserve herring was invented in the early fifteenth century. This invention gave rise to a growing fishing industry, with more shipbuilding and the export of salted herring. The fishing industry has lost its important role in the whole of the Dutch economy, but still maintains its image as a basic industry for the country.

Many future Dutch cities, like Deventer, Kampen, Harderwijk, and Groningen, participated in the Hanseatic League, an early attempt to monopolize trade in the region ranging from the River Seine and the Baltic states to the Danube. Later on, the leading positions were taken over by Amsterdam and, even more importantly, Rotterdam.

In the sixteenth and seventeenth centuries, Dutch traders sailed all over the world to find new products, customers, and markets. What had started as the opening of new markets later led to official colonialism in what are now Indonesia, Surinam, and the Dutch Antilles. In the eighteenth and nineteenth centuries, tropical products like coffee, cocoa, tea, and spices were transported to the Netherlands, while textiles were sent from the Netherlands to the colonies. After World War II, Indonesia became an independent republic, and in 1975 Surinam earned independence. The Dutch Antilles are still within the Dutch Kingdom.

After World War II, the consecutive government coalitions of Labour and Christian political parties built up an extensive network of social security. As a consequence, taxes and premiums for social benefits increased from 33.7 percent of GDP in 1960 to over 61 percent of GDP in 1983. From that time on, coalitions of the now merged Christian parties (the Christian Democratic Alliance) and the Liberals have been more or less successful in decreasing total government expenditure as a percentage of GDP. In the mid-1990s, it dropped to almost 50 percent. The coalition of Labour and Liberals effectively continued these austerity policies.

In 1947 the Netherlands formed an economic union with Belgium and Luxembourg, the Benelux, which can be regarded as the forerunner of the European Economic Community. As a trading nation, the Netherlands has been in favor of free trade and, in the framework of the European Union, in favor of expansion. The further unification of Europe is not part of public debate. It is no surprise that a small country like the Netherlands is strongly in favor of "majority rule" instead of the current veto held by each individual country. In 1991, under the Dutch chair, the Treaty of Maastricht was signed. This treaty was geared to creating a single-currency community, the European Monetary Union (EMU). EMU entry requirements for countries were derived from economic performance in certain areas, such as budget deficit as a percentage of GDP, relative inflation, and public debt as a percentage of GDP. The Netherlands was in favor of the strict application of these requirements.

GDP per capita in 1994 was US $21,733, which puts the Netherlands somewhere in the middle of the EU countries, with Denmark in the lead and Greece as the poorest country. Inflation is a very low 2.1 percent, while economic growth is relatively high in EU terms at 2.0 percent. The unemployment rate is 7.2 percent, which is low within the EU framework. As mentioned earlier, the participation rate in the labor force is quite low. For some ten years, preceding the launch of the euro in January 1999, the Dutch guilder was closely linked to the German Deutschmark, creating an informal monetary union between the two countries. This policy of the Dutch Central Bank arose from the importance of Germany for the Dutch economy and the belief in a strict monetary policy, independent of the government.

Throughout its history, the Netherlands has been a trading nation. Its geographical location near highly industrialized neighboring countries helps to maintain the strong Dutch position in international trade and related service industries like banking and insurance. With exports and imports of over 55 percent of its GDP, the Netherlands ranks as one of the most open economies in the world. Over 75 percent of exports go to other member countries of the EU.

Dutch agriculture (dairy products and horticulture) has been very successful due to the close cooperation of skilled farmers, highly sophisticated research institutes, good education, and the government. Presently, the country is one of the major world exporters of agricultural products. The country has some 5 million cows, 15 million pigs, and 100 million chickens. For each hectare of agricultural ground, 7 more hectares outside the country are needed to produce the fodder for all these animals. From outer space, astronauts reported that they could see the sun reflected in the enormous area of Dutch glass houses (hothouses). Products exported range from condensed milk, butter, and cheese, to potatoes, tomatoes, cucumbers, and lettuce, and to poultry, eggs, and cut flowers. Presently, 50 percent of European horticulture under glass is situated in the Netherlands. Many of the advanced technologies used in agricultural production are exported to other countries such as the former eastern and central European countries and countries in the Third World.

At present, the Dutch economy is one of the better performers in Europe. The OECD, however, has suggested that the country should increase its potential growth by abolishing minimum wages and by cutting the link between wages and social benefits. These issues are still politically very hot – perhaps too hot to be handled effectively by the current coalition. The feminine characteristics indicated by Hofstede suggest, perhaps, that the tension between the soft caring side of Dutch society and the harder economic side of political necessity will increase. However, as the former president of the Central Bank, Mr Duisenberg, says, the reduction of the budget deficit should continue till it reaches a maximum of 1 percent of GDP, taking into account the cost increase for the ageing population. Mr Duisenberg became the first president of the European Central Bank.

Bibliography

Central Statistical Office (CBS), *Statistisch Jaarboek.*
Cock Buning, A. de and Verheijen, L. (1987) *The Netherlands in Brief*, Foreign Information Service, Ministry of Foreign Affairs.
Commission of the European Communities Country Studies, *The Netherlands.*
Hampden-Turner, C. and Trompenaars, F. (1994) *The Seven Cultures of Capitalism*, London: Judy Piatkus.
Hofstede, G. (1991) *Cultures and Organisations: Software of the Mind*, New York: McGraw-Hill.
Horst, H. van der (1996) *The Low Sky*, The Hague: Scriptum.
OECD Economic Surveys, *The Netherlands.*
Schama, S. (1987) *The Embarrassment of Riches*, New York: Knopf.
Somers, F. (1994) *European Community Economics*, Harlow: Longman.
Wedford, R. and Prescott, K. (1992) *European Business*, London: Pitman.
Woltjer, J.J. (1992) *Recent verleden* (Recent Past), Amsterdam: Balans.

The Netherlands: Distribution of turnover in industry
Composition of exports, 1997

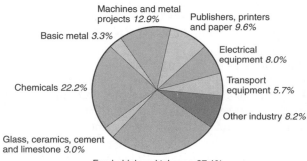

Machines and metal projects *12.9%*

Publishers, printers and paper *9.6%*

Basic metal *3.3%*

Electrical equipment *8.0%*

Chemicals *22.2%*

Transport equipment *5.7%*

Other industry *8.2%*

Glass, ceramics, cement and limestone *3.0%*

Food, drink and tobacco *27.1%*

Total: Fl288bn (Euro 130.9bn)

Source: Statistics Netherlands (CBS)

PART II

The former EFTA countries:
The failure of loose federation

Editor's introduction: Switzerland

Look at any political map of western Europe and you will find in the center a gray spot that looks much like the "empty quarter" in the Middle East. What is this irreducible patch in the middle of the surrounding European Union? Why does it resist merging with the rest of western Europe? Switzerland is a sort of independent island in the midst of the EU which is proud of its independence. In fact, as Alexander Bergmann points out, Switzerland defines itself in opposition to its surrounding neighbors. Yet, Switzerland participates in almost any European institution you would care to think of, through a series of special agreements. As a result, Switzerland is both inside and outside of Europe.

What then are the issues for further thought?

♦ Among the traditionally neutral European nations (Switzerland, Austria, Sweden, and Ireland), only Switzerland has remained outside the EU. Why?
♦ What are the strengths and weaknesses of Switzerland *vis-à-vis* the EU?
♦ To your mind, what conditions must be met for the Swiss to want to join the EU?

Switzerland

Area: 41,286 sq km

Languages: German (64%), French (19%), Italian (8%), Romansch (1%), Others (8%)

Currency: Swiss Franc (SFr)

Population: 7.1m (average 1996 official estimate)

Constitution

National government
Federal Council (the executive authority) of seven members elected for a four-year term by, but not necessarily from, the Federal Assembly. The president and vice-president are elected for a one-year term which is not immediately renewable. Since 1959 the Federal Council has contained two members each of the Social Democratic party, the Radical Democratic party and the Christian Democratic party, and one member from Swiss People's party. The Federal Council was re-elected in December 1995

National legislature
Bicameral Federal Assembly (parliament), comprising the National Council and Council of States. National Council of 200 members directly elected by proportional representation using the Hagenbach-Bischoff quota, except in the smallest cantons where the single representative is elected by the plurality (first-past-the-post) system. Council of States of 46 members representing the cantons. Any law passed by both houses may be submitted to a referendum if demanded by eight cantons or 50,000 citizens

State legislatures
Each of the 26 cantons and half-cantons has a parliament elected by universal suffrage and a government whose organisation varies from canton to canton. In five, the principle of universal sovereignty is exercised directly through assemblies of all voters. The cantons are sovereign in all areas not specifically entrusted to the federal government

Main political parties
Radical Democratic party (RDP); Social Democratic party (SDP); Cristian Democratic party (CDP); Swiss People's party (PP); Liberal party; Ecology party; Independent Alliance

Economic summary	1997 (estimate)	1998 (forecast)
Total GDP, nominal ($bn)	253.9	270.6
Real GDP growth (annual % change)	0.6	1.9
GDP per head ($)	35,733	37,898
Inflation (annual % change in CPI)	0.5*	1.0
Average wages (annual % change)	0.9	1.5
Industrial production, ex construction (annual % change)	3.5	5.7
Unemployment rate** (% of labour force)	5.2*	4.9
Three-month Euro-deposit (%)	1.5*	2.1
Reserves excluding gold, December ($bn)	35.0	n.a.
Federal government budget balance*** (% of GDP)	−1.7	−2.0
Current account balance ($bn)	19.6	18.8
Merchandise exports ($bn)	88.6	94.1
Merchandise imports ($bn)	−89.7	−95.7
Trade balance ($bn)	−1.1	−1.6

* Actual ** National rate *** Confederation

Main trading partners (share of total trade to world 1996)

EXPORTS

Germany	France	US	Italy	EU 15	Efta 4
23.3%	9.4%	9.0%	7.7%	61.4%	0.6%
32.8%	12.0%	6.6%	11.3%	80.2%	0.3%

IMPORTS

6

Switzerland and Europe

Alexander Bergmann
HEC (Hautes Etudes Commerciales), Lausanne, Switzerland

Although small, Switzerland is a complex country; indeed, a country of contradictions. For example, after Israel, it is the most heavily armed country in the world, but it has had no war since longer than anyone can remember. Switzerland is reputed to be quite xenophobic, but it has the highest percentage (over 18 percent) of foreigners in Europe except Luxembourg. It is a country in which everybody knows and observes everybody else, leading to considerable pressures for conformity, but it is also a country of stubborn, secretive individualists. It is equally reputed to be rather sexist (it granted women the right to vote and to be elected only in 1971), but it has today a percentage of women in public office which is exceeded in Europe only by the Nordic countries. It is rather inward looking (*Kantonlisgeist*), but also very international, with over 50 percent of GNP derived from international operations. It is almost the only country in the world not to be in the United Nations, but it hosts the UN and several of its specialized organizations in Geneva. It has been viscerally anti-communist, but this did not prevent it from doing business with practically all communist countries. It is profoundly "free market," but only 20 percent of the prices are set by market mechanisms (55 percent by public authorities and 25 percent by cartels). It is a materialistic country (its richness is not a matter of luck!), but it is also the cradle of the Red Cross and of numerous other humanitarian and philanthropic organizations.

Finally, it has so far refused to follow the example of all of its neighbors and join them in a united Europe, but it is the home of some of the most fervent Europeans and hosts the archives of Jean Monnet (the "father of Europe") as well as those of Robert Schumann. Just after World War II, Switzerland was a privileged meeting place for those Europeans who hoped to promote European unity. It is no accident that Winston Churchill made his famous plea for the union of the people of Europe at the University of Zurich in 1946. Indeed, Switzerland has a peculiar, unique, and very ambiguous relationship with Europe. It is in the heart of Europe and is somewhat an island in Europe. It is possibly the most and at the same time the least European of countries. In Switzerland, you find some of the most inveterate isolationists, but also some of the most passionate Europeans.

In this chapter, we will examine this small, contradictory nation in the center of Europe from several viewpoints. First, we will discuss the forces for unity with Europe, turning thereafter to the factors separating the Swiss from other Europeans. We will also explore what Switzerland has to offer the European Union and vice versa.

Let us begin by looking at Switzerland as part of Europe, and even Switzerland as the heart of Europe. Geographically, Switzerland occupies a central position among France, Germany, Austria, and Italy. Strategically, it commands the major transit lines from north to south. Historically, it is part of the central kingdom established by the partition of the Carolingian Empire – the only unified, albeit partial, Europe that ever existed. It remained part of the Holy Roman Empire until the Treaty of Westphalia in 1648. Culturally, it takes part in two of the four major European cultural families, the Germanic and the Latin (the other two being the Anglo-Saxon and the Slavic). As for its value orientations, in a study evaluating various European countries on two dimensions (dynamism–inertia and traditional values–hedonism), Switzerland found itself at the very center – that is, at the intersection between the two scales. Economically, about half of its national product comes from dealings with and in foreign countries, almost two-thirds of which are European.

Switzerland's historic, economic, and cultural development is intimately linked not only to that of its neighboring countries – that is, Germany and Austria, France and Italy – but also to many other European countries. Thus, let us take only a few recent examples. While Switzerland has been traveled by numerous celebrities, such as Casanova, Goethe, Victor Hugo, Lord Byron, Turner, and Felix Mendelssohn, and has hosted others for longer periods, such as Sainte-Beuve, Charles Dickens, Franz Liszt, Nicolas Gogol, and Marie Curie, and, more recently, Stravinski, Rainer Maria Rilke, Thomas Mann, Nietzsche, Balthus, and Yehudi Menuhin (but also Mussolini), the development of its tourism is largely due to the interest that English vacationers took in the Swiss Alps around the turn of the century. Other VIPs have elected to take residence in Switzerland, whether they come from show business, like Charlie Chaplin, Audrey Hepburn, Alain Delon, and David Bowie, or from sports, like Jacky Stewart and Alain Prost, or are industrialists, like Horten, Gunther Sachs, Baron Thyssen, and so many others. Still others took refuge here: Lenin, De Coubertin (this is why the International Olympic Committee is still in Lausanne), Ignacy Paderewski, Bertold Brecht, and various European royal families, such as the Spanish, after the Spanish Civil War, the Belgian during World War II, and the Romanian, Albanian, and Yugoslav after their countries turned to communism. Switzerland also gave a new home to many less illustrious refugees from Hungary and Czechoslovakia after the 1956 and 1968 revolutions. Furthermore, the country entertains privileged relations with other neutral countries, such as Liechtenstein (with which it has a monetary and postal union), Austria, and Sweden. Let us also not forget that the cradle of one of the families that most marked Europe over the centuries, the castle of Habsburg, is in Switzerland. Moreover, two of the three most important European rivers, the Rhône and the Rhine, have their source at the Gotthard, as do one of the major confluents of the Danube, the Inn, and the biggest Italian river, the Po.

Switzerland is today the only country in Europe where multiculturalism (four languages and cultures have official status!) seems to work without major friction. Thus, it has repeatedly been considered a model for Europe. Its political organization of bottom-up federalism, which respects and protects the regional particularisms and leaves a maximum of competencies to local authorities, has equally been proposed as an example to be imitated by a proposed "Europe of regions."

Switzerland apart from Europe

However, while it is impossible to dissociate Switzerland from Europe, Switzerland has from its very origin tried to differentiate itself and to maintain some distance from Europe.

Indeed, Switzerland was created by an act of revolt by what were to become three Cantons against the domination of the Habsburgs, the emperors of the Holy Roman Empire, of which Switzerland was then a part. Ever since, the glue that holds Switzerland together has been not only common interest (specifically, economic interest), but also common fear of its more powerful neighbors. Swiss neutrality, internationally recognized for well over 300 years, is an important feature of its identity and is still a rallying point for most Swiss.

This original negative definition of what Switzerland stands for – that is, independence from foreign influence and the will not to be German or Lombard or Savoyard – has always prevailed. Entry into the European Union therefore poses a problem of identity for Switzerland that no other country faces in the same way. Indeed, while there was never any doubt that even smaller countries would preserve their identity after joining the EU, this is not so obvious for Switzerland. If it is no longer necessary to stand united to defend the country against bigger, stronger neighbors, what is Switzerland for? Let us not forget: Switzerland is a country and a state, but not a nation. Its unity does not come from a common language, a shared culture, a single religion, the belonging to a single ethnic group, etc. Swiss unity resides in its political will and in political institutions, and this clearly has implications if those institutions change.

This phenomenon may explain the result of the referendum of December 1993, by which a majority of Swiss rejected the adhesion to the European Economic Area (EEA), more than other factors, such as the fear of losing certain cherished privileges (for instance, that of a semi-direct democracy) and of having to make a number of legal and institutional changes. Another, lesser factor was the fear of being forced to carry an over-proportional burden in financing European institutions and projects, given Switzerland's wealth. The refusal to join was probably primarily an anti-German vote. The majority came from the German-speaking part of the country (which accounts for almost 75 percent of the population). This part of Switzerland liberated itself from the domination of a "German" emperor 700 years ago, and is especially sensitive to German hegemony after two world wars. The Swiss Germans do not want to be German (nor the Italian Swiss Italian or, to a lesser degree, the French Swiss French). They also do not want to be part of a Europe that might be dominated by a coalition of big countries, including Germany.

The vote against joining the EEA was only the first of three referendums that bore out the will of the country not to open up to Europe and to stay outside the European community. The EEA referendum was followed by another, refusing the financing of two new tunnels through the Alps to facilitate the traffic between northern and southern Europe, and a third, opposing the lifting of restrictions on ownership of land by foreigners.

The fear of losing one's identity in an integrated Europe may also be at the base of another development that parallels this integration process chronologically. For a number of years, the Swiss Germans have tended to increasingly speak their dialect, and to refuse to speak "High German" (as the Germans call it) or "Written German" (as the Swiss call it). Thus the Swiss are losing the capacity to do so. They have even begun using Swiss German dialect in written contexts, a trend that is particularly visible in advertising. Thus, it is conceivable that, within a generation, Swiss German will have evolved from a dialect to a genuine language. This process, more than almost anything else, could assert a Swiss – at least a Swiss German – identity in the face of a growing threat to that identity. The latter stems from the increasing economic and political interdependency of Switzerland with its neighbors. One trend accepts economic *rapprochement*; the other accentuates cultural distinctiveness.

Reasons for Switzerland to keep distance from Europe

While this largely unconscious fear of loss of identity and of its *raison d'être* may be the strongest barrier to Switzerland joining a united Europe, it is by no means the only one. The first of these other barriers is proverbial Swiss pragmatism. The Swiss do not have big dreams or big projects. They have come to realize that big projects involve big risks (as well as big pay-offs). They prefer incremental progress to sweeping changes, the effects of which are difficult to foresee and to control. Note that this mentality has not prevented them from recently adopting, in one sweep, new legislation that followed European positions on some 100 different issues.

The Swiss also do not like fuzzy projects, and such is the Swiss image of Europe. It is still not clear – indeed, it is increasingly unclear – what Europe really wants to be. It wants economic prosperity, certainly; but what beyond that? Does it want political clout and independence? Does Europe want to be a world power? Does it stand for social progress and, if so, of what kind? Does it strive for cultural synergy, whatever that might be? The Swiss feel uncomfortable with so many unanswered questions. They want to know what they are getting into.

A second reason that makes the Swiss balk at Europe is their long tradition of hands-on democracy. This tradition makes them quite uncomfortable with what has been recognized as the democratic deficit of the EU: that is, a Parliament with almost no authority, a Council of Ministers rendered non-operational by the requirement of unanimous consensus, and a powerful administration. The Swiss are already skeptical about their own federal institutions, preferring that matters be treated locally where the citizens can influence them directly. They are even more skeptical of an additional layer of power, which seems to totally escape their control.

Joining the EU seems to imply, at best, participation in costly and inefficient institutions and endless palavers. This visceral dislike of such institutions is one of the major reasons why Switzerland has not joined the United Nations. At worst, EU membership implies being subject to an enormous centralizing bureaucracy. The Swiss believe in the superiority of their political and economic institutions – and not without reason. They take themselves to be living proof that small is beautiful and that it makes sense to decentralize, to seek consensus (or at least compromise) rather than confrontation, and to spread responsibility and burdens as widely and as equitably as possible. This characteristic has led, on the one hand, to a social security system that keeps mandatory insurance and deductions at a minimum and that leaves a maximum to the responsibility of the individual; and, on the other hand, to what is called the "militia system": rather than professionals in politics, in economic associations, and in the military, there is a Parliament of citizens who continue to hold other jobs, officials of unions and employers' or professional associations who carry out their duties in their spare time, and an army in which all men between the ages 18 and 45 serve almost every year.

A third reason, actually a whole bundle of reasons, is economic. For some 25 years, Switzerland has been successful in concluding over 100 treaties with the European Community – later the EU – which has guaranteed it, on specific issues, almost the same status as member states. Why not continue along the same lines? Economic exchanges with EU states have continued to grow. More capital than desired continues to come into the country. This capital pushes up the value of the currency, thus increasing the price of Swiss products in foreign markets. Switzerland is still doing better economically than any European country taken individually or than Europe as a whole. It is still, by all standards, one of the world's richest countries. Indeed, in popular parlance, to describe a country elsewhere in the world as rich, clean, and orderly, one often calls it the "Switzerland of . . ." Asia (Singapore), Latin America (Costa Rica), the Near East (Lebanon), etc.

Joining the EU also seems to lead to exposure to a flood of immigrants – immigrants whom Switzerland would no longer be able to select on grounds of their contribution in labor or capital, who would obviously try to profit from the wealth of the country and thus diminish it for everybody. But this is not all: Switzerland would also expose itself to undesirable imported phenomena, such as unemployment, inflation, or major tax hikes. Indeed, it still has an unemployment rate that is less than half of the EU average. It has one of the lowest inflation rates anywhere, and its tax burden on citizens is considerably below that of its neighbors. Specifically, Swiss VAT is about one-third of that in several European countries.

However, the most disturbing aspect of EU membership seems to be the necessity to align the Swiss price structure. In this area, everybody could lose, at least at first blush: salaries could be reduced (they are currently well above those practiced elsewhere); the Swiss franc could be devalued (it is currently considerably overvalued, as any Swiss on vacation abroad cannot fail to notice); and the outrageous real estate prices could tumble.

Switzerland has been a well-protected country not only militarily, but also economically. Most Swiss markets have been protected from foreign competition, especially the labor market. Although the percentage of foreigners is high, they tend not to compete with Swiss in the labor market, but generally do work that the Swiss either do not want or are unable to do. The agricultural and construction markets are also protected (the latter, in particular, for streets and public buildings).

Finally, the Swiss fear forced adjustment in many areas, such as social security, agriculture, and transportation. Their system of social security is quite unique. The price of milk is fixed by the constitution. Trucks of over 40 tons are not allowed on Swiss streets. The Swiss do not want to change all this, for the very reasons that led them to regulate these areas in the first place, but also simply because they do not want others to tell them what to do.

To sum up, economically, it appears to many Swiss that the risks of joining the EU are high and difficult to contain, while the advantages seem much less obvious and certain.

A last reason for opposition to Europe is political. Belonging to Europe would mean the end of Swiss neutrality – the very neutrality that allowed Switzerland to stay out of the two disastrous world wars. These wars were started by Europeans and were, after all, mainly European wars. Once it might have been attractive to join Europe to protect Switzerland from communist aggression. However, with the specter of such aggression fading, what remains is the danger of being drawn into a military-political adventure when Europe (under American leadership or on its own) sets out on "peacekeeping/ making" expeditions. As times are increasingly turbulent and unpredictable, it seems to many Swiss safer not to take sides, and to maintain relationships of benevolent or friendly distance with as many countries as possible.

What Europe could offer Switzerland

While many of these fears have been used by opponents of the Swiss signature of the treaties of Rome and of Maastricht, not a week passes without articles in the press, both popular and specialized, claiming the necessity and inevitability of Swiss participation in European institutions. These articles present arguments in favor of following the examples of Sweden and Austria, offer new opinion polls that show a more favorable attitude toward Europe, and propose that Switzerland engage in negotiations leading to integration into the EU. These articles have become the more pressing as bilateral negotiations with Brussels over specific issues, such as transit through the Alps or the residence of foreigners, meet failure after failure.

There is a growing feeling in Switzerland of marginalization and isolation. Not long ago, it was a shock to many Swiss to get off an airplane in Paris or London and to have to join different lanes and be treated differently by immigration officers from citizens of EU member states. Today, the Swiss have changed their own immigration procedures so that one no longer finds one lane for Swiss citizens and another for all others, but rather one for Swiss and EU citizens and one for the rest of the world.

This kind of shock subsists for those Swiss who want to study or work in one of the EU member countries and who face restrictions. Their diploma is not automatically recognized. They are excluded from all EU-funded scholarships. They have difficulty obtaining a work permit, etc. These restrictions do not apply to citizens of EU countries. They make it very difficult, if not impossible, for Swiss citizens to realize their plans – even if they want to work for a Swiss company operating in an EU member state. The Swiss, who claim to be "separate, but equal," are discovering that they will suffer inequalities if they continue to set themselves apart.

It was considered to be a humiliation that Switzerland, which had still been admitted as an observer to the Europe–Mediterranean conference in Barcelona in 1995, was denied participation in the Europe–Asia summit in Bangkok in 1996. Furthermore, in Brussels, Swiss negotiators who make every effort to convince their European partners of the sincere wish of their government to tighten the Swiss–EU relationship find that representatives of the EU are less and less willing to accept Switzerland as the special case

(*Sonderfall Schweiz*) that the Swiss have always claimed be, and who are increasingly uncompromising: either Switzerland joins the EU like everybody else; then one can make temporary adjustments during a transition phase; or Switzerland stays out of the EU and will be treated like any other third country. Moreover, EU officials show less and less understanding with a Swiss delegation and a government that agree on certain points one day and then retract the next because they have been disavowed by a popular vote.

The political consequences of the Swiss hesitation toward Europe are clearly negative. In the past, Switzerland played an important role on the diplomatic scene. It has mediated in many conflicts and has represented other countries when their representatives were personae non gratae. It was respected for its neutrality and reliability. Now, this reputation has suffered. Swiss neutrality is increasingly considered an expression of its lack of solidarity and an excuse for the refusal to shoulder real responsibilities. Swiss politics appear to be not forward, but rather backward looking; and Switzerland's reliability as a partner is being questioned.

The economic loss of staying out of the EU does not touch all sectors, but it is nevertheless considerable. The major Swiss multinationals not only sell up to 98 percent of their volume outside of Switzerland, but also produce much of it abroad, often in EU countries. They are therefore not greatly affected. But the small and medium-sized companies, which export exclusively and do not have the means to reach much beyond Europe, are severely handicapped. Not only are they excluded from public markets and hit with tariffs, but also they have to comply with elaborate, time-consuming procedures, with European norms and standards that are different from those in Switzerland, and with all sorts of other complications. These factors clearly spell competitive disadvantages for them.

Europe could offer these small and medium-sized companies the market that their high degree of specialization requires. Europe could also provide the best workforce possible, rather than limiting the choice of workers to those available in Switzerland.

Moreover, Europe could give Swiss youth a feeling of freedom and of being on the move. Swiss youth today often feel locked in and locked out, and that their perspectives are limited. The feeling of living in an open rather than a closed, blocked society could not fail to make that society more dynamic. Furthermore, young people could participate and have a say in shaping the environment to which they currently feel only subjected.

What Switzerland could offer Europe

Switzerland has more to offer to Europe than its small size might suggest. It has more to offer than beautiful mountains, pure water, milk and chocolate, or watches. It could make valuable contributions in political, economic, social, as well as cultural areas. No more than anybody else can it give lessons to the rest of Europe. However, many of the principles of its political organization could be used as a model – and indeed some have already. The Swiss economy is highly diversified and one of the most successful and stable in Europe, if not in the world. The integration of such an economy into the EU could only benefit the whole. Switzerland has a unique social welfare system, which provides safeguards without becoming a welfare state. Thanks to its multicultural character,

Switzerland is optimally suited to be a turntable in cultural exchanges among other European countries and to promote cultural synergy.

In the political realm, the Swiss could contribute to Europe, beyond the traditions of Switzerland as the oldest and one of the most stable world democracies. It also has a long tradition of handling differences and conflicts through compromise and consensus rather than through confrontation and competition. Furthermore, Switzerland possesses a deep attachment to federalism, which respects and values local and regional differences rather than suppressing them. This approach allows problems to be treated where they occur, at the lowest level possible, and has the advantage of involving the people who know the facts and who are most directly concerned. The country holds an equally deep attachment to a neutrality based on non-interference and the refusal to embark on any form of conquest and colonialism. Swiss neutrality, however, does not exclude actions of solidarity, particularly of a humanitarian nature. Indeed, such actions may be possible only if impartiality is guaranteed, as the Red Cross, a Swiss creation, has shown again and again.

A particularly interesting aspect of Swiss political traditions is its militia system. As Machiavelli – who admired it – observed, it is the expression of the principle of equality. Everyone participates in the affairs of state, and above all in the army, the very symbol of state power. Initially limited to the army, the militia system has spread to politics and to other areas of public and private affairs, where it promotes not only equality (the right to participate), but also solidarity (the duty to do so). Indeed, Switzerland continues to have a militia army and a militia parliament; and most professional associations, unions, sports clubs, and learned societies function with officials who work on a voluntary basis (again, alongside another job and without being paid, or paid much).

As citizens of the oldest modern democracy, the Swiss are extremely sensitive to questions of individual rights, the respect of minorities, and popular control of government. As members of the EU, they would undoubtedly play the role of guardians and defenders of these principles. Having a long tradition of federalism and subsidiarity, the Swiss are allergic to centralization and would oppose any drift of power from local institutions to a large and distant European bureaucracy. As part of a small country, they would naturally be opposed to a central European state and would thus strengthen the opposition to any member state (or a coalition of states) wishing to dominate the others. Switzerland could and would therefore contribute much to promote a balance among the interests of all members of a united Europe.

Switzerland has for centuries been a haven of peace, internationally as well as domestically and socially. It also has a long tradition of dealing with the entire world. Many of its citizens emigrated while Switzerland was still a poor country, but kept their attachment to their country of origin. Let us not forget that the League of Nations had its seat in Geneva and that Switzerland today hosts the International Labour Office, the World Health Organization, the UN Commissariat for Refugees, the World Trade Organization, the International Postal Union, the International Bureau of Telecommunications, the World Meteorological Organization, the International Office of Intellectual Property, the Bank for International Settlements, several international labor unions (such as the powerful International Metal Workers Federation, the International Federation of Chemical and General Workers, and the International Union of Food and Allied Workers' Associations), as well as the International Red Cross, the International Olympic

Committee and one European institution, the Centre européen de recherche nucleaire). It would be against its history to subscribe to any form of European nationalism, imperialism, and *Grossmachtpolitik*, or to isolationism and protectionism.

As mentioned earlier, Switzerland is one of the most heavily armed countries in the world. The army is well equipped and well trained, but it has purely defensive objectives and is not only tightly controlled by political leaders, but extremely well integrated into the population. Switzerland does not have an army; it *is* an army. Does Europe not need this kind of army – defense ready and non-aggressive; accustomed to function with soldiers who speak different languages, and who serve as mere citizens and not as part of some supposedly elite caste?

Economically, Switzerland is a (little) giant. It has a smoothly functioning, highly diversified economy. It remains one of the most competitive countries in the world, and is by most economic indicators one of the richest.

Some of its major companies hold top positions among the international competition in their respective sectors of activity: Nestlé (food), Novartis and Hofman-La Roche (pharmaceuticals), Firmenich and Givaudan (fragrances), Holderbank (cement), Rolex, SMH, etc. (watches), Buhler, Buhrle, Georg Fischer, Landys-Gyr, Netstal, Sulzer, Thornos, etc. (machines, machine tools), Marc Rich, André (trading), Danzas, Kuhne & Nagel, Panalpina, and Swissair (transportation), Credit Swiss, Swiss Bank Corporation, and Union Bank of Switzerland (banking), Rentenanstalt, Swiss Re, Winterthur, and Zurich (insurance and reinsurance), and Adia and SGS (services). While these companies are the most visible, the real strength of the Swiss economy lies with its small and medium-sized companies, such as Bobst, Castolin, ETEL, Galenica, Kudelski, LEM, Logitech, Microfil, and Sicpa, which have been very successful in exploiting niches in which they occupy enviable and profitable positions.

These and other companies are generally well managed and dispose not only of one of the best-trained and most highly motivated workforces, but also of production techniques and processes that are ahead of most of their European competitors (as shown by a study of 116 Swiss companies by IBM and IMD).

Some of the characteristics of what might be called the "Swiss way of management" seem to have contributed to the competitiveness of the Swiss economy. They could inspire companies in other European countries, which have a culture that is, after all, closer to the Swiss than to the Japanese. These characteristics can be summed up under the following headings:

♦ The Swiss have a high degree of individualism, translating into a high respect for the individual, who is given a large sphere of autonomy. Superiors tend to intervene only on a subsidiary basis. Colleagues try not to meddle with what is not their responsibility. Likewise, there is much decentralization, with not only the acceptance but the encouragement of a maximum of differentiation among different units. These units are given a wide margin of maneuver to adapt to local conditions. Accompanying the decentralization is a firm determination to remain independent, through a high level of self-financing, strong protection against takeovers, controlled growth, etc.
♦ The whole becomes "organic complementarity," meaning that all work is equally respected as long as it is well done. Also, power is easily accepted as long as it is

functional and exercised with competence and restraint. Managers must not claim any privileges, but do their job as a duty. They must refrain from ostensibly displaying their power and wealth, must be accessible to everybody, must be ready to pitch in and get their hands dirty if necessary, must consult and listen, and so on. There is a strong pressure toward integration and conformity, compromise and consensus. Conflict is suppressed, competition limited.

♦ Prudence, leading to the defense of acquired positions, is likewise quite Swiss. It is more important to hold on to what one has than to conquer new territories. In addition, there is distrust of what is new and unproved, and trust in the value of experience and continuity. Development is preferred to research; adaptation and continuous improvement to innovation. There is also a preference for constant incremental, local change in order to avoid revolutionary, general upheavals. All is accompanied by high cost consciousness and thrift, modesty and avoidance of waste, as well as a high level of discretion to avoid embarrassment if things turn sour, and jealousies if they go well. There is an almost total lack of transparency and limited communication. The Swiss involve as few people as possible and communicate only on functional topics, showing much understatement and extreme politeness.

♦ The Swiss prize pragmatism: that is, a willingness to adapt ends to means and to stay away from projects that are too big or from battles they cannot win. They have an acceptance of the world as it is, even if is not as they would like it to be. Thus, hierarchy, long working hours, and restraint on salary increases in difficult times are not seriously contested. There is an absence of dogmatism. One is flexible in the application of principles, and never applies imported "textbook" models and methods without having adapted them. There is a definite preference for the concrete and the practical over what is abstract and theoretical; a "no nonsense" culture and some skepticism with regard to people who think too fast and talk too well. The observer also notices a dominance of production and of directly productive work, with a strong aversion to administrative staffs and headquarters, in addition to a valorization of the small, which is controllable and concrete. Finally, there is a tendency not to force an issue, but to seek a compromise as the only reasonable way to deal with conflicting interests.

Switzerland cannot claim the same success on the social side as in the economic area. Indeed, many social indicators are much worse than what one might expect: the suicide rate is high, as is the number of alcoholics, drug addicts, and mentally ill. The divorce rate is high and the birth rate low.

While the Swiss are obviously not able to eliminate the causes of these problems, they are good in dealing with their consequences. Health care is excellent, and countless self-help groups and associations deal with people who have specific problems of all kinds. This is a sign that the social tissue is still largely intact – an assertion that is also borne out by the fact that the streets are safe and that the number of socially excluded is low.

While it is not clear whether the Swiss could do more for Europe socially than not to create additional problems, Switzerland could again serve as a model in education and training, where its system is envied by many.

The Swiss system of general education is known for its quality. It has attracted students from all over the world to its public and private schools. But the Swiss system of professional education is probably even more remarkable and has its equivalent only in Germany. It consists of professional schools in practically all trades, which work hand in hand with the state and with companies. In fact, the latter even organize some of the courses that complement the "learning by doing," which are otherwise offered by the schools. Thus apprentices are provided with a combination of courses and practical experience over three to five years, which enable them, once they have passed exams and graduated, to exercise any skilled activity in their profession. This system has not attracted foreign students, but it has provided the Swiss economy with a skilled labor force that is one of its major assets.

As for universities, Switzerland cannot boast quantity, but quality. Its ten universities and the Federal Institute of Technology are as good as any comparable institution in Europe. In certain fields, these institutions have a reputation that sets them apart from and above others. It would certainly not only be an advantage to the Swiss, but to Europe, if the Swiss universities participated fully in all European research programs and in the exchange of faculty and students, particularly at the graduate level.

Conclusion

While joining the EU would certainly open up certain opportunities to Switzerland, at present it does not seem existentially necessary. EU membership even seems to imply certain dangers and thus arouses fears that must be taken seriously.

In many respects, the Swiss seem to be better off than their European neighbors, and Switzerland is as interested in world trade as in Europe. Some have even seriously proposed seeking membership in the North American Free Trade Association. Many Swiss feel that the country is too small – with 7 million inhabitants, it would be the smallest in the EU – to be able to have any real influence on the European institutions and regulations to which Switzerland would be subjected. (This fear is not really justified, since, at least on paper, the EU privileges the small states.) They feel that Switzerland would even be weaker than other small countries because it is not a country with a single people and one culture. Indeed, the integration into Europe might bring about the progressive disintegration of Switzerland. These people are the opponents of EU membership (the "Nein-Sager").

On the other hand, there are those who are in favor of joining the EU due to fatalism or realism. They feel that European integration is a development too powerful to be ignored or escaped. History does not stop at the borders of the country! Even if Switzerland stays outside the EU, it will be and indeed is already affected by it. Switzerland will have to adapt, but will have no direct chance to influence what it has to adapt to. These people think that, even if the Swiss economy is complementary to that of Europe and specializes in satisfying needs that others neglect, thus avoiding head-on competition, it is too big to follow such a strategy. It might be possible for Liechtenstein and Monaco, which live on fiscal and financial services, luxury tourism, health care, etc., but not for Switzerland.

There are also enthusiastic supporters for joining Europe. They feel that neutrality does not have to mean passiveness, that direct democracy and federalism in their present form are altogether outdated, since they do not facilitate the solution of present and future problems – which are the same for Switzerland as for its neighbors. They fear that, by standing alone, Switzerland will become a museum or an enclave of the past like the Amish. They want to have an exciting project for Switzerland – a vision of a Europe with a mission of humanism, humanitarianism, progress, and solidarity.

This enthusiasm is made difficult by the fact that Europe has chosen an unexciting, gradual interpenetration of its economies rather than the spectacular, immediate creation of a new state with a common vision, army, anthem, etc. Moreover, the media present the functioning of the European institutions as a constant bickering and horse-trading, leading to painful and often unsatisfactory compromises, rather than as an irresistible movement toward unity, generating not only economic, but also cultural and spiritual wealth. It is difficult to fall in love with a supermarket.

The existence of these three groups has produced a constant ebb and flow between overture toward and rebuffs of Europe. Thus, one can safely predict, on the one hand, that Switzerland will eventually be part of Europe, but on the other hand, that it will hesitate a long time before doing so.

It is somehow ironic that Switzerland, which was formed much in the way the European Union is forming, is today so reluctant to repeat the process at a higher level. The same forces that obliged Switzerland to unite and that brought the Cantons to transfer a part of their sovereignty to the Confederation and, later, to form a Union; those same forces that pushed the Swiss cities and counties to create a common market, a common currency, a common law, and finally a political union with a single foreign policy and an integrated army, etc.; those same forces are operating today in and on Europe. If Switzerland, which by its history could seem predestined to lead such a development, does not want to play the role of a catalyst, we cannot see how it can, in the long run, withstand these forces and stay apart.

Switzerland and Europe: Key dates

1291   With an oath to stand together in the defense of their liberties, representatives from three Swiss counties create what is to become Switzerland.

1513   The three original Cantons had been joined by ten others (the last of the 22 Cantons that make up Switzerland today came into existence only in 1979).

1648   Swiss independence is officially recognized in the Treaty of Westphalia, ending the Thirty Years War.

1815   Swiss independence and neutrality are recognized to be in the interest of all of Europe and are formally guaranteed at the Congress of Vienna, reorganizing Europe after the fall of Napoleon.

1866   The "First International" (Congress of Labor) assembles in Geneva.

1946   Winston Churchill pleads for the United States of Europe at the University of Zurich.

1946   The European Union of Switzerland regroups Swiss federalists.

1947   The Congress of the Union of European Federalists is held in Montreux.

1948   Participation of 30 Swiss delegates in the Congress of Europe at The Hague.

1952   Inauguration of the European Research Center for Nuclear Physics (CERN) in Geneva.

1955   Creation, by Jean Monnet, of the Action Committee for the United States of Europe, with its seat in Lausanne.

1960   Switzerland is a founding member of the European Free Trade Association (EFTA). The Swiss government takes a stand against the adhesion of Switzerland to the Common Market. This position is followed by Parliament as well as by most professional associations.

1963   Switzerland joins the Council of Europe, which meets in Strasbourg.

1974   Switzerland rejects by a popular vote the introduction of European daylight savings time and refuses to align its time (because of the supposedly negative impact on cattle); the inevitable is finally accepted by Parliament one year later.

1975   Switzerland is a founding member of the European Space Agency.

1979   Switzerland becomes a member of Euratom.

1984   Switzerland participates in the European research programs JET, Esprit, and Eureka, but not in Erasmus, which promotes the intra-European mobility of students and scholars. Hundreds of projects are submitted; many are accepted.

1991   Switzerland is a founding member of the European Bank for Development.

1993   A popular vote stops the initiative of the government to have Switzerland join the European Economic Area.

1995   A popular vote forces the government to cancel its promise to the EU to build a new tunnel under the Alps to facilitate traffic between northern and southern Europe.

1995–6   Switzerland is admitted as an observer to the Europe–Mediterranean conference in Barcelona, but is denied participation in the Europe–Asia summit in Bangkok.

1996   To reconcile the Europhiles and the Europhobes, several politicians demand the formal withdrawal of Swiss candidacy to the EU (the candidacy is "frozen") and revival of the project of adhesion to the European Economic Area (of which there is hardly anything left).

Bibliography

Bergmann, A. (1994) Le "*Swiss Way of Management*", Paris: ESKA.

Boltanki, L. (1996) *Le Bonheur suisse*, Paris, Editions Minuit.

Courvoisier, J.-C. (1989) *La Suisse jubilaire et l'Europe naissante*, Lausanne: L'Aire.

De Rougemont, D. (1965) *La Suisse ou l'histoire d'un peuple heureux*, Paris: Hachette.

De Tscharner, B. (1989) *Quelle Europe? Quelle Suisse?,* Lausanne: Centre de recherches européennes.

Frochaux, C. (1969) *Heidi ou le défi suisse*, Lausanne: Editions La Cité.

Kahil, B. (1995) *Suisse – Europe: mesurer le possible, viser à l'essentiel*, Lausanne: Centre Patronal.

Lempen, B. (1985) *Un Modèle en crise: La Suisse*, Lausanne: Payot.

Liniger-Goumaz, M. (1993) *Paroles d'helvète. Europe: L'acœnt suisse*, Geneva: Les Editions du Temps.

Michaud, G. (1947) *Histoire de la Suisse*, Lausanne: Payot.

Reszler, B. (1986) *Mythes et identité de la Suisse*, Geneva: Georg Editeur.

Steinberg, J. (1980) *Why Switzerland?*, Cambridge: Cambridge University Press.

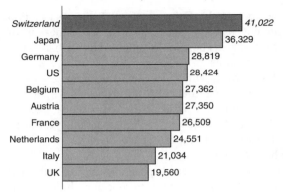

Switzerland GDP per head 1996 ($)

Switzerland	41,022
Japan	36,329
Germany	28,819
US	28,424
Belgium	27,362
Austria	27,350
France	26,509
Netherlands	24,551
Italy	21,034
UK	19,560

Stock market 1997

	Size ($bn)	Rise/fall
New York	8,879	31%
Tokyo	2,085	−17%
London	2,068	22%
Frankfurt	825	41%
Paris	674	29%
Zurich	*575*	*55%*
Amsterdam	468	43%
Milan	345	64%
Brussels	137	30%
Vienna	20	16%

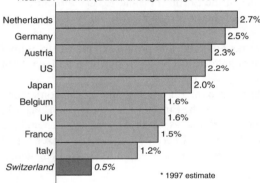

Real GDP Growth (annual average change 1990–97*)

Netherlands	2.7%
Germany	2.5%
Austria	2.3%
US	2.2%
Japan	2.0%
Belgium	1.6%
UK	1.6%
France	1.5%
Italy	1.2%
Switzerland	0.5%

* 1997 estimate

Sources: The Economist; UBS; Swiss Stock Exchange; Credit
Suisse; OECD; Datastream/ICV

Unemployment rate (% of labour force)

Industries where Swiss companies are world leaders
SFr bn

Industry	*Company*	*Market capital*
Food	Nestlé	101
Pharmaceuticals	Novartis	184
	Roche	162
	Ares-Serono	8
Speciality chemicals	Ciba	12
	Clariant	11
Electrical engineering	ABB	18
Textile machinery	Saurer	2
	Rieter	2
	Sulzer Rüti	n.a.
Cement	Holderbank	10
Watches	SMH	7
Elevators/escalators	Schindler	3
Temporary employment	Adecco	8
Testing and inspection	SGS	4

Source: FT research market and Vontobel stock guide, March 1998

Editor's introduction: Sweden

Sweden has been something of a pulsar on the European scene, sometimes bursting into full blaze, as during Charles XII's military campaigns on the continent, but more often content to remain in its Scandinavian fastness. Certainly, within its own region, Sweden has played the dominant role almost without exception, and indeed colonized Norway and Finland. On the other hand, Sweden's recent history has been one of westward-leaning neutrality. At the same time, Sweden is a major European arms manufacturer. And so the contradictions reign.

By and large, Sweden can be viewed as the strongest force in a generally isolated region. Of the four Scandinavian nations (Sweden, Norway, Finland, and Denmark), only Denmark is geographically attached to the Continent. Thus, the psychological as well as physical isolation of Sweden is a national constant. Yet, Sweden chose to throw in its lot with the European Union for sound economic, political, and cultural reasons. Although on the periphery, Sweden is part of Europe and intends to remain so.

Given this background, what issues might be explored further concerning Sweden?

- Although a part of Europe, Sweden has traditionally had difficulty understanding its southern European neighbors, as the breakdown of the proposed Volvo–Renault merger attests. Can this great cultural misunderstanding be overcome?
- What does Sweden bring to the European Union? What does Sweden hope to obtain from the EU?
- Will participation in the euro bring Sweden closer to its EU partners?

Sweden

Area: 449,964 sq km

Languages: Swedish (Finnish and Lapp spoken by northern minorities)

Currency: Krona (SKr)

Population: 8,854,322 (End 1998)

Constitution

National government
Cabinet headed by prime minister resposible to the Riksdag

National legislature
Unicameral Riksdag (parliament) of 349 members directly elected for a four-year term; in the event of an early dissolution, the new parliament serves only the remainder of the previous parliament's term

Main political parties
Social Democratic party (SDP, 131 seats); Moderate party (known as Conservatives, 82); Left party (43); Christian Democratic party (CD, 42); Centre party (18); Liberal party (17); Green party (16)

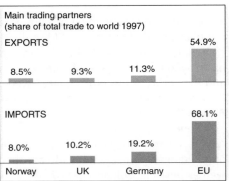

Main trading partners
(share of total trade to world 1997)

	Norway	UK	Germany	EU
EXPORTS	8.5%	9.3%	11.3%	54.9%
IMPORTS	8.0%	10.2%	19.2%	68.1%

Sources: Economist Intelligence Unit; Datastream/ICV

Economic summary	1998	1999 (forecast)
Total GDP ($bn)	224.2	269.0
Real GDP growth (annual % change)	2.8	2.4
GDP per head ($'000)	25.3	30.3
Inflation (annual % change in CPI)	−0.1	0.9
Industrial production (annual % change)	4.4	2.2
Unemployment rate (% of workforce)	6.5	6.2
Government expenditure (percentage of GDP)	61.3	60.4
Current account balance ($bn)	5.9	6.4
Exports ($bn)	85.5	91.5
Imports ($bn)	66.6	69.7
Trade balance ($bn)	18.9	21.8
Budget balance (% of GDP)	0.5	0.6

7

♦ ♦ ♦

Sweden in Europe

Christer Nedstrom
City of Stockholm, Sweden

Historical background

Sweden has had a most interesting history from a European perspective, moving from a small, poor agricultural country far up in the polar zone of Europe, to expand into a super-power for a short period of time. During the Thirty Years War in Europe (1618–48) and during the reign of King Charles XII (1697–1718), Swedish armies victoriously swept over Europe, of which very large areas were parts of the Swedish Kingdom in that period.

Then came a period of recession. The Swedes went back to farming and their country fell back into the shadow of history. During one period of the nineteenth century, the country was hit by an extremely deep recession for several years, which led to mass emigration, mainly to the US. Over some 15 years, more than one-third of the Swedish population left the country for more prosperous lands outside the home country.

In the latter part of the nineteenth century, industrialism made its appearance in Sweden, thus starting a new epoch for the country, bringing development and prosperity. Much of the wealth that came with industrialism was based upon the ability to exploit the natural resources of the country, such as water power, wood, and iron ore. In the process of developing and exploiting these natural resources, much modern technology and many inventions were born, some of which still hold leading positions and competitive power in the modern world.

However, it is interesting to note that, even if the raw materials were at hand in Sweden from the dawn of history, the knowledge to exploit and to develop new processes had to be imported from other European countries. As a consequence, many craftsmen and specialists were asked to move to Sweden from other parts of Europe, mainly from Wallonia. So it can truly be stated that Sweden, as early as the seventeenth century, was building relations and exchanging experiences with other European countries, in a European cooperation that one might see as a predecessor to the present EU membership. However, most Swedes seem to have forgotten this part of their own European history.

Swedish entrepreneurs and inventors, such as Lars-Magnus Ericsson (telephone equipment) and Alfred Nobel (gunpowder), gave birth to a new age of Swedish industrial development and to a transformational period for the whole of Swedish society. The country started its journey from a traditional rural country to become one of the leading industrial countries in Europe. At the same time as the industrial development occurred in Sweden – and, of course, based upon and financed by that development – the Swedish social welfare state was built step by step.

Another very good reason for the positive development of the country is, no doubt, that Sweden to date has managed to avoid war for more than 200 years, unlike most other European nations. This fact has had – and still has – great implications for Swedish attitudes toward the European Union. There is a strong conviction, shared by all political parties and by the population at large, that the reason for having achieved this rare position is the firm Swedish policy of neutrality. It is because of this conviction that you will find a common opinion among the Swedes that any political decision that might question Swedish neutrality must be closely scrutinized before being accepted.

A typical Swedish character?

With the above-mentioned background, one may ask if the history of the country has influenced or created a special Swedish character. The answer is undoubtedly yes.

You can still find in the mind of many Swedes a generally conservative approach to life and to new ideas in general. This attitude is typical for a country of farmers and of people who only recently, historically speaking, left the land. Even if the last two generations have voted for and supported mainly social democratic governments, you can still find a generally conservative attitude to change. For instance, Swedes have a strong tendency to reject proposals that put their social security at risk.

Still today a lot of Swedes feel like "the country cousin" when meeting continental Europeans. The Swedish language is not understood by others, and the rural cultural background, customs, and habits of the Swedes are not as elegant as those of the French, for example. This has led Swedes to adopt a rather provincial general attitude toward themselves, and to pursue a wait-and-see policy toward foreigners, their habits, and lifestyles. Swedes are consequently regarded – by themselves and by non-Swedes – as a rather shy people, as they are not outspoken and animated like Latin Europeans. They most often do their best to give short, straight answers to questions, trying not to leave "loose ends" or too much scope for interpretation.

On the other hand, it would not be totally incorrect to argue that the memories of the period when Sweden played a dominant role on the European stage still have an influence on Swedes today. It is interesting to note that this influence is mainly felt among the young and unemployed generation. It is not without reason that the right-wingers and skinheads of today are celebrating the death of Charles XII, trying to revive the pride and greatness of the Sweden of those days. This group of people represent just a very small fraction of the population, and their ideas are supported by only a very small minority among the Swedes. Still there is, underneath the normally cool and tolerant surface of the Swedes, a feeling of pride. This is pride in having turned a nation of farmers into an industrialized nation of excellence in many different areas. The point here is that the Swedes have managed to do this on their own. This may very well be one reason why so many Swedes still think that they do not need the EU, since they have demonstrated that they can manage on their own.

Modern history: Sweden's approach to Europe after World War II

Some ten years after the beginning of the European postwar period, two trading political constellations were created in Europe: the European Economic Community (EEC) in 1957 and the European Free Trade Association (EFTA) in 1959. EFTA can be simply described as a legally rather loose organization with its emphasis on trade and better trade conditions among its members. The EEC had to some extent the same goal, but from the beginning it had much higher political ambitions, as is clearly demonstrated by the transformation of the EEC into the EU – the European Union – of today.

Initially, EFTA was the larger of the two, but as time went by, more and more of its members left the organization to seek membership of the EEC, which grew stronger and became more influential. The growing power of the EEC can partly be explained by two major factors:

♦ The two politically and financially strong nations of Europe – Germany and France – were both members, as well as founders, of that organization.
♦ The whole structure of the two organizations was very different. The EEC had a legal framework and decision-making procedure that was very strict and legally binding for its members, while EFTA was very loose in its legal structure and had no system to make the organization "speak with one voice."

As a natural consequence of the development described above, and based upon political considerations by the Swedish government, Sweden realized slowly that membership of EFTA alone would most certainly, long term, not be the most fruitful solution for the country's development. As another consequence of this analysis, and as a first step toward improving trade with the rest of Europe, Sweden initiated negotiations for the first time with the EEC in 1961. These negotiations did not lead to any decisions and in 1963 they were considered as finished. In 1967, a second effort was made by the Swedish government to apply for negotiations on membership with the EEC, but not even this time did the negotiations lead to any result.

In 1970, Sweden again approached the EEC for negotiations on closer cooperation, but the very strong link to Swedish neutrality prevented a positive result of the negotiations. During the following years, numerous contacts were made by the Swedish government, but no real solutions for closer cooperation were found. In 1990, the EFTA and EEC countries began talks about creating a larger trade area – the European Economic Area – including 19 countries and forming a single internal market. This new structure of the European market was in place and became effective from 1994.

During the last period of the negotiations of the EEA agreement, it was quite clear that the Swedish position and the general debate on the nation's relationship to the "New Europe" were shifting. Increasingly, the debate had turned toward a new objective – a situation of full membership in the European Union.

The question of Swedish EU membership

No country in Europe that has been or is in the process of applying for membership of the EU has changed position as rapidly as Sweden. The social democratic government needed only a few months to shift position from the long-held, traditionally negative attitude toward membership, to the enthusiastic conviction that membership was now the only solution.

In the spring of 1990, the prime minister, Ingvar Carlsson, started the membership process by a series of public statements, indicating that, based upon the great political changes taking place in the rest of Europe, Swedish membership was "no longer unthinkable." During this one year, Sweden and its largest political party had totally changed their positions. The result of that change was great confusion in the Social Democratic Party and in the political community of Sweden. One year later, in late July 1991, the Council of Ministers of the EU officially recognized that Sweden had applied for membership and that negotiations could start.

During the period 1991–4, negotiations took place which also involved the applications by the close neighbors of Sweden, Finland and Norway. The historical background and common interests among these three countries played an important role in the political process. Important also were the relations between Sweden and the newly freed Baltic states, with which Sweden had signed bilateral trade agreements. These agreements could not be regarded as an obstacle in the negotiations.

In 1994, the negotiations were finished and the parliaments in each of the three countries had decided to ask for a final "yes" or "no" in national referendums. Although the outcome of the referendums was to be regarded as "consultative," all the governments had promised to follow "the voice of the people." Finland started the process in the early fall of 1994 by producing a clear majority for membership. A few weeks later Sweden voted, and the result turned out to be a very small majority (some 52 percent) in favor of membership. A few weeks after Sweden's verdict, Norway, which had already held a referendum in 1971, said "no" a second time. The reason was partly that the wounds from the 1971 referendum, which had deeply divided the nation, had not yet healed. Another reason was the very positive development of the Norwegian economy, mainly based on the income from the Norwegian oil fields in the North Sea, leaving Norway in a unique situation for Europe: with no national budget deficit.

Thus the traditional unity of the Nordic countries was broken, leaving Norway out of the Union, but still to some extent a partner via the EEA agreement. On January 1, 1995, Sweden became a full member of the European Union.

National attitudes toward the EU

As has been clearly demonstrated above, Sweden has undergone several rather dramatic changes in modern times:

- There has been a general development from a sovereign, rather isolated rural nation into a highly industrialized country involved in a web of international obligations.

- A shift has occurred in political standpoints in matters that historically and traditionally were regarded as sacred, such as the policy of neutrality.
- There has been almost non-existent unemployment in modern times.

All these changes have not taken place without tension, conflict, and question marks. The underlying reasons for these question marks are that most Swedes have not been mentally prepared for such dramatic upheavals. The speed of change *per se* has been so swift and so new to most Swedes that they have not had time to study and to fully understand the European transition process – and even less to follow, to accept, and to adapt to it.

- The Swedes have lived for centuries rather isolated in a region that was not always even looked upon as a part of Europe. Still they managed, alone, to develop their country in a very positive way. And now, through EU membership, they are integrated into thousands of decision-making processes in areas where they were never involved before.
- Sweden has been left outside the horrible disasters of war for more than two centuries – a fact that the Swedes have come to look upon as a natural situation. This is most certainly the main reason why Swedes have not really understood the very basic idea of the EU as a peacekeeping mechanism. Now, through EU membership, the Swedes are being integrated into a common foreign policy, which might lead to a common defense policy, which in turn might lead ultimately to a common European army. This is a very dramatic prospect for the Swedish public in general as well as for their politicians.
- The Swedes have managed to build up a social welfare system that, during the 1960s and 1970s at least, was regarded as the model for a modern industrialized country, as there was practically no unemployment. Now, through EU membership, they seem forced to accept an unemployment rate of 12–15 percent and rather dramatic cuts in the social welfare system.
- Sweden has experienced very few political changes of any magnitude, thus creating political stability and calm in the country. The same is true of relations between employers and employees in the Swedish labor market. Now, through EU membership, politicians from other countries and in other forums will strongly influence things that were previously handled by the Swedes internally.
- Over three centuries, the Swedes have developed a very high degree of self-determination at the local and regional levels. There is a unique tradition in Swedish history, going back to the time of the Vikings, which is that decisions are taken, after discussions and hearings of all concerned in the matter, at the lowest possible level. This tradition is in sharp contrast to habits in other European nations and to the centralized decision-making process within the EU. Now, through EU membership, this traditional right to self-determination seems to be at stake.

An ordinary Swede today might well say something like: "All of a sudden, cornerstones in our beliefs and habits must be abandoned. New beliefs and values will be pressed upon us by others, as a consequence of our membership of the European Union. Now we have become part of the EU harmonization process and must adapt our behavior in almost all aspects of life to strange, unknown, and unwanted EU standards! Political decisions are no longer made at home, and we will most certainly not even be allowed to keep our own currency!" It is therefore not surprising that the weak support for EU membership in the

1994 referendum has now become a 75 percent negative attitude. This negative attitude is mainly based upon a series of disappointments. Many politicians in favor of EU membership promised that it would create jobs, reduce prices on food, reduce interest rates, and create substantial growth of wealth in general. Few of these things have so far materialized. On the contrary, people more and more have the impression that the costs of membership, bureaucracy, and lack of openness within the EU institutions are millstones around their necks.

National interest in the EU

The general Swedish attitude toward the EU, given what precedes, might seem negative. Indeed, there is a genuine risk that major national interests may suffer if this attitude is not changed. One of the reasons for the present lack of support is that the dominant political party for the last few decades, the Social Democrats, is still deeply divided in its own opinion. At the same time, the two parties that have always been against membership, the Environmentalists and the Leftists, have steadily grown in popularity.

Sweden is, and has always been, very dependent on exports for its goods and services. The domestic market is very small: the total Swedish population is today just under 9 million. Some 80 percent of the production by the 15 largest Swedish corporations in manufacturing is exported, thus contributing to a positive trade balance and a natural growth of wealth for the entire nation. If Sweden should leave the EU, it would put Swedish corporations outside the EU internal market, thus creating new trade barriers to the rest of Europe – the single most important market for Swedish industry. Devastating consequences for the Swedish export industry, the backbone of the wealth of the nation, would follow.

The Swedish economy is very small compared to most other economies in the industrialized world. The Swedish currency, the krona, has suffered from attacks by international financial raiders over the last few years, thus forcing the national government to intervene, at high cost. Moreover, several devaluations have been made by different Swedish governments during the last few decades. Short term, these devaluations have solved a national problem, at the cost of a long-term mistrust by the international financial market. Therefore, the highest priorities are to rebuild international confidence in Sweden's economic stability and to ensure that Sweden takes part in the creation of different systems to secure international economic and financial stability. Being a member of EMU and joining the common European currency, the euro, will most certainly be a good path toward these goals.

Traditional Swedish foreign policy has been built upon neutrality in wartime situations. This policy still stands. However, the international political environment has changed so dramatically and so rapidly that it is at least possible today to discuss a new Swedish foreign policy.

Given the weak economy of Sweden, and the recent dramatic cut in Swedish national defense, the time may now have come to re-evaluate Swedish neutrality, and perhaps even to discuss membership in NATO. For the past few years, Sweden has been a member of the European Partnership for Peace (EPP), which in itself can be regarded as a first step on the path to reconsidering traditional political standpoints on neutrality and a starting point for deeper cooperation with other nations in foreign affairs.

To be able to create a strong position in Europe for Sweden, the single most important activity is a clear demonstration of a new and much stronger national political leadership than has been demonstrated for the last few years. Of course, the future of Sweden as a nation must be viewed as far more important than the future of the political parties. In the interest of the nation, the leaders of the political parties must find ways to overcome the internal struggle for power. In sum, Sweden, a small country that is extremely dependent on international trade and still with a rather weak economy, has too much at stake not to support the development of a united Europe.

The role of the regions

There is a long tradition in Sweden of well-developed and strong regional and local self-determination. This historical fact has played an important role in creating internal strength, but also in forming the critical attitudes toward the EU held by many Swedes. The EU has been looked upon as an organization representing centralization and "too much power in Brussels," which is in sharp contrast to Swedish tradition. Given the Swedish tradition of strong self-determination, there is now a debate in Sweden about whether it is possible to go even further in delegating regional and local decision making.

For more than 400 years, Sweden has been divided into 24 counties, or *lan*, which are headed by a governor, appointed by the national government in Stockholm. These governors are normally chosen among elderly politicians, and their position is very often a reward for good and long-time service in the interest of the nation. The institution of county governors has been seen as something natural and in line with Swedish traditions. However, during the last few years this traditional system has been scrutinized and put under debate, as it is perceived as old-fashioned and even undemocratic.

Today, many Swedes are not at all satisfied with the fact that their governor comes from another region and, on top of that, that he or she is appointed by the central government in Stockholm. People want to have more direct influence on the choice of their governor, and there is a common opinion that he or she should come from the region in question. At the same time, the national government itself is considering whether there still is a need for all 24 counties, which were set up a few hundred years ago and were tailored to the structure of Sweden at that time. New regional structures have already been decided upon, in which three to five traditional counties have been merged into one large one, with a regionally appointed governor. The trend is very clear: there will be more such mergers of counties in Sweden. As a consequence, the traditional power of the capital city will diminish.

This process of ever deeper decentralization, a living example of applied subsidiarity, is now demonstrated even when it comes to the larger cities of Sweden. In the two largest cities, Stockholm and Gothenburg, the traditional way of governing the city has been replaced by a system in which each city has been divided into several independent boroughs, which have been given a high level of autonomy and their own "local mayor."

Although Swedes are regarded as rather conservative, they are open-minded and willing to accept change when they can see practical reasons behind it. Therefore there is a strong support in Sweden of the EU principle of subsidiarity. It is true to state that there is a real momentum in Sweden for increased regional autonomy. As a proof of this development, there are today five representative offices in Brussels from five different regions of Sweden, monitoring their own areas of interest and building their own networks. The tasks for these offices may vary, but they all have in common the promotion of cooperation with other regions in the EU, lobbying the EU institutions, and finding sources to co-finance development programs and projects. As there are Permanent Representations from each EU member country in Brussels, representing the respective national governments, one might think that there could be a risk of conflict between the two levels, the national and the regional. In the case of Sweden, the situation can best be described as complementary, as the two levels have different masters and different objectives.

The trend of increased regional autonomy is also visible from a larger European perspective, as the EU is working hard to materialize the principle of subsidiarity, giving more influence and political power to the regions at the expense of the EU institutions in Brussels. The best proof of this attitude is the creation of the Committee of the Regions.

Sweden is a very large country. It is more than 1,700 kilometers in length, which means that there are also natural regions based on pure climatic conditions. Far up in the north, north of the Polar Circle, is the region of the Laplanders, one of the few nomadic peoples of Europe. Here people have to adapt their lives to extreme changes of climatic conditions, going from days of almost total darkness during the winter period to the light summer nights, when the sun never sets. This is one of the few areas where you can find what is described by the EU as "arctic farming" with very tough living conditions. This Arctic region is very sparsely populated, with a general density, outside the cities of the region, of 1,000 to 5,000 inhabitants per 100 square kilometers. In the far south of Sweden, you can find the total opposite: a soft and welcoming landscape, very fertile and with a rich and varied agriculture and industry. In this region, the density of the population is some 30 times as high as in the north!

Such large differences in living conditions, of course, also create different lifestyles and general habits. It is therefore difficult to say that you can find one, common, culture or lifestyle that is dominant and which can be described as national and typical for the whole of Sweden. Furthermore, the dialects are so different that it is almost impossible for a typical Swede from the northern part of the country to understand his fellow citizen from the southern part. Indeed, Sweden is in this respect a typical example of the classical north–south conflict, with more vivid and emotional lifestyles in the south than in the north. This situation is visible in many other European countries, like Italy, Spain, and even Germany. In Sweden, the most industrialized and most productive areas are situated in the south of the country.

Growing number of immigrants

In the 1960s, the Swedish labor market attracted immigrants mainly from the other Nordic countries and from Turkey, Yugoslavia, and Greece. In the 1970s and 1980s, they were refugees, usually from countries outside Europe. That means that new ethnic groups are becoming common in the Swedish population.

Table 1   *Negative attitudes to immigration in Sweden, 1969–87*

	1969 (%)	1981 (%)	1987 (%)
None	27	61	60
Moderate	56	36	37
Strong	17	3	3

In 1989 the distribution of countries of origin as a percentage of the total numbers of immigrants in Sweden was as follows: Finland, 27%; Yugoslavia, 9%; Iran, 8%; Norway, 8%; Denmark, 6%; Turkey, 5%; Chile, 4%; Poland, 3%; Germany, 3%; Great Britain, 2%. The attitudes among the Swedes to immigrants have changed as time has passed. Table 1 shows the development from 1969 to 1987.

In short, Sweden is a nation in transition from its strong Nordic roots and sometimes glorious history to a new role within the European Union. Still a bit shy, Sweden is nonetheless playing a full and vigorous part in building Europe.

Bibliography

Gyllenskioll, E.C. (1987) *EG – i gar, i dag och i morgon* (The European Community – Today and Tomorrow), Lund: Studentlitteratur.

Hamilton, C.B. (1991) *Europa och Sverige* (Europe and Sweden), Stockholm: SNS Forlag.

Kitzinger, U. (1993) *The Challenge of the Common Market*, Oxford: Blackwell and Mott Ltd.

Tsoukalis, L. (1993) *The European Community: Past, Present and Future*, Oxford: Blackwells.

Viklund, D. (1991) *Atta Forsta EG* (Understanding the European Community), Stockholm: Norsteds Juridikforlag.

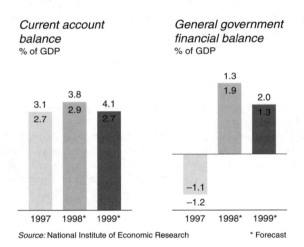

Real GDP
Annual % change

November forecasts

Inflation
Annual % change in
CPI (Dec to Dec)

Unemployment
% of workforce
(excluding government
training schemes)

Current account balance
% of GDP

General government financial balance
% of GDP

Source: National Institute of Economic Research　　　　　* Forecast

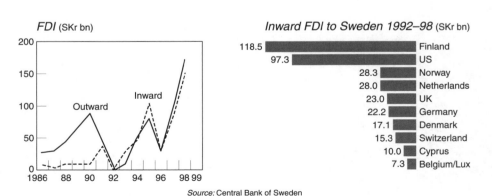

FDI (SKr bn)

Inward FDI to Sweden 1992–98 (SKr bn)

118.5	Finland
97.3	US
28.3	Norway
28.0	Netherlands
23.0	UK
22.2	Germany
17.1	Denmark
15.3	Switzerland
10.0	Cyprus
7.3	Belgium/Lux

Source: Central Bank of Sweden

PART III

Central and eastern Europe:
From disintegration to unity?

Editor's introduction: Russia

Janus-like, Russia looks both east and west – and has for centuries. Of course, Janus-type personalities can be perceived as perfidious or schizophrenic. Indeed, these two observations on the Russian character have often been made by westerners. Moreover, the criticism intensified after Russia's effective default on its debt in the summer of 1998. However, the reality of Russia is not perfidy, but duality. Russia is both European and Asian, sophisticated and barbaric, and the list of dualities continues.

Author Nigel Holden develops these contradictions and others with the deftness of the true expert. He highlights the sources of the fascination that Russia has always exerted over west Europeans and suggests common ground for business understanding between Russians and westerners. Despite the steady view of Russia as a whole given by Holden, many issues remain open for exploration.

- How does Russia, the recent master of an empire, view the advancement of a voluntary political and economic association of free states (the EU) and of a voluntary military association (NATO) toward its borders?
- Will Russia seek integration with western policies and economics, or seek refuge in its mystical and oriental traditions?
- How can the "fit" that Holden describes between Russia and western Europe be made better?

Russia

Area: 17,075,400 sq km
Languages: Russian and local languages
Currency: Rouble (Rbs)
Population: 147.5m (mid-1997 estimate)

Main trading partners (share of total trade to world 1997)

	EXPORTS (%)	IMPORTS (%)
EU	32.0	28.9
Germany	7.5	9.8
Ukraine	8.3	5.8
Belarus	5.3	6.8
Poland	2.9	1.6

Sources: Economist Intelligence Unit; IMF; EBRD

Constitution

National government
The government is appointed by the prime minister

National legislature
The constitution created a two-chamber legislature: the lower house, the State Duma, with 450 deputies elected on a territorial basis; and the upper house, the Federation Council, with 178 deputies, two from each of Russia's 89 republics and regions

Main political parties
The most important parties are:
Communist Party of the Russian Federation (CPRF); Our Home is Russia (OHR); Liberal Democratic party (LDP); Yabloko; Agrarian Party of Russia (APR); Russia's Democratic Choice (RDC); Women of Russia; Congress of Russian Communities (CRC)

Economic summary	1997	1998 (estimate)	1999 (forecast)
Total GDP ($bn)	446	329	n.a.
(Roubles bn)	2,586	2,740	n.a.
GDP deflator (annual % change)	16.6	11.3	80.0
Industrial production (annual % change)	1.9	−5.2	n.a.
Unemployment rate (% of workforce)	10.9	12.4	14.0
Money supply, M2 (annual % change)	28.4	21.0	32.6
Gross reserves inc. gold ($bn)	17.8	12.2	n.a.
Current account balance ($bn)	−0.8	−1.4	14.0

8

◆ ◆ ◆

Coping with Russia as a bad fit

Nigel J. Holden
Copenhagen Business School, Denmark

All our enterprises begin with words and evaporate in words.
> Alexander Nikitenko, nineteenth-century literary censor (quoted in Hingley, *The Russian Mind*, 1978)

Everybody knows that Greeks and Orientals like high-flown language, and indeed make a cult of insincerity. (This is why Romans find it so difficult to come to a true measure of Easterners; we do not realise that for them rhetoric is an end and pleasure in itself, frequently unrelated to action, never moving beyond a purely verbal significance).
> Alan Massie, *Augustus*, 1995

Introduction

This chapter on Russia is primarily written for managers and other business professionals who are curious to understand the workings of the Russian business mind. Evidence considered later suggests that business involvement between foreigners and Russians frequently becomes stressful and antagonistic for both parties. The aim of this contribution is to attempt to explain how such frictions and misunderstandings occur and what perhaps – though it may be a big perhaps – can be done about it.

The chapter is in two main sections. The first presents a view of Russia and Russians from a historical perspective, but with an emphasis on the ambivalence of Russian attitudes to the West. The underlying premise is that Russia has, for at least five centuries, been "a bad fit" (Davies, 1996), first in the European context, then in the era of global ideological confrontation called "the Cold War" and again in the present period, which awkwardly and inadequately classifies post-Soviet Russia as "a transitional economy." In the second main section, we focus on the nature of the clash of minds – more bad fit – between non-Russian and Russian business people.

It should be explained that this chapter hardly touches on the monumental quest of introducing market-economy thinking and practices. Readers interested in this topic have no shortage of excellent works and commentaries at their disposal. The author of this contribution takes the view that only restricted insights into the post-Soviet Russian mindset derive from observing the evolution of Russia's proto-capitalist structures and institutions. Wider insights surely come from probing those features of Russian life which, well before this present era and even before the Soviet one, have always captured the foreign imagination: "the quaint, the bizarre, the incongruous" (Hingley, 1978). This chapter, taking its cue from that, is an attempt to reveal Russia's quaintness, bizarreness, and incongruity as a direct source of insight into the Russian business mentality. It is hoped that this admittedly unusual approach may prove beneficial to practitioners, while making a useful contribution to the growing literature on psychic distance, which is concerned with understanding the impact of factors that impede the smooth flow of information between firms and markets in cross-cultural contexts (for a discussion of psychic distance, see: Hallén and Widersheim-Paul, 1984; Holden and Burgess, 1994; Johanson and Wiedersheim-Paul, 1975).

An ancestral suspicion: history, geography, and climate

No discussion of Russian life past or present can preclude mention of "the brutally harsh climatic and economic conditions of the Russian climate" (Vlachoutsicos and Lawrence, 1996), on the one hand, and the mind-boggling vastness of Russian territory, on the other. For it is in this "unpatrollable eternity" (Fallowell, 1994), in this "ungraspable formlessness" in which "everything falls apart, is diluted, drowned" (Kapugcinski, 1994) that we perhaps find the most potent influences on the Russian mind and temper.

Geography and climate have not only conspired to keep Russia out of step first with Europe and then with "the West," but also shaped the Russian value system with its emphasis on the primacy of the collective for sheer survival. In these traditions, we find two consistent traits of Russian life, which were by no means diminished in the Soviet era: first, the governance of the collective by tough leadership; second, the performance of work in energetic bursts.

This latter point is especially important. The rigors of the climate meant that traditionally Russians could work only for limited periods – in late spring and summer. For the rest of the time they were indolent. But when the work could be done, it was done with a vengeance. Although the industrialization of life in the Soviet period inevitably disrupted the traditional seasonal pattern of work, the centralized planning system never really evened out the balance between periods of slackness and periods of intense activity. The periods of intense activity were frequently associated with the latter stages of an official planning period, the most important such deadline marking the end of a five-year plan. Interspersed were the periods of slackness, when men and machines were idle: there was variously skiving, waiting around for supplies, and producing things in a lackadaisical fashion (sometimes for the black market). Under this "tradition of mechanistic growthmanship" (Dyker, 1992) a consequence was that many projects were never completed by the official deadlines through chronic supply inefficiencies. By the late 1980s, for example, about a third of capital investment in construction was being poured into projects that would remain uncompleted (Dyker, 1992).

Both the traditional Russian and the Soviet way of working in intensive bursts has been widely noted. Hingley (1978) discusses this question, and it is worth quoting him:

Are the Russians energetic or lazy? Abundant evidence can be quoted to show them as both. Where one observer stresses their "dynamic energy" and "enthusiasm for work," another says that they cannot bear to exert themselves.

That the Russian tends at any moment to be a prodigy of laziness or of energy – that he works, if at all, in spasms of momentary enthusiasm – is a common observation. This pattern is often linked to the peasant psychology of a nation largely consisting until recent years of farm labourers accustomed to toil in a northern latitude where field work is concentrated with a short period, thus demanding greater efforts than milder climes impose. To this brief, violent spurt of annual labour the Russian peasant long ago gave the name strada (etymologically, "suffering"). It is from the strada, according to the historian Klyuchevsky, that the people derives its talent for "short, concentrated bursts of excessive exertion. Hence the routine of brisk, frenzied, effective toil followed by the autumn's and winter's enforced idleness. No other nation in Europe can put forward such concentrated spasms of labour as the Russian."

Are the Russians energetic or lazy? Are they European or Asiatic? Are they with us or against us? According to the great Russian Christian philosopher, Nikolai Berdyayev (1874–1948), Russia has the capacity to intrigue the world with its inner mysteries and repel it in equal measure with its sheer barbarity (Berdyayev, 1918/1990). Ever since its first contacts with western Europe in the sixteenth century, Russia has bemused and perturbed visitors with its bizarre combination of the familiar and unfamiliar; indeed, early travelers "did not know how to interpret" the mysterious Muscovites, as Russians were then known (Hingley, 1978). Over the centuries, the Russians have been variously described as not knowing their strength and having no powers of self-restraint, as combining European intelligence with Asiatic genius (a nineteenth-century opinion), as longing for freedom and – curiously – a sense of crampedness at the same time, and taking perverse delight in their lack of social polish *vis-à-vis* some of their more genteel neighbors to the west. In 1939, Winston Churchill famously described Russia as "a riddle wrapped in a mystery inside an enigma." Post-Soviet Russia continues to bemuse and perturb us, but the late twentieth-century scenario has enhanced both the familiar and unfamiliar with many a deadly twist.

To those without much knowledge of the country and its people, Russia's not infrequent anti-western swipes and postures are a particular source of bafflement. Was Russia not supposed to be getting visibly pro-western after the country had been liberated from the shackles of communism? So how is it that Alexander Rutskoi, a former vice-president of the Russian Federation, could dismiss western aid – millions of dollars, ecus and yen – as nothing more than "free cheese in a mouse trap" (quoted in Steele, 1994)? Are there really Russians in high places who believe that the main work of western organizations based in Moscow, like the Ford Foundation, the Soros Foundation, and US Peace Corps, is "to thwart Russia as a state"? The Federal Counter-Espionage Agency, the successor to the KGB, thinks so (*Financial Times*, 1995).

Is there really a strong Russian conviction that the EU Tacis program, which accounts for about 70 percent of technical aid to the former Soviet Union, is being used by European companies "as a stepping-stone to the 'exploitation' of the Russian economy" (*Economist*, 1993)? Did a former Russian ambassador to Washington really describe his country's foreign policy in the so-called post-communist honeymoon period as "infantile pro-Americanism" (*Economist*, 1995b)? And is it really true that Russia has revitalized a top-secret Soviet program to harness underground nuclear shock-waves in order to unleash earthquakes and tidal waves against potential enemies, such as Americans on the other side of the San Andreas Fault (*Russia Express*, 1996)?

For those with a knowledge of Russian history, much of this is uncomfortably redolent of Russia's deep-seated wariness of the West: the conviction that western aid and investment as well as western-sponsored management training initiatives in Russia are a ploy to weaken still further the Russian economy and to keep Russia in a state of semi-colonial tutelage to the West. Russians seem to forget that western businessmen only see ruin for their investment if the Russian economy were actually to buckle under (which nearly occurred in summer 1998), and I have yet to meet a western management educator who is a self-confessed purveyor of a lethal anti-Russia preparation code-named "management know-how."

The fact is that every person professionally involved with Russia needs to be fully aware of the occasional zaniness and vigor of Russian perceptions about the motives of western governments and companies. We may call them "hang-ups," but a 1993 issue of *The Economist* expressed it better by referring to Russia's "ancestral suspicion" of the West. Russians look into their history and often see betrayal and abandonment by the West. Today in Russia, then, there is more than a passing feeling that the West cannot be trusted. Nor is this mood restricted to politicians and bureaucrats. The following vignette, quoted by authors Wilson and Donaldson (1996), speaks volumes about prejudices just below the surface: "The foreign boss of a growing company told a Russian sales representative that profit would go toward sorely needed equipment purchases, then later to salary hikes. 'I know what you're doing,' she protested. 'I've read Marx. You're an exploiter.'"

Every western professional who seeks insights into developing relationships with Russian counterparts needs to be very clear on the potency of this ancestral suspicion. It is against this background of ancestral suspicion and the corresponding deep-seated western wariness of Russia that western managers operate and develop their business relationships. This brings us to a major insight and challenge to western managers operating in Russia. The most important relationship that western managers have is the one with Russia itself. Unless they can cope with Russia, they will not be able to manage relationships with Russians.

Whither Russia?

Russians now live in a country which "does not correspond to any previous 'Russia' in history" (Applebaum, 1995). This new Russia is the product of what Yergin and Gustafson (1994) term Russia's "triple transition," which followed the disintegration of the Soviet Union in December 1996. The three transition processes were as follows:

* From dictatorship to democracy.
* From centralized economy to free market.
* From four-century-old empire to nation-state.

The awesome scale of Russia's transformation and the very swiftness with which the

Communist Party lost its grip still astound us. That colorful and perceptive chronicler of post-Soviet Russia, Duncan Fallowell (1994), tried to capture the Russian sense of after-shock with a comparison with post-imperial Britain. "If Britain finds it difficult to grasp quite how it fell from being the dominant world power to a funny little island in less than half a lifetime, how much greater must be the Russian amazement at their fall from super-power to quasi-third-world bankrupt in 6 years flat."

Toward economic integration?

No one knows where the new Russia is heading. It is only a partial comfort to know that most commentators, both western and Russian, seem to agree that Russia will not go back to totalitarian ways. Not that consensus among specialists has the force of accurate pre-diction. After all, how many of those same commentators, a decade ago, would have pre-dicted a virtually bloodless collapse of the Soviet Union? After the disintegration of the Soviet Union in 1991, experts were only too quick to suggest that Russia, true to form, would be unreformable, and that its leaders would be incapable of transforming the wreckage of communism into viable companies and market institutions. In the words of *The Economist* (1995b), at the tail-end of the Gorbachev era: "The overwhelming con-sensus among Soviet economists and foreign Sovietologists then was that the Russians were different: they had entrepreneurial ability, they harboured an unusually strong sus-picion of wealth, and they had no interest to become rich. Homo Sovieticus was only dis-tantly related to economic man."

When the Soviet Union collapsed in 1991, most forms of private business activity were illegal. Five years later, Russia had some 2,500 licensed commercial banks, 600 invest-ment funds, and 40 million shareholders. The liberalization of prices and privatization of some 6,000 medium-sized and large enterprises within 18 months created a private-sector market that accounts for more than 60 percent of GDP. To put that in another way: pro-portionately, Russia's state-owned sector is now smaller than Italy's.

This is a remarkable transformation, even though there is a long way to go to the sus-tained deindustrialization of the Russian economy, without which a true market economy cannot come into being. The battle for deindustrialization means:

- The breaking-down of gargantuan enterprises into smaller productive units, which specialize in the manufacture and marketing of products that people want to buy.
- The creation of a diverse service sector.
- The spread of consumer markets.
- The creation of conditions attractive to investors (see Sachs (1994) for an admirably lucid discussion of these issues).

The complex act of rebalancing resources and priorities can take place satisfactorily only in a politically stable environment (which Russia both is and is not) and against a background of continued infrastructural improvement. Fortunately, and this is easily overlooked, Russia's legacy from the Soviet period has not been too bad in this latter respect. Russia, in comparison with other former socialist countries, has a serviceable national electricity grid, national and regional road and rail networks, a country-wide system of airports, and – vital for business development – a national telephone system, which people are no longer afraid of using.

This last point is but one highly significant indicator of how life has changed almost beyond recognition for the peoples of Russia. But the big question is: will the advance to a market economy be all worth it in the end? The dilemma is well posed by Mikheyev (1996):

> Everything has changed: how people earn a living, buy things, address each other, choose their homes and vacations, educate themselves, seek medical assistance, and socialise. The changes have been greater for some than for others. Social status, living standards, and quality of life are now defined differently: different social problems, ills, and fears now preoccupy people. But have these changes been for better or worse? A great debate rages on this issue.

Within five years, Russia created a business culture comprising two dominant, but opposing tendencies, if we are to believe Wilson and Donaldson (1996). On the one hand, there are those who hanker after the old days of socialism with all its mapped-out security and its lumbering centralized economy, which could build a power-station faster than a barber's shop, and who presumably miss the dreary, empty stores and the 9 billion (no misprint for million) hours of queuing per year (Skurski, 1983).[1] These people are attached to the old style of doing things and often work in the generally unreconstructed realms of officialdom. While disapproving of Russia's "descent into capitalism," they rapidly gain from it, making handsome sales from foreign and Russian business people alike out of their insider knowledge of the oppressive bureaucracy.

On the other hand, there are the new movers and shakers of Russian society: the new entrepreneurs, who may be revamped Soviet bosses, or the young thrusting yuppie class, which is buying up portentous residences and cruising around the cities in Mercedes and BMWs. Of course, not everyone belongs to one group or to the other. Where, for example, do we place those PhD biochemists who are now vastly overqualified car salesmen, barmen and bouncers, whose "highly trained minds are now roaring round the rim of despair?" (Fallowell, 1995).

Another way of looking at this polarization is to say that one part of Russia is cautious, conservative, and suspicious of the West, which is merely continuing its policy, well established in the Cold War, of trying to unhinge Russia; while another part of Russia wants change and looks upon the West as an essentially positive support and source of ideas. But have we not been here before? Are we not seeing the late twentieth-century version of the nineteenth-century division of Russians into the modernizing westerners (*zapadniki*) and the Russia-is-special Slavophiles? Alas, for the rest of the world, not to mention Russia, the 1917 Revolution failed to resolve this dilemma about Russia's special direction. The dramatic collapse of the USSR in 1991 merely exposed afresh the Russian "love–hate hysteria about the West" (Hingley, 1978).

A bad fit: national attitudes toward the place of Russia in the world

What are we to make of all this? After all, since the demise of Soviet power, Russia has lost its empire, its international political influence has shriveled, it is no longer the great counterpoise to the western way of life, no longer a beacon for the world non-aligned movement. The short answer is that Russia is experiencing a severe identity crisis. Russians are hypersensitive about their status with those whom they formerly regarded as equals in terms of world power and prestige, and they are feeling vulnerable that, for the first time in nearly 500 years, Russia's borders have shrunk. In other words, Russia is reappraising its place in the world. The point not to overlook here is that these processes of reappraisal and readjustment are not just political: they have a transcendental dimension, focusing on a deep-seated Russian sense of special mission.

Perhaps the first inkling in the West of this Russian sense of special mission became noticeable after the Napoleonic Wars, when Russia established itself as a "mercurial and meddlesome" ally (Kissinger, 1994) of Great Britain and Austria. This political recognition by the two other great imperial nations of Europe not only whetted the Russian appetite for territory, but also intensified Russian awareness of its special, Eurasian destiny.

Russia's non-conforming outsider specialness was articulated by Pyotr Chaadayev, a leading nineteenth-century philosopher: "We do not belong to any of the great families of mankind, neither to the East nor to the West" (quoted in *Economist*, 1996a). The theme was taken up by the Russian translator of John Stuart Mill and Karl Marx, who argued that "Russia can lay down a new historical path from that taken by Europe" (quoted in *Economist*, 1996a). Both Tolstoy and Dostoyevsky were of the same persuasion. (Was it not Dostoyevsky who described the Russia of his day as "sublime chaos"?) But perhaps the most eloquent and certainly the most mystical advocate of the Russia-is-special school was the philosopher Berdyayev, who wrote in 1918 that "from earliest times there has been a premonition that Russia is predestined to something great, that Russia is a special country, unlike any other."

In the Soviet era, this thinking took on a new garb: the USSR (i.e. the Sovietized successor to the Russian Empire) was "the world's first socialist state," the slayer of Hitlerism with minimum support from its western allies, and the bulwark against world capitalism. Whatever else it was, the Soviet Union was always an alternative. Present-day Russia, which is steadily showing signs of non-conformity with western aspirations, is continuing the tradition of being a meddlesome outsider nation.

The issue of whether we should regard Russia as more European than Asiatic, and to what degree, is one of the great debates of history. The author of this chapter ventures his own point of view. Russia, in terms of its high culture, has shown western tendencies; in matters of statecraft, it has shown a penchant to Asiatic despotism. But it will be safer to quote a real historian on the question of Russia's status *vis-à-vis* the West and, in particular, Europe. In his much acclaimed study of the history of Europe, Norman Davies (1996) has written: "For more than five hundred years the cardinal problem in defining Europe has centred on the inclusion or exclusion of Russia. Throughout modern history, an Orthodox, autocratic, economically backward but expanding Russia has been a bad fit."

The term "bad fit" is excellent shorthand for describing the peculiar dilemma of Russia's place in the world. In the Soviet era, the description "bad fit" would have had plenty of ideological overtones. It would have been seen overwhelmingly in terms of Cold War political relations and military posturing. In today's world, its internal politics and foreign policy are causing Russia to be called "an especially awkward customer" (*Economist*, 1993) by western governments, and the West's intelligence community is haunted afresh by Cold War rhetoric with "an awful sense of déjà-vu" (*Financial Times*, 1996a).

These days it is not just governments who are experiencing Russia as a kind of unreconstructed bad fit. Western management educators, consultants, and investors are constantly reminded of Russia's reluctance, inability, or unwillingness to develop "isomorphic management structures and practices" (Whitley, 1990) with actual or potential business partners' organizations. Western experiences with Russian counterparts often speak of clashes of opinion, mutual misperceptions of motives, abortive discussions, and so forth. No small literature is being built up on "chilling tales of failure and frustration" (Dunayeva and Vipperman, 1995).

Consider these instances and observations. Management training program for Russians have been described as "a cross-cultural mine-field" (*Financial Times*, 1993). German companies "are getting the impression that they are being treated like criminals intending to buy up Russia cheap" (Kravchenko, 1995). Richardson (1995) has observed that "every negotiation is an occasion for Machiavellian intrigues, manoeuvring and posturing." Russians and westerners do not share a common language of business and management, literally and metaphorically: literally, because the Russian language has not developed the necessary concepts and terminology (see Holden *et al.*, 1997; Holden, 1995). This in turn may help to explain why business negotiations between Americans and Russians have been likened to "a dialogue of the deaf" (Dunayeva and Vipperman, 1995).

Being a bad fit, Russia has also been not so much behind and backward as out of phase with the countries and societies against whom Russia has traditionally measured itself. This is surely the price that Russia has paid for being by-passed by the great shaping influences of "the Reformation, the Enlightenment, the Age of Discovery; and modern market economics" (Kissinger, 1994). This explanation may help to account for the fact that no small number of observers – even Russian ones – are describing Russia as a premodern society.

Russia: a premodern society?

At first glance, the suggestion that Russia is premodern seems pejorative, almost insulting, but how else are we to consider this country? Has not Solzhenitsyn (1991) written that Russia "has cruelly forfeited the entire twentieth century," while other writers emphasize that Russia has lost its way as a result of the trauma of the collapse of the USSR from superpower to bankruptcy and virtual Third World economy? Russia today is "a pre-democracy" (Yergin and Gustafson, 1994). According to a Russian historian, quoted in Remnick (1994), "a medieval mind-set has lasted until very recently. We are leaving the Middle Ages." Even Richard Poe (1993), a vastly enthusiastic "Russia-preneur," to use his own idiosyncratic self-designation, concedes that Russia "never left the Middle Ages."[2]

Premodernity is admittedly a tricky concept; the modern western mind finds it difficult to handle; we will not find any reference to it in the current literature on international management (you will find more discussion of postmodernism). But we believe it to be a vitally important heuristic for understanding the Russian mindset. Premodernity is in fact part of the bad fit: it jars with the western world, which Russia both admires and envies; it is a major factor creating clashes with foreign business counterparts. It is an element of what Vlachoutsicos (1995) terms "the inner logic"[3] of Russian managerial thinking and behavior; for this inner logic, which operates like "an obstructive fist" in the transformation of the Russian economy, is a still potent expression of the Russian collective value-system, whose origins can be clearly traced back to the Kievan state (1054–1238).

Another facet of Russian premodernity of outlook may be their tendency to make "dogmatic assertions about the unknowable," a ready tendency that takes the breath away of even Hingley (1978), a seasoned connoisseur of the Russian mind. (For a wonderful array of Russian dogmatic exotica, see Fallowell's semi-autobiographical *One Hot Summer in St Petersburg* (1994).) Another creditable authority noting the same tendency is a biographer of Tolstoy, who noted how the great author, on a brief fact-finding journey to Germany, was convinced that the German system of public education was seriously flawed (Wilson, 1989). Tolstoy's ability to roundly criticize these deficiencies, while making a virtue of the fact that Russia did not have any system, is reminiscent of Soviet rebuttals of, say, "the excess production" in capitalist societies, whereas millions of Soviet citizens were being perennially deprived of most basic consumer items in the USSR as a matter of state policy.

By this point, it will be unequivocally clear that it is an immense challenge to describe even in a partially meaningful way the Russian mindset – the mindset of a nation that has produced some of the world's finest composers and novelists (and in Pushkin, perhaps the finest poet of the nineteenth century); which embarked on, and eventually recoiled from, one of the most psychologically disruptive political and social experiments of the twentieth century; which sends manned space stations orbiting the Earth; which relishes earthy proverbs and munches ice-cream in biting winter cold. Even more humbling is Hingley's (1978) caveat that one should "never ... assume in advance that an unknown citizen of Russia ... will necessarily exhibit even a single characteristic, however minor, from any amalgam which may be claimed as typical of the group as a whole."

If the reader feels that he or she knows much less about Russia than when starting to read this chapter, then that, paradoxically, is progress!

The culture of Russian business practice

Reviewing the above list of foreigners' impressions of Russians as business negotiators, we cannot fail to be struck by four facets of the Russian mindset, which not only are culture specific, but also tend to go against the grain of western logic about good business practice. The four factors, which will be discussed individually below, are as follows:

♦ Russians' relative unbusiness-mindedness.
♦ Their proneness to boredom and dislike of "dry" business relationships.
♦ Their inclination to view negotiation as a process for securing absolute advantage over a business partner.
♦ The quest for equivalence – as opposed to equality – with their western business partners.

The relative unbusiness-mindedness of Russians

The apparent Russian lack of flair for, or interest in, business has received attention from many authors (e.g. Aslund, 1993; Chamberlain, 1995; Holden and Cooper, 1994; Remnick, 1994; Smith, 1990; Wilson and Donaldson, 1996; Yergin and Gustafson, 1994). Russians, it seems, frequently tend to see business as exploitative, deceptive, and vulgar. There is, as far as I know, no study on the competences of Russians as business people (although Handelman (1994) provides much detail on the wheeling and dealing activities in the shadow economy). The list cited above of impressions made on their western counterparts can be taken to support the conviction that Russian business people lack not merely formal skills, but the instincts for business that long years under communism have not eradicated in countries such as the central European "tigers" – namely, Poland, Hungary, and the Czech Republic – and, more to the point perhaps, in China.

It is customary to ascribe this seeming commercial maladroitness to Russia's seven-decade exposure to communism and two pre-revolutionary factors: an enduring disdainful attitude to money and money-making, and the failure of late-Imperial Russia to develop an interlocking system of capitalist institutions supporting the growth of industry. But this is only part of the story. This explanation does not take account of the Russian character or, to be more precise, the opposing poles of the Russian character.

First, although it is highly persuasive to assume that Russia's new entrepreneurs are dominated by the need to make a profit, this must be tempered with a recognition that this is not so clear-cut. In 1991, just before the collapse of the USSR, the German *Manager Magasin* reported a Russian businessman as saying: "Anyone who thinks that the chance to profit must electrify every Soviet manager fails to understand our logic." This informant seems to exemplify that strain of Russian businessperson who has "a from-the-heart idealism, a compulsive urge to be seen to do good, to seek philosophical justification for wealth" (*Sunday Times*, 1992; quoted in Holden, 1992). This is no ideal theorizing. As two leading French researchers have noted, there is still a resistance about breaking with the Soviet model of enterprise management, under which *le bon directeur* dispenses accommodation and sports facilities for his workers (largess that must somehow come out of revenue earned by the enterprise); while the workers, fearful for their livelihoods, beg the bosses with pleas of "don't forget our children" (Berelowitch and Wieviorka, 1996); to which the bosses probably respond with more compassion than bosses in the West, behind whose backs there lurk only shareholders and creditors.

Second, we need to note the existence of another strain of the idealistically oriented Russian businessperson – the intellectually well-rounded specimen, who, it seems, likes to operate as an independent soul. With this type in mind, a Russian business magazine in 1990 described the new-style business manager as "a special person, educated, quick-witted, dynamic, and paradoxical as it may sound, [with] a certain degree of dilettantism" (*Delovye Svyazi*, 1990). The use of the word "dilettantism" requires a brief explanation, for it conjures up something quintessentially Russian: it connotes the much-cherished freedom to be exuberant combined with the compulsion to switch enthusiasms, to embark on a new project – and leave other things half finished (Holden, 1992).

Thus, when attempting any characterization of Russian business people, we need to take account of the mercurial side of the Russian character: that impulsive element in their make-up which inclines them to change mood, attitude, and agenda – possibly simultaneously!

Boredom and the need for emotional solidarity

Russians have a tendency, once they cannot immediately see the point of anything, to become distracted and look massively bored (they look massively bored because they are!). In business, two things bore Russians:

♦ "Dry" relationships with business partners.
♦ Matters of detail.

Russians do not take to "dry" relationships with foreign business partners (Mejevitch, 1993; Holden, 1995): interactions with a low emotional voltage. It may not be too much of an exaggeration to say that, whereas a western businessperson wants to get close to a business partner to understand how to service the partner's needs better, the Russian businessperson wants closeness for emotional solidarity.

This particular need not only dominates the Russian frame of reference; it also overrides the importance of long-term benefits, which may be central to the foreign partner's negotiating stance. This means that pronouncements about mutual long-term benefits may not have much emotional and psychological appeal to Russians, unless there is an adjustment of the social distance between the Russian and the non-Russian business partner.

The Russian way of handling human relationships in business involvements is not, say, the Japanese way, which always requires a punctiliously tactful observance of social distance. For Russians, social distance must be obliterated, and business entertainment, smoothed with vodka, can help achieve precisely that, and fast too. No wonder that many foreign business people believe that the explicit purpose of Russian business entertainment is to achieve inebriation all round (Holden *et al.*, 1997). This, of course, is merely continuing a centuries-long tradition of Russian befuddling of foreign visitors (see, for example, Massie (1992) on Peter the Great's epic drinking bouts, and Holden *et al.* (1997) on toasting as a form of business communication in Russia).

The second thing to bore Russians are the actual technicalities and intricacies of business, including the accompanying paperwork, which get in the way of doing a deal now (Wilson and Donaldson, 1996). This reluctance to handle detail in preference to the grand design may be connected with traditional Russian gigantomania, which the Soviet system "exploited" and even magnified with its tendency to proceed with (prestige) projects without adequate information at the working level – and hope for the best. To quote an experienced informant, Russian managers "like to make big decisions – fast" (Holden *et al.*, 1997). Once the big decision has been made, it will as a rule be left up to subordinates to sort out the detail, which can place those subordinates in an invidious position (Wilson and Donaldson, 1996).

The quest for absolute advantage

Not only in international economics, but also in their political and military behavior too, Russian posturing is based on a quest to secure and keep absolute advantage. Russians, claim Wilson and Donaldson (1996), "often see negotiating as a zero-sum game. That is, one side cannot win without the other side losing." They add that "a win-win situation [is] alien to their past experience." It does indeed seem that there is in the Russian mind little or no place for the concept of relative advantage. In 1947, US Secretary of State Dean Acheson bemoaned the fact that "the business of dealing with the Russians is a long, long job" (Yergin and Gustafson, 1994); his boss, President Truman, had experienced the same at the Potsdam Conference two years earlier (see McCullogh, 1992). And it took McDonald's no less than 14 years to negotiate the opening of the first Moscow fast-food restaurant. If ever a capitalist enterprise deserved an Order of Lenin for sheer perseverance!

The Russian negotiator is inclined to take up a fairly *a priori* rigid position – so rigid, in fact, that he or she has limited scope to maneuver and hence make concessions. Accordingly, it is up to the negotiating partner to make concessions – which is seen by Russians partly as a sign of the former's weakness and flexibility. Understanding this general Russian position is essential knowledge for the foreign business partner. It means, of course, that foreign partners must ensure that there is sufficient slack in their negotiating position, including their pricing tactics, to go through the motions of making concessions, which is singularly reminiscent of business negotiations with the USSR's centralized foreign trade corporations (see, for example, Kennedy, 1985).

The idea of equivalence

It is perhaps hardly surprising that Russians have a reputation for being hard bargainers, but not for being adroit negotiators. And the foreign businessperson who assumes that negotiation with the Russians is a game that is concerned with achieving "da" has failed to grasp the Russian mindset. Insight into this mindset requires some awareness of troublesome topics such as traditional attitudes to money and money-making, ambivalence to the West, and a need for a business relationship to comprise intellectually and emotionally satisfying elements. Without this awareness, the western businessperson may not appreciate that the Russian way of seeking accommodations with foreign business partners is based on the conviction that it is the foreign partner who should be the more flexible – indeed, demonstrably more flexible – in making adjustments to the relationship.

It is in this aspiration that we find what Vlachoutsicos (1995) illuminatingly describes as the Russian desire for equivalence as distinct from equality in their relationships with western business partners. At the heart of this desire for equivalence is a Russian conviction that Russians are no less intelligent, educated, or competent than people elsewhere, but that Russia has a lot of problems which make it difficult at the moment to harness all its talents. At the same time, Russia still has undisputed potential as an economic and technological powerhouse. It is, the Russians will point out, the selfsame potential that transformed a largely backward agricultural country into the second most powerful country on earth in a matter of decades, defeated Nazi Germany single-handedly (*sic*), launched the world's first artificial satellite, created a scientific establishment which in its heyday (in the 1970s) comprehensively rivaled achievement in the western world (Graham, 1994), and presented over many decades a fully fledged alternative model of global economic development.

The fact that the communist leadership sacrificed millions of Russians and non-

Russians in the gulag (see Conquest, 1990), kept the rest behind the country's borders, and deprived them of what we consider to be basic necessities of life over several decades – all this does not diminish the Russian argument. The Russian businessperson who uses the example of Russia's launch of the first sputnik (in October 1957) to impress a would-be joint venture partner from the UK is using a past – and world-famous – technological achievement to demonstrate contemporary potential. The Russian knows that his enterprise is not technologically equal to the UK firm now, but believes that it has the potential to be. This posture requires of a foreign business partner a recognition of equivalence in the situation. Awareness of a Russian need for equivalence is one thing, but building this need into a viable business arrangement is something else.

Thus the advice that "Western managers should expect to approach their Russian counterparts as equals" (Veiga *et al.*, 1995) sounds sensible enough, but it is misplaced. Likewise the assumption guiding a cross-cultural management program in Moscow, which allows "Russians and Americans to learn from one another and preserves the best from both cultures" (Dunayeva and Vipperman, 1995), seems to miss an essential component of the Russian mindset.

Grasping the potency of Russians' need for equivalence is one of the cross-cultural keys – perhaps the major one – to their mindset. If, however, the distinction between equivalence and equality is still not clear, then this explanation may help: there is only one time-honored way in Russia of achieving equality with foreigners, at least in the short term, and that is to ply and quite possibly anesthetize them with vodka.

It will be useful to add a comment on the coping strategy which suggests that the western businessperson, seeking to accommodate the Russian wish for emotional congruence, needs to address his or her Russian partners grandiloquently with an appeal to their hearts. Here the western negotiator must develop an understanding for the Russian love of language in its poetic and rhetorical modes, especially at social gatherings. The Russians prize eloquence, which they (perhaps deceptively) see as a hallmark of a civilized person; they enjoy grandiloquence because it appeals to the romantic and sentimental element of their character. Toasting at meals, when the vodka flows, is when Russian and foreigner alike can indulge this cherished facility with words. For the Russians, hearty feasts, carefree merrymaking, and lavish toasting are all very much part and parcel of doing business (Holden *et al.*, 1997). The Russians actually have a word that connotes all this revelry. The word is *otdykh*, which is literally translated as "rest" or "relaxation." But, as anyone familiar with Russian life will tell you, Russian-style relaxation is not for the fainthearted. And you may be certain of one thing: when the Russians are in entertainment mode, the very last thing on their mind will be your joint business plans.

For good order's sake, I must point out the importance of the participation of interpreters, whose capacity for perpetuating mutual miscomprehension is "impossible to exaggerate" (Johanson, 1994; see also Holden, 1995). Foreign business people who do not know Russian must be aware of two ways in which Russian interpreters can undo much good. First, there is a serious deficiency of standardized terms in Russian for describing market-economy business and management phenomena. Interpreters are frequently unfamiliar not only with the relevant terminology in English, but also with the assumptions, principles, and practices of management to which that terminology refers (see Holden, 1995). Thus they often fail to follow the western logic behind whatever they are translating; the result is a misconstruing of facts, assumptions, and attitudes. Second, interpreters have a habit of "freezing out" the emotional element – and often humor as well – in the discussions in which they participate. Foreigners with a good knowledge of Russian will despair at this. Interpreters have a habit of simply delivering verbal cardboard!

Conclusion

In writing this contribution on the Russian mindset, I have been guided by a number of notions – I dare not call them truths. Such notions include the powerful concepts of equivalence and Russia as a bad fit. In my exposition, I have tried to take account of the fact that Russians as a people are highly emotional in their reactions and in their needs. Curiously, in a vast amount of management writing, and not least in the growing field of cross-cultural studies, the manifestation of emotion is rarely discussed as a major cultural variable. Presumably the reason is that emotion simply becomes conflated with too many other things.

But in the case of Russians, their emotions are virtually on permanent display. Indeed, no study of Russians which discounts the fact that an emotional manifestation is an integral part of their normal reaction to events and pressures is likely to ring true. But the problem facing foreigners in their professional contact development is that Russian reactions frequently appear to be contradictory. Thus it is a major factor influencing the psychic distance dividing foreign and Russian business people. At this point, it is perhaps judicious to leave the reader in the very safe hands of Ronald Hingley (1978), who provides a brilliant explanation of this complicated issue. He comments:

> Since the Russians have already been observed oscillating between the extremes of life-enhancement and life-denial, it will not be surprising if they also exhibit other opposed characteristics. Broad, yet narrow; reckless, yet cautious; tolerant, yet censorious; freedom-loving, yet slavish; independent, docile, tough, malleable, kind, cruel, loving, hating, energetic, lazy, naïve, cynical, polite, rude – they will be found veering in all these directions at some time or other; as what people will not?

And now the crux: "The Russian speciality is a tendency for a single individual or group to alternate between one extreme position and its opposite; or even, somehow, to occupy two or more mutually exclusive positions simultaneously." You have been warned!

Notes

1. The figure of 9 billion hours is based on Soviet statistics for 1975, quoted by Skurski (1983): "Sociologists and economists estimate that the country averages 35 billion hours annually on shopping and that 25 per cent is spent waiting in line."
2. Norman Davies (1996) quotes Eric Fromm (*The Fear of Freedom*, 1942) on the distinction between the medieval and modern worlds: "What characterises mediaeval in contrast to modern society is the lack of individual freedom." As early as the nineteenth century, Russia was known as a "prison-house of peoples." In 1912, according to Soviet sources in the 1930s, there was a total 183,949 prisoners in enforced detention. Under Stalin, around 40 million Soviet citizens were "repressed" from 1929 to 1953, of whom 20 million died in the labor camps. There were about 6,000 such camps, mostly located in the least hospitable regions of the Soviet Union. The source of this information is Conquest (1990).
3. The expression "inner logic" has been used by Vlachoutsicos with the author. His publications cited in this chapter refer to "internal logic."

Bibliography

Applebaum, A. (1995) *Between East and West: Across the Borderlands of Europe*, London: Papermac.

Aslund, A. (1993) "The gradual nature of economic change in Russia," in Aslund, A. and Layard, R. (eds), *Changing the Economic System in Russia*, London: Pinter.

Babaeva, L. and Chirikova, A. (1995) "Business leaders talk about themselves," *Delovie Lyudi*, January.

Berdyayev, N. (1918; reprinted 1990) *Sudba Rossii*, Moscow: MGU.

Berelowitch, A. and Wieviorka, M. (1996) *Les Russes d'en bas: Enquête sur la Russie post-communiste*, Paris: Éditions du Seuil.

Chamberlain, L. (1995) *Volga, Volga: a voyage down the great river*, London: Picador.

Conquest, R. (1990) *The Great Terror: A Reassessment*, London: Pimlico.

Crystal, C. (1994) "Making Russian managers," *International Business*, February.

Davies, N. (1996) *Europe: A History*, Oxford: Oxford University Press.

Delovye Svyazi (1990) "Rynok – zhestokii uchitel, tem i khorosh," no. 6, pp. 12–15.

Dunayeva, D. and Vipperman, C. (1995) "Similar but different: why do Russian and American business-people, even when they speak the same language, so often seem to be engaging in a dialogue of the deaf?", *Business in Russia*, June.

Dyker, D. (1992) *Restructuring the Soviet economy*, London: Routledge.

Economist (1993) "EC aid to the East." April 10.

Economist (1995a) "Nag, nag: Russia and the West," April 8.

Economist (1995b) "Survey of Russia's emerging market," April 8.

Economist (1996) "Is Russia different?", June 15.

Fallowell, D. (1995) *One Hot Summer in St Petersburg*, London: Jonathan Cape.

Financial Times (1993) "A cross-cultural minefield," August 2.

Financial Times (1995) "Moscow suspicion grows: Kremlin factions are at odds over policy," January 19.

Financial Times (1996a) "Spy follies," May 8.

Financial Times (1996b) "Russia insists it will expel UK 'spies' May 15.

Graham, L. (1993) *Science in Russia and the Soviet Union*, Cambridge: Cambridge University Press.

Hallén, L. and Widersheim-Paul, F. (1984) "The evolution of psychic distance in international business relationships," in Hagg, I. and Wiedersheim-Paul, F. (eds), *Between Market and Hierarchy*, Uppsala: University of Uppsala.

Handelman, S. (1994) *Comrade Criminal: The Theft of the Second Russian Revolution*, London: Michael Joseph.

Hingley, R. (1978) *The Russian Mind*, London: Bodley Head.

Holden, N.J. (1992) "Creating the new Russian manager: implications for designing a cultural intervention," *Creativity and Innovation Management*, vol. I, no. 2, pp. 95–101.

Holden, N.J. (1995) "Management education in Russia: issues in course design, development and evaluation. A report with special reference to the Russian construction industry," Manchester: Brooke Publications Limited.

Holden, N.J. and Burgess, M. (1994) *Japanese-led Companies: Understanding How to Make Them Your Customers*, London: McGraw-Hill.

Holden, N.J. and Cooper, C.L. (1994) "Russian managers as learners: implications for theories of management learning," vol. 25. no. 4, pp. 503–22.

Holden, N.J., Cooper, C.L. and Carr, J. (1997) *Coping with the New Russia: Management Cultures in Collision*, Chichester: John Wiley.

Johanson, J. and Wiedersheim-Paul, F. (1975) "The internationalisation of the firm – four Swedish case studies," *Journal of Management Studies*, vol. 12, October, pp. 305–22.

Johanson, M. (1994) "Viking Raps: a case study of joint venture negotiation in the former Soviet Union," in Buckley, P. and Ghauri, P. (eds), *The Economics of Change in East and Central Europe*, London: Academic Press.

Kappel, G., Rathmayr, R. and Diehl-Zelonkina, N. (1992) *Verhandeln mit Russen: Gesprachs- und Verhaltensstrategien für die interkulturelle Geschaftspraxis*, Vienna: Service Verlag.

Kapugcinski, R. (1994) *Imperium*, London: Granta Books.

Kennedy, G. (1985) *Negotiate Anywhere: Doing Business Abroad*, London: Business Books.

Kissinger, H. (1994) *Diplomacy*, New York: Touchstone.

Kravchenko, Ye (1995) "A land of great expectations/Russia bureaucracy even has the Germans beaten," *Business in Russia*, November, pp. 58–61.

McCullough, D. (1992) *Truman*, New York: Touchstone.

Manager Magasin (1991) "Trends+Signale Sowjietunion," July, pp. 109–17.

Massie, A. (1995) *Augustus*, London: Sceptre.

Massie, R.K. (1992) *Peter the Great: His Life and World*, London: Abacus.

Mattock, J. (1996) *Russia: An Essential Guide for the Business Traveller*, London: Kogan Page.

Mejevitch, V. (1993) "An investigation into the emergence of customer orientation in the construction industry of St Petersburg," unpublished MSc dissertation, Manchester School of Management, UMIST.

Mikheyev, D. (1996) *Russia Transformed*, Indianapolis, IN: Hudson Institute.

Poe, R. (1993) *How to Profit from the Coming Russian Boom: The Insider's Guide to Business Opportunities and Survival on the Frontiers of Capitalism*, New York: McGraw-Hill.

Puffer, S. and McCarthy, D. (1995) "Finding common ground in Russian and American business ethics," *California Management Review*, vol. 37, no. 2, pp. 29–46.

Remnick, D. (1994) *Lenin's Tomb*, London: Penguin

Richardson, P.E. (1995) *Russia Survival Guide: The Definitive Guide to Doing Business and Traveling in Russia*, Montpelier, VT: Russian Information Services, Inc.

Russia Express (1996) "Russians cling to dream of nuclear earthquake weapon," no. 182, October 14.

Sachs, J. (1994) *Poland's Jump to the Market Economy*, Cambridge, MA: MIT Press.

Skurski, R. (1983) *Soviet Marketing and Economic Development*, London: Macmillan.

Smith, H. (1991) The New Russians, London:Vintage.

Solzhenitsyn, A. (1991) Rebuilding Russia: Reflections and Tentative Proposals, London: HarperCollins.

Steele, J. (1994) *Eternal Russia*, London: Faber and Faber.

Sunday Times (1992) "Psst, wanna Moskovich?," January 12.

Veiga, J., Yanouzas, J. and Buchholtz, A. (1995) "Emerging cultural values among Russian managers: what will tomorrow bring?," *Business Horizons*, July–August, pp. 20–26.

Vlachoutsicos, C. (1995). Work in progress entitled "Constraints and opportunities of the Russian enterprise manager," Athens: Hellenic Foundation for European and Foreign Policy.

Vlachoutsicos, C. and Lawrence, R. (1996) *Behind the Factory Walls: Decision Making in Soviet and US Enterprises*, Boston: Harvard School Press.

Wilson, A.N. (1989) *Tolstoy*, London: Penguin.

Wilson, D. and Donaldson, L. (1996) *Russian Etiquette and Ethics in Business*, Lincolnwood, IL: NTC Business Books.

Whitley, R. (1995) "Eastern Asian Enterprise Structures and Comparative Analysis of Forms and Business Organization," in Ghauri, P. and Prasad, S. (eds), *International Management: A Reader*, London: The Dryden Press.

Yergin, D. and Gustafson, T. (1994) *Russia and What it Means for the World*, London: Nicholas Brealey.

Rouble
Against the dollar (Rbs per $)

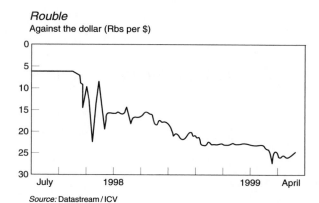

Source: Datastream / ICV

Foreign direct investment in 1997
% of GDP

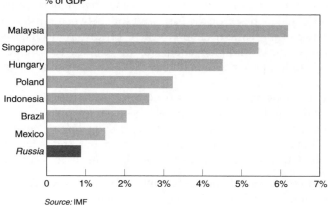

Source: IMF

Real wages and wage arrears

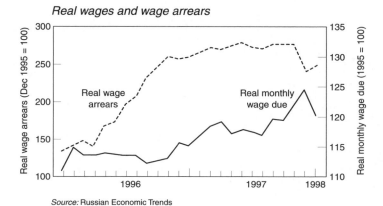

Source: Russian Economic Trends

Editor's introduction: Ukraine

Is Ukraine one nation, two, or none at all? Of course, the Ukrainian government would argue the first case, going back to the Rus in Kiev – the original hub of Russia itself. The two-nation theory could be based on the east–west split between Russian and Ukrainian speakers and between the eastern cultural sphere of Russia and the western former Habsburg lands (i.e. the Austro-Hungarian Empire). Finally, for over a half century Ukraine was really only a province (republic) of the Soviet Union, and thus no nation at all.

In this context, the geography of Ukraine becomes crucial. The east–west cultural fault line is fundamental to understanding the problems – cultural, political, and economic – of modern Ukraine. Given its divisions, Ukraine is struggling to create and assert a national identity in the shadow of its great Russian neighbor. This is no mean feat.

Given this cultural dichotomy, what are the Ukrainian issues to be developed further?

- Can Ukraine approach the EU and NATO without provoking Russia?
- Can Ukraine knit together its two distinct cultural identities?
- Can Ukraine rebuild an economy that has virtually disappeared since independence?

Ukraine

Area: 803,700 sq km
Language: Ukrainian (official), Russian widely spoken
Currency: Hryvna (Hm)
Population: 50.48 million (Jan 1 1998)

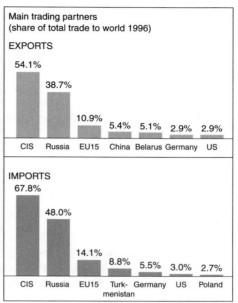

Economic summary	1996	1997 (estimate)
Real GDP growth (annual % change)	−10.0	−3.2
Industrial output (annual % change)	−5.1	−1.8
Agricultural output (annual % change))	−9.5	−1.9
Inflation (av. annual % change in CPI)	80.0	16.0
Gross average monthly wage in industry (annual % change)	92.0	20.0
Broad money (end year, annual % change)	35.0	28.0
Treasury bill rate (three-month maturity, end year, %)	62.0	41.0
General government balance (percentage of GDP)*	−3.2	−5.8
Current account balance ($bn)	−1.1	−1.5
Exports ($bn)	15.5	15.3
Imports ($bn)	−19.8	−20.1
Trade balance ($bn)	−4.3	−4.8
Foreign direct investment, net ($bn)	0.5	0.7
Gross reserves excluding gold ($bn)**	2.0	2.2
External debt (% of GDP)	20.8	20.5

* Includes municipalities and extra budgetary funds   ** Foreign exchange reserves of monetary authorities

Sources: EBRD; EIU

9
♦♦♦

Ukraine

Pavlo Sheremeta
International Management Institute, Kiev, Ukraine

Introduction

If you ask what the largest country in Europe is, you will probably not get the right answer. Assuming that Russia is a Euro-Asian country, the correct answer to the question is Ukraine. Despite the fact that Ukraine reappeared on the European map only in 1991, many recognize its huge potential and strategic importance for European economic and political stability, and envision its role as a bridge from western and central Europe to Russia and the Middle East. Others still see it as a kind of Russian "domain." What is this country? Why is its image confusing? Is it possible to predict what Ukraine will become in the future?

The land and the people

Ukraine is located in eastern Europe and borders on Belarus in the north; Russia in the east; and Poland, Slovakia, Hungary, Romania, and Moldova in the west. It has direct access to the Black and Azov Seas in the south. The territory of Ukraine approximately equals those of Great Britain, Belgium, the Netherlands, and Italy combined. The population of Ukraine is approximately 52 million people, which is the fifth largest in Europe. There are four cities with over 1 million inhabitants. Ethnic Ukrainians constitute about three-quarters of the population; ethnic Russians, one-fifth.

Historical background

Confusion concerning Ukraine starts with its name. Most historians believe that this name literally means "frontier land" and appeared in the sixteenth century, while others believe that the name is much older, dating from the twelfth century, and that it derives from the Ukrainian word *kraïna,* which means "country." The history of Ukraine as a European entity begins with the medieval princedom of Kiev (or Kyiv in Ukrainian), an ancient city on the Dnipro river. It stands at the crossroads of old north–south river and sea routes from Scandinavia to Greece and east–west routes from Europe to central Asia. This strategic location guaranteed the country intensive external affairs and a prominent role in Europe. For example, Prince Yaroslav Mudlyi (Yaroslav the Wise) married his three daughters to three European kings in the eleventh century.

The Kiev princedom was absorbed by Grand Duchy of Lithuania in 1362. The Union of 1569 that brought Poland and Lithuania together in one state put all Ukrainian lands under the direct control of the Polish crown. At the same time, numerous merchants, notably Italians from Venice and Genoa, settled on the Black Sea coast, especially in Crimea. But it was not until 1648 that an uprising led by Bohdan Khmelnytskyi led to the re-establishment of the Ukrainian Hetman state in the form of a Cossack republic. The way in which the Cossacks conducted their internal affairs is now seen by many in Ukraine as an attempt to develop a true democracy and a law-governed society. The "hetman" was a prototype Ukrainian president who was democratically elected by the free Cossack citizens.

The Cossack state badly needed allies in order to survive and was compelled to sign a military treaty with the Moscow tsar in 1654, which guaranteed a great degree of autonomy for Ukraine. This autonomy, however, disappeared step by step, as eastern Ukraine was forced to enter the Russian Empire. Another unsuccessful attempt to assert Ukrainian independence from Moscow occurred under Hetman Mazepa, who joined the Swedish king Charles XII in his unsuccessful war against Peter the Great. As Cossack institutions were disbanded, Ukrainian noblemen began to play an important role in the administration of the Russian Empire, perhaps because of their higher level of education and more western outlook (Fernandez-Armesto, 1994).

The larger part of western Ukraine remained within Poland until 1772, then within the Austro-Hungarian Empire until 1918, and again within Poland from 1921 to 1939. In this way, Ukraine was involved in European politics, economy, and culture, which not only preserved but even developed its sense of national identity. The Greek Catholic (or Uniate) Church, which has been predominant in the western Ukraine since the eighteenth century, is the best example. It recognizes the supremacy of the Roman Pope and yet preserves the Ukrainian Orthodox religious and national traditions.

This sense of national identity in the western and central part of the country acted as a catalyst for two bids for Ukrainian independence in the twentieth century. The first one was unsuccessful in 1917–21, when the short-lived Ukrainian People's Republic was occupied by the Red Army. The communist rule established thereafter was devastating for Ukraine. Until 1990, fully 95 percent of Ukraine's economy was controlled by Moscow, which was also responsible for the distribution of over 90 percent of the republic's production. Less than a quarter of Ukraine's national income remained in the republic – the rest was returned to the center. Enterprises controlled by Moscow often repatriated 90 percent of their profits to Russia (see Krawchenko, 1993: 87).

The consequences for those few who overtly promoted the use of the Ukrainian language and culture in Soviet Ukraine were grave. They were usually treated as anti-Soviet criminals, if not outright outcasts or deviants. Although Ukrainians constituted only about 16 percent of the Soviet Union, they on average made up 40 percent of gulag prisoners (Lapychak, 1996: 6). The traditionally Ukrainian-speaking rural population in the eastern and central regions was devastated by the collectivization campaign and an artificially induced famine in the 1930s. Ukrainian-speaking western Ukraine, annexed by Stalin only after World War II, was brutally marginalized. Exasperated, 90 percent of Ukrainians voted for independence in 1991.

Three important historical factors have influenced and will continue to influence the place and role of Ukraine in Europe. Obviously, Ukraine is not a newcomer to the map of Europe. With or without national independence, Ukrainians were active participants in European affairs. Similarly, Ukraine is not a new democracy. Finally, Ukrainian politics and culture are and will continue to be influenced by the long historical division of the nation. This is the major reason why Ukraine has not yet chosen a clear common vision for itself, which in turn gives rise to a confused image of Ukraine in the world.

Regions of Ukraine

Ukraine is too big and too diverse to talk about universally accepted aspirations, business values, and culture. A brief tour of Ukrainian regions may be helpful in understanding this point.

The east is an overindustrialized and overpopulated area, dominated by the coal-mining basin of Donbas and the industrial city of Kharkiv. Most of the enterprises in this area are economically inefficient. For example, Ukraine's coal industry, largely concentrated in the east, employs approximately 800,000 people. In the past five years, mining output has fallen by over 40 percent. A Ukrainian miner produces an average of 112 tons of coal a year, compared with 250 tons in Russia, 420 tons in Poland, 2,000 tons in the UK, and 5,000 tons in the US. Up to half of Ukraine's 250 mines will need to be shut down in the next ten years to restore the industry's competitiveness (World Bank, 1996: 48). At the same time, coal mining firms provide a wide variety of social services, including kindergartens and housing. These are often overstaffed as well: kindergartens, for example, often have one employee for every three children.

Rapid restructuring may result in a dramatic increase in unemployment and could have potentially disastrous social consequences. The national government, being frightened of the latter, is trying to prolong the transition, granting subsidies to these companies, pursuing the policy of slow and gradual change. Most economists agree that this transition is much too slow and results in wasted national resources and time. The basic problem remains almost untouched and social dissatisfaction is growing dangerously. Add to this situation the fact that this part of Ukraine is the least Ukrainian in its character, since it was populated in the nineteenth and twentieth centuries by the workers of many different nationalities, and one understands that potential unrest in this region is still a significant threat to political stability.

Further to the west, the Dnipro river cuts Ukraine into two parts. Approximately one-quarter of all Ukrainians live on the banks of this river, producing almost one-third of the Ukrainian GDP and most of the country's export products. About 60 percent of cumulative foreign investment is also concentrated in this region. This concentration of industry and money inevitably results in a concentration of power. Not only Kiev, the capital of Ukraine, is located here. For example, in 1997, both the president and prime minister came from the large city of Dnipropetrovsk, located on the Dnipro river. There is no reason to comment on the origins of the national government bureaucracy, which is much more stable than the top officials.

In central Ukraine, one sees vast fields of very productive black soil in the steppes. This is the heart of Ukraine and its culture. It is the region that once gave rise to the well-known image of Ukraine as a bread basket. It is also the region that will decide whether Ukraine will ever again become a bread basket. In other words, will Ukrainian agriculture be based on private property and become much more productive? The jury is still out on this question.

To the south there is the Black Sea shore, which is dominated economically and politically by the city of Odessa with its distinct culture, and the Crimean peninsula. Crimea is the only region in Ukraine in which ethnic Ukrainians constitute less than half of the population. Crimean Tatars, who were forced to move from Ukraine to central Asia by Stalin, are returning and resettling in their historic motherland. Relations between the central and regional governments remain tense amid the demands by Crimean Russians for increased autonomy (Crimea already has the highest degree of autonomy among Ukrainian regions) and closer links to Russia. There is talk of establishing free economic zones in both Odessa and Sevastopol.

Finally, western Ukraine was part of Poland, Austria, and other central European countries much longer than it was part of the Russian Empire or the USSR. The sense of national identity as well as people's aspirations for independence are strongest here. Lviv is the biggest and, by far, the most important city in the western Ukraine, and is considered by many the cultural capital of Ukraine. Lviv was important not only for Ukrainian culture throughout its history – you may find this city on Polish maps under the name of Lwow, on Austrian maps as Lemberg, and on Russian/Soviet maps as Lvov. A significant Polish minority resides in the Lviv region; Hungarian and Slovakian ones are in Transcarpathia; Romanians are in Bukovyna.

In summary, Ukrainian regions differ very much from each other in economy, history, and culture. The further west you go, the more nationalistic and pro-European people tend to be. However, nowhere does Europe top the political agenda. The economic and social problems of transition concern people most in the east. They seem to be willing to seek any viable solution, even at the expense of Ukrainian independence. Moreover, these people voted for independence precisely for economic reasons – they expected that national independence would make their lives more prosperous. On the other hand, Ukrainian statehood is the principal issue in the west, and people are willing to wait for better times if the strengthening of the independent Ukrainian state is at stake. In any case, only an improved economy can bring political and social stability to Ukraine.

Ukraine's ambiguous foreign policy

In regard to Ukraine's foreign policy, inconsistency must be one of the key words. To some extent this ambivalence is needed to maintain independence from Ukraine's huge eastern neighbor, Russia. In many ways, the policy is working. Other than the Baltic states, Ukraine was the first ex-Soviet republic to establish its own army in 1992. The army is now Europe's largest (after Russia's). Ukraine has managed to undermine Russian regional ambitions without infuriating that country. But Ukraine's ambivalence toward Russia also reflects the country's ambivalence about itself and its place in the world (*Economist*, 1996). As we have seen above, the country is split between an industrialized, more Russified east and a nationalist, more rural west. Translated into foreign policy, the result is what might politely be described as neutrality or, perhaps, confusion and a policy vacuum. Ukraine is not actively seeking membership of NATO and is cautious about its expansion – partly because such moves might strengthen the pro-Russian camp in the Ukrainian army, already heavily Russified. Yet Ukraine has refused to sign the Tashkent treaty, the Russian-led military alliance within the Confederation of Independent States.

Ambivalence explained

Usually it is the urban political and business elite that defines a vision for a nation, following its economic and political interests. The elite makes every effort to communicate this vision to the nation. National identity is also created by elite social groups who develop and politicize objective cultural markers (Krawchenko, 1993: 89). Although it possesses a modern social structure with a quarter of the employed population holding higher or specialized secondary degrees, Ukraine's traditional problem lies in the fact that its urban elite was and remains weak. Part of the explanation for this phenomenon comes from the history of cities in Ukraine. Urban centers in Ukraine have not been fully Ukrainian since the seventeenth century. At best, the cities were surrounded by Ukrainian villages. Indeed, only in the last few generations have cities in Ukraine even had a Ukrainian majority.

Historically, the cities in the east were ruled by Russia, and Russian culture dominated. In the west, the cities were dominated by either the Austrian Habsburgs or the Poles, and these cultures dominated. The next major group, the small traders and craftsmen, were often Jewish. All the major cities, notably Odessa and Lviv, had large Jewish populations. Ethnic non-Jewish Ukrainians lived in the surrounding villages.

Those ruling in the city made every effort to ensure that Ukrainian culture did not expand outside the village. The numerically few on top had every reason to fear the development of a unified Ukrainian consciousness. United, the Ukrainians could threaten their privileged positions. Publishing in Ukrainian was often discouraged, if not suppressed. Some cities had prohibitions against Ukrainians even staying in the city overnight. Those most clearly associated with Ukrainian nationalism became prime targets for repression – a policy continued after the communist takeover. Political and religious leaders espousing Ukrainian nationalism were systematically liquidated. The small rural landowners were killed off during the period of forced collectivization.

However, in the last three decades this traditional pattern has been completely reversed. More Ukrainians have moved into the cities to work in the new factories that the communists built in their headlong rush to industrialize. Others left the villages to escape the drudgery of work on collective farms. Many of the young came to the city for education and stayed on. Ukraine has attained independence and Ukrainian culture has become dominant. Given these changes, the culture should develop as others have. The blockages that for so long prevented this dynamic have now been removed. For the moment, the village has come to the city. It will take time for this change in residence to have its effect on Ukraine's culture.

The interests of the newly formed and strengthening economic elite are also being linked more tightly to the emergence and future of a separate Ukrainian state. The existence of this state guarantees the elite's survival and the chance to develop their business in the new economic situation that is evolving in eastern Europe.

Values of the extended family

The extended family is alive and well in Ukraine. What does such a family offer to an individual? By drawing lines of commitment and trust around a large group of people, the extended family reduces the risk that each individual faces. It works like insurance. By sharing during the good times, the individual gets support during the bad. And the value of an insurance policy is directly proportional to the risk in the environment. If individuals perceive the environment to hold little threat, they are more likely to do without the cost and bother of the group. Alternatively, in an environment seen as unpredictable and full of irrational danger, it is better to have lots of people committed to helping you – just in case.

If one looks at the truly awful historic suffering of the people of Ukraine, it is not surprising that they cling to any institution offering such protection. In the absence of effective social welfare, insurance companies, etc., family is the only such institution remaining.

The fertile black soil in most of Ukraine was another factor that promoted family values – this time, at the expense of community ones. Unlike Russians and Nordic Europeans, Ukrainians did not need to unite into a strong community to overcome a hostile natural environment. The Ukrainian peasantry had never known the system of the "repartitional commune," and were undoubtedly more individualistically minded than their northern neighbors (Rudnytsly, 1987: 15). For centuries, the Ukrainian family was a self-sufficient unit of the economy.

If you put together the importance of the extended family and the strong ties to the village, Ukrainian culture comes into better focus. Contrary to other collectivized societies, the villagers did not lose the knowledge of how to grow and preserve food. For all but the worst times, they have tended their garden plots and even raised a few animals. As factories have closed, more people have moved back to the land, where they can at least contribute to this process. But it was the extended family that allowed Ukrainians to share what was available, so that few became destitute and homeless. The strong ties to the land – to the village, in particular – have allowed this extended group to produce most of the food needed to limit malnutrition even when many were earning no wages. The extended family is the safety net that has held Ukrainian society together.

Reality and impact of transition

We have described above what has differentiated Ukraine and its business environment for centuries from its neighbors. Let us now take a look into the not so distant past: the socialist economy's legacy and paths of transition chosen by Ukraine in comparison to other countries in the region. The interplay of these factors, in combination with the long-term national characteristics described above, define a newly formed business culture in Ukraine.

The heritage of the socialist economy is well known and has been thoroughly analyzed. Therefore, let us restate its major consequences only. The main goal of the socialist economy, as developed in the Soviet Union and copied later throughout the region, was to meet targets set by central planners in these countries. The plan designated output targets, inputs, and investment. It usually promoted heavy industry, energy, and investment goods at the expense of services and consumption goods. Under central planning, companies did not stress quality, variety, customer satisfaction, or profits, even less innovation. Being protected from competitive pressures, they operated in shortage economies where everything they produced was grabbed up immediately. Most managers were production engineers. Their performance was judged in terms of output rather than customer satisfaction. Profits and losses were distributed among firms, making financial performance irrelevant. Lacking a bottom line, managers fought frequent input shortages by stockpiling inventories and labor.

Ukrainian enterprises were no different in principle. However, their obedience to central planners based in Moscow, rather than to national ones, magnified the problems of overinvestment in industries that later, with a switch to world prices, became value subtracting – the input prices were higher than those of their final products.

The first element of transition is to move from the centrally planned management of subsidies and transfers to strong, profit-oriented incentives, ensuring financial discipline, and allowing for risk. The experience of central Europe shows that enterprises' actual adjustment to market forces is closely linked to the credibility of government commitment to reform. The Ukrainian government lacked this commitment until 1995. As a result, many bankrupt companies in Ukraine are still unwilling to reduce their workforce significantly, hoping for government financial aid and choosing to require workers to take unpaid leave, rather than undertaking real restructuring. Also, government continues to play too direct a role in managing the economy. Therefore, political contacts are an indispensable short-term competitive advantage. Managers tend to develop these contacts at the expense of long-term competitive advantages such as innovation and productivity.

The second vital element of transition is creating and allocating property rights. Ukraine was late in this process too. Management–employee buyouts were preferred as the most frequent mode of privatization. These buyouts are somewhat fast and easy to execute, both politically and technically. Theoretically, such buyouts should have been better for corporate governance, since insiders have better access to the information needed to monitor managers than outsiders. Nonetheless, experience has shown in transitional economies that management–employee buyouts more often undermine corporate governance than strengthen it. Product and especially capital markets cannot yet be relied upon to enforce discipline. Thus, controls on management as agents are underdeveloped.

Insiders are often incapable of bringing new skills and capital to the firm, and in fact may prevent outsiders who can do this from investing. Research in Ukraine shows that owners who bought their smaller business units at competitive auctions invested more and obtained better performance than insiders who got their shops at near-give-away prices, although even the insider-owned firms did better than state-owned shops (World Bank, 1996: 49). So management–employee buyouts and insider ownership are likely to evolve at least partially to ownership by outside investors (banks, investment funds, or other domestic or foreign investors). The Ukrainian government's encouragement of the creation of so-called financial-industrial groups is a step in the right direction.

Finally, creating legal frameworks for private sector development is critical. Basic economic laws (property rights, contract laws, company and foreign investment laws, bankruptcy laws, and competition laws) have been adopted in Ukraine. Nobody claims that they are perfect or sufficient. These laws will be improved as a result of both approaches: "top-down" through government initiative and foreign technical assistance, and "bottom-up" through private demand. The main problem, however, lies not in perfecting existing laws, but in finding reliable mechanisms to enforce them. Private companies have little hope of success in court and instead count heavily on trust in choosing business partners. Firms look for customers who pay quickly and suppliers who ship quickly, and work with them on a continuous basis. They are distrustful of new customers, who are carefully screened and often forced to pay up-front. All of this blocks new firms from entering the market. Long-term inter-company contracts are almost non-existent, because such contracts are especially hard to guarantee. The vacuum in legal enforcement mechanisms also opens a door for more violent mechanisms, such as organized crime.

Ukraine on its way to EU membership?

To simplify the matter, one might compare the European Union to a club. Thus, there are three fundamental preconditions for Ukraine as a potential applicant to be admitted into this club. First and most obvious, there should be a strong public will to join the club. Secondly, a new member should abide by the rules of the club. Finally, a club member has to be able to pay the fees and duties. Let us consider these conditions in turn.

As I have argued above, membership of the EU is not considered a top priority by the Ukrainian population at large. The EU seems to be rather too remote, too unreal. There are other more pressing issues, such as dealing with economic crisis and strengthening national governmental institutions. However, Ukrainian leaders emphasize the importance of the country's integration into European structures. President Kuchma said, in his address to the European assembly on April 23, 1996, "Our strategic aim is to become a full member of the EU."

Ukraine received the status of special guest in the Council of Europe following the declaration of independence in 1991. After the signature of a partnership and cooperation treaty between the European Union and Ukraine in 1994, their relations intensified. Ukraine was accepted into the Council of Europe in October 1995 – a significant milestone in the process of Ukrainian integration in Europe.

This integration process is extremely important not only in the context of the recognition and strengthening of Ukrainian independence. It also has another significant aspect. Economic transformation has trailed far behind political transformation in Ukraine. In other words, Ukraine has been quite successful in turning itself into a stable democratic state. Its record in turning its economy into a growing market-based one is much worse. This gap creates a potential internal threat to stability, as people gradually become dissatisfied with their daily lives, many of them blaming necessary political reforms for their dissatisfaction. Under such conditions, Ukraine's participation in European structures becomes a stabilizing factor, an anchor that makes the overall transition process irreversible.

Let us consider the second condition for EU membership – abiding by democratic rules. Formally, Ukraine is doing well in this field. It has just adopted a new constitution, which guarantees democracy and all basic human rights. Ukraine had its first transition of power from one freely elected president to another in 1994 – quite an accomplishment in eastern Europe in the twentieth century! There have been no military conflicts. Thus, there is every reason to believe that Ukraine will continue its political transformation, which is already well advanced. Well established in the capital and in the major cities, however, this transformation has yet to enter and reform every aspect of public life, especially at the local level. Building and strengthening local governance and democratic local decision making has become a top priority.

Finally, the failing Ukrainian economy is itself the most serious obstacle to European Union membership for Ukraine. Indeed, this is the most serious threat to the country itself. Economic reforms came late and were painfully slow. However, three years of confusion and mismanagement after 1991 have been followed by domestic trade and price liberalization, a reduction in import barriers, macroeconomic stabilization, and limited privatization. Professor Anders Aslund, senior associate at the Carnegie Endowment for International Peace and economic advisor to the government, believes that Ukraine is progressing well toward becoming a free-market economy. "The reforms are true this time," he says (*Euromoney*, 1996). But he warns that investors and agencies should be patient. Involvement of European business in the process of economic transition is invaluable and obvious.

Conclusion

Famous Ukrainian historian Ivan L. Rudnytsky described Ukraine's geopolitical role in the following way:

> Ukraine, located between the worlds of Greek Byzantine and Western cultures, and a legitimate member of both, attempted, in the course of its history, to unite the two traditions in a living synthesis. This was a great work, although it must be admitted that Ukraine has not fully succeeded in it ... The final synthesis miscarried, and Ukraine succumbed to excessive pressure from outside, as well as to internal disruptive tendencies. In this sense, it may be said that the great task, which appears to be the historical vocation of the Ukrainian people, remains unfulfilled, and still lies in the future. (1987: 9)

So our verdict is not unique at all – economic growth as an outcome of economic reforms should turn Ukraine into a stable and democratic country. As a result, a stronger urban middle class will develop. The new middle class will undoubtedly have a pro-European outlook based on its economic and political interests in European integration. Similarly, Europe should be much more interested in integrating Ukraine into the EU as global competition becomes stiffer. In the end, Ukraine has more than 50 million well-educated people and good industrial potential. So it is not politics, as at present, but economics that will reinforce centripetal trends in the future. A new Ukrainian middle class and its future leaders should finalize the integration process and thereby turn Ukraine into an east European geopolitical and economic stronghold and a big trading partner – the role Ukraine played a millennium ago.

Bibliography

Economist (1996) "Disorienting Ukraine," February 17.
Euromoney (1996) "An ideological retreat on economic policy?," April.
Fernandez-Armesto, F. (ed.) (1994) *The Times Guide to the Peoples of Europe*, London: Times Books.
Krawchenko, B. (1993) "Ukraine: the politics of independence," *Nation and Politics in the Soviet Successor States*, Cambridge: Cambridge University Press.
Lapychak, C. (1996) "The Quest for a Common Destiny," *Transition*, September 6.
Rudnytsly, I.L. (1987) *Essays in Modern Ukrainian History*, Edmonton: Canadian Institute of Ukrainian Studies.
World Bank (1996) "From plan to market," *World Development Report*.

Foreign direct investment in Ukraine, 1990–5 (cumulative, %)

Kiev, Dnipro	26
Cherkasy, Dnipro	9
Dnipropetrovsk, Dnipro	8
Odessa, South	14
Donetsk, East	14
Lviv, West	6
Other cities	24

Source: *Business Central Europe,* March 1996.

Editor's introduction: Hungary

To imagine the Hungarian national psyche, suppose yourself to be strapped to the road in the center of a busy intersection on a major truck route. Due to its pivotal position on a major invasion corridor from east to west, Hungary has in fact been regularly invaded and occupied. The invader-occupants who come to mind most readily are the Ottoman Empire (160 years), the Austrians (some 300 years), and the Russians (a mere 50 years). As a result of being frequently crushed and occupied, Hungarians have come to be of a rather pessimistic frame of mind.

On the other hand, the land itself is rich and beautiful. Even (or perhaps, particularly) during the communist era, life was good, thanks to the mild climate, the excellent indigenous wines, and the fine food. Hungary might be described as the France of central Europe, given the quality of life it traditionally offers. Moreover, in their discreetly ingenious way, the Hungarian people have nurtured a pleasant lifestyle, even under adverse circumstances and harsh occupants.

However, Hungary today is faced by yet another harsh occupant: capitalism. The traditional unity of the Hungarian people against the occupying power has been broken, as they struggle among themselves for capitalist gains. Can capitalism be successfully adapted to the Hungarian way of thinking? Undoubtedly. In fact, the process is well under way.

In this light, what are the issues for further discussion in Hungary?

- How can the highly skilled and literate workforce combine its romantic Hungarian yearnings with the tough demands of a global, capitalist economy?
- How can the successes of Hungary under communism (good schools, quality of life, etc.) be maintained in the capitalist era?

Hungary

Area: 93,030 sq km

Language: Magyar (Hungarian)

Currency: Forint (Ft)

Population: 10,153,000 (mid 1997)

Main cities and population: (Jan 1 1997)

Budapest (capital)	1,886,000
Debrecen	208,000
Miskolc	178,000
Szeged	166,000
Pécs	161,000
Györ	127,000

Constitution

National government

A coalition government, led by the prime minister, Viktor Orban, and consisting of the Federation of Young Democrats-Hungarian Civic party, the Hungarian Democratic Forum and the Smallholders' Party, took office in June 1998

National legislature

Unicameral parliament of 386 members, of whom 176 are elected from single-member constituencies. Constitutionally, supreme power is vested in parliament. The Constitutional Court has powers to overturn parliamentary decisions and governmental decrees deemed contradictory to the constitution

Economic summary	1997	1998
Total GDP ($bn)	44.7	46.7
Real GDP growth (annual % change)	4.4	4.6
GDP per head ($)	4,462	4,620
Inflation (annual % change in CPI)	18.3	15.0
Average wages (annual % change)	22.3	20.0
Industrial production (annual % change)	11.1	11.0
Unemployment rate (% of workforce)	10.4	9.4
Unit labour costs (annual % change)	−3.9	−0.2
Foreign exchange reserves ($m)	8.4*	9.7***
Government balance (as % of GDP)	−4.9	−4.9
Total foreign debt ($bn)	23.7	22.9
Current account balance ($bn)	−1.0	−1.6
Merchandise exports ($bn)	19.6	22.0
Merchandise imports ($bn)	21.4	24.4
Trade balance ($bn)	−1.7	−2.4
Three-month inter-bank rate (%)	20.1**	18.5†

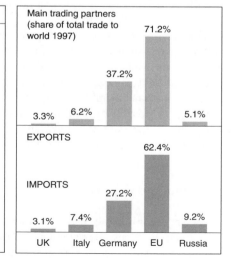

Main trading partners (share of total trade to world 1997)

EXPORTS

	UK	Italy	Germany	EU	Russia
	3.3%	6.2%	37.2%	71.2%	5.1%

IMPORTS

	UK	Italy	Germany	EU	Russia
	3.1%	7.4%	27.2%	62.4%	9.2%

* December   ** End December   *** July   † End November

Sources: Economist Intelligence Unit; EBRD

10

♦♦♦

Hungary
From goulash communism to goulash capitalism

Robert Kovach
Pepsi Cola Bottling, Warsaw, Poland
János Vecsenyi
Budapest Bank, Hungary

Introduction

North Atlantic Treaty Organization (NATO) leaders agreed in June 1997 that Hungary, Poland, and the Czech Republic would be invited to join the alliance. A few days later, the summit of the European Union in Amsterdam accepted a list of five nations including Hungary to participate in a series of membership negotiations. These are milestones on the path to a return to the Euro-Atlantic world, where Hungarians have always felt they belonged.

The changes that have taken place in the countries of central and eastern Europe and the (former) Soviet Union are unprecedented in recent history. The restructuring of socialist economies toward a market-driven economy has captured the attention of observers worldwide. Hungary, the land of "goulash capitalism," was one of the first to establish east–west joint ventures, privatize its industry, and be granted associate membership of the EU. The Hungarians were central and eastern Europe's pioneers in adopting democratic and pro-market reforms.

The changes that have taken place, and the history of being in the center of central Europe, have shaped Europe's impression of Hungary and Hungary's impression of Europe. Not content to be second-class citizens in a free world, the Hungarian people (Magyars) have undergone enormous challenges and sacrifices, striving in order once again to become members of Europe and business contenders. However, unless the country's companies can realize the potential of Hungary's excellent educational system and improve the state of Hungarian workers to a par with western European countries, there is a danger that this process may be stalled.

The land and the people

There are slightly more than 10 million people in Hungary today, 20 percent of them in the capital, Budapest. Its neighbors include Austria, Slovakia, Ukraine, Romania, Serbia, Croatia, and Slovenia. It is often said that Hungary is a small country with a very large culture, as these "displaced Magyars" are and feel themselves to be Hungarian. Some of the most well-known Hungarians are Béla Bartók, the composer; Puskás, the soccer player; Rubic, the father of the Rubic's cube; von Neumann, the inventor of the computer; and János Kádár, the communist leader of the Hungarians in the last 30 years of "goulash communism," just to mention a few who have trademarked the country in the last few decades of the twentieth century. Hungary is unique in central Europe in that it is 97 percent ethnically homogeneous.

A brief history

The origins of the Hungarian people lie somewhere in the central Asian steppes. One of the small groups of Finno-Ugric peoples, the Magyar and Onogur split off at least 4,000 years ago, to seek new territory because of overpopulation in the region. The Magyar probably became known as Hungarians among foreigners because of their close association with the ancient Bulgar Onogurs (therefore, Ungarn, Hongrois, Hungarian), who were their neighbors in the region of Bashkiria from around AD 500 to 800.

Continuing their move westward, the consolidated Magyar tribes, under the leadership of Arpad, conquered the Carpathian Basin between AD 895 and 896. Seeking ever more powerful alliances, the early Hungarian kings established contact with western Christianity, culminating in the coronation of the first Christian king, Stephen, in 1000. Through missionaries sent by the Pope and the military force of the king, the pagan Magyars were converted to Christianity. The church, representing an ideological change, served also to change the social and political face of the region and helped establish Hungary as a feudal state, along with the emerging Bohemian, Polish, and Russian states.

For nearly 250 years, Hungary held its own kingdom under increasingly strong kings, who were receptive to economic and cultural exchanges with both Byzantium and the Holy Roman Empire. Then, in 1241, came the Mongol invasion. Devastating and destroying everything in their path, the Mongols scoured the Carpathian Basin for 12 months, leaving only 20–40 percent of the settlements standing and few people alive. The refusal of Pope Gregory IX and Emperor Frederick II to come to King Bela's aid in 1241 marked the beginning of a deeply ingrained belief, borne out again and again through the centuries, that only Hungarians can be trusted to help Hungarians.

The Mongol Invasion, considered the first of three national catastrophes for Hungary, also marked the end of the longest period of Hungarian self-rule – over 700 years. The throne of Hungary was variously occupied, bargained for, and stolen by rulers from Bohemia, Bavaria, Luxembourg, Austria, Poland, and Naples for the next 200 years. But, by the end of the late fifteenth century, Hungary had become one of the richest and most powerful Renaissance centers in Europe. The second catastrophe then arrived in the form of the invincible Ottoman Turks.

The king and most of the ruling noble class were slaughtered in the first major battle against the Ottomans in 1526, in effect leaving the country leaderless. The Turks occupied and ruled most of the country for the next 150 years, destroying more than half the Christian population and its buildings and institutions. The western slice of what remained of Hungary elected Ferdinand as the Habsburg king of Hungary in the hope that his powerful family could stop further Ottoman advances. The Habsburgs, seeing Hungary as a buffer for their own lands and interests, maintained that rule until 1918.

Although the Habsburgs were able to reunite the Hungarian lands after the Ottoman Turks were defeated by the Holy Alliance in 1699, they were never able to completely subjugate Hungarian culture. Inspired by the American and French Revolutions, the first half of the nineteenth century became a period of Hungarian nationalistic fervor. The War of Independence of 1848, though unsuccessful, paved the way for eventual Habsburg concessions, resulting in the Compromise of 1867 and the creation of the Austro-Hungarian Dual Monarchy.

What followed was a rapid economic development, culminating in the celebration of the Magyar Millennium in 1896: 1,000 years after Arpad first rode into the Carpathian Basin. This event marked the zenith of Hungarian culture in the arts and architecture, followed rapidly by economic improvement and the development of internationally reputed musicians, scientists, and writers. In 1849 Scottish engineer Adam Clark built a suspension bridge across the Danube between Buda and Pest, and hence Budapest was born. Tungsram, the Hungarian light bulb company, was founded in 1896 at the height of these exciting and intoxicating times.

Then the third catastrophe struck. Its effects are still so immediate in the minds of most Hungarians that the entire culture at times seems permeated by resentment. Thrust into World War I as part of the Austro-Hungarian Empire, Hungary found itself on the wrong side of victory. In 1920, at Versailles, the Treaty of Trianon carved away two-thirds of Greater Hungary. The loss of territory and people was perceived as unconscionably unfair, especially since it effectively removed 89 percent of iron production, 84 percent of forests, and nearly half the food-processing industry. Some 62 percent of the railroad network was lost, with treaty provisions strictly limiting the building of new ones.

Interwar Hungary became an economically stagnant, bitterly right-wing country, ripe to be drawn into the orbits of Mussolini and Hitler, who promised – and temporarily delivered – the restoration of Greater Hungary. Once more, Hungary was on the wrong side of victory. Hitler's decision to spare Vienna by sacrificing Budapest at the end of the war resulted in the near total destruction of the city, as the last Nazi stronghold. The Soviet army first liberated and then occupied Hungary for the next 45 years. It is still difficult to sort out the effects of the war and subsequent Soviet occupation on the culture and society of Hungary. Despite a failed revolution attempt in 1956 and the moderate political and economic reforms of 1957 and 1968, two full generations of Hungarians knew only a socialist, centrally planned and controlled system.

The central planning and central management were politically and not economically oriented. The undervaluation of the individual, the authoritarian management, and the good relationship of management to the Communist Party all fostered negative work attitudes. Meanwhile the seeds of change were planted in the market reforms of 1957 and 1968 by János Kádár, the Communist Party leader from 1956 to 1988 and the father of the "Kádár regime" and goulash communism. Change gradually began to extend and grow. The apogee came in 1989. The October 23, 1989 announcement of the change of the political status of the country from People's Republic to Hungarian Republic signified that the silent revolution was gaining momentum. This event was followed by political changes in 1990 and the first free political election. Since then, the business environment has advanced rapidly.

The economic tradition of the "old" system

Under a centrally planned economy, the entire management function was strictly hierarchical. The basis of the command system was the general economic plan developed by the state. The plan was circulated among the individual ministries and departments. They, in turn, assigned it to the corresponding enterprise or other appropriate organization. The plan was then passed on to the subordinate enterprises, plants, factories, or organizations, which further divided the plan among specific workshops, brigades, services, etc. These had to carry out the plan developed at the ministry, regardless of their specific needs or any changes that had taken place since the planning started.

During the 40 years between 1948 and 1988, many efforts were made to reform the socialist system. The most influential reform was implemented in 1968. Economic development slowed. The reform wing of the Communist Party leadership initiated a series of reforms in the economic system by implementing the New Economic Mechanism.

In the New Economic Mechanism, direct interventions were replaced by economic regulators: price policy and price control; financial policy of the state-budgetary revenues and outlays; enterprise profit through income and other taxes; regulation of personal income (wages); credit policy; foreign trade policy; investment policy. The managers of state-owned companies were afforded greater autonomy in organizing production and framing their strategy and investment plans. To realize these plans, however, managers continued to depend on the decisions of the central bureaucratic organs, since more than 80 percent of the net income went to the state budget, which was then reallocated by governmental organs.

The New Economic Mechanism eliminated the centrally planned economic system, but could not create a real market economy. The decentralization of economic control was not accompanied by a change in the centralized function of the political system. The totalitarian political system, as revealed later, was a fundamental cause of the fact that the results expected of the elimination of central planning were not achieved.

The oil crisis of the 1970s and the slow reaction in changing the economic structure and level of energy consumption aggravated the economic situation of the country. Political managers could balance this situation only by obtaining ever-increasing credits. In 1980 the debts of the country amounted to US$10 billion ($1,000 per capita). The serious economic situation called for new solutions in the country's economic management. The reform movement gained new momentum in 1978 with growing concern for the country's deteriorating trade position. Reforms were aimed at improving the efficiency of Hungarian industry in order to increase exports, especially to the West. In 1982 the passage of the Small Business Act was the first step to allow private business again in the country.

Profit orientation was still, for most state-owned enterprises, divorced from the reality of working life. Without real market competition and market prices, no attention was paid by managers to real human resource needs or to the quality of the products, programs, or services provided.

As individual salaries were low under this system, it was fashionable to steal from the company. A commonly heard phrase, "We pretend to work because they pretend to pay," characterized the general mood. For example, a bonus system was introduced, but it was subverted and resisted. In some factories, bonuses were distributed equally to all workers, and it did not matter how hard one worked or how lazy one was. Some managers withheld a secret percentage of the bonus funds, in order to individually negotiate rewards for extra work. The negotiated amounts were confidential. The result was that the workers became distrustful of management and suspicious of each other.

The ideological values encouraged the status quo, opposed a future orientation, equated entrepreneurship with cheating and criminal activity, and defeated the desire to change and improve performance. Leaders of high-performing organizations were typically not reinforced for their efforts as any profits made were skimmed off to subsidize lower-performing organizations. Therefore, the workers tended to avoid surpassing average performance. The system failed as the need for change increasingly became obvious.

While it may be tempting for a foreigner to attribute many of these policies to managerial incompetence, this would certainly be a mistake. These practices evolved within complex systems that were largely successful in achieving their real objectives: political control and production quantity. Under the socialist system, thousands of Hungarian workers, working in state enterprises, were vastly underutilized. Some experts estimate that the old system used as little as 10 percent of the productive capacity of its workers.

The transition

The third major milestone in the transition in the economic system after 1968 and 1982 was in the period of 1988 and 1989, when fundamental economic laws paving the way to the capitalistic world were accepted, ironically, by the communist parliament. To develop the private economy, the Corporation (Business Associations) Law created seven different types of enterprise ownership: unlimited partnership, deposit partnership, limited company, business union, joint enterprise, and the two most popular forms in Hungary, the limited liability company and the joint stock company. The Corporation Law was aimed at enabling an easy, unhindered flow and reallocation of capital in the economy. All citizens were allowed to form joint companies and economic associations at will. This law, implemented in 1989, offered new legal forms for entrepreneurs starting their business activity, based on the Small Business Act of 1982.

To facilitate direct investments of foreign capital in Hungary and to protect foreign investors against nationalization or expropriation of investment, a Foreign Investment Law was issued in 1989. Tax benefits were given to foreign investors to encourage foreigners to transfer technology to Hungary.

As it decreased the proportion of the state-owned enterprises, the Business Transformation Law also offered a new path to ownership transformation of companies. New rules were provided for the transformation of state-owned companies into business associations, declaring simultaneously the principle of general (legal) succession.

Furthermore, it provided for the transformation of a company into another type of firm, including by mergers and splitting. Supporting the privatization of large state-owned enterprises, the State Property Agency was formed in early 1990. A new accounting system was also introduced to develop mutually acceptable accounting and book-keeping practices. The basic book-keeping methods and contents of the balance sheet follow the rules of the Generally Accepted Accounting Principles of the western countries.

In order to diminish the role of government in the economy, new institutions were formed to reduce the enforced vertical relations between the central bureaucratic organizations and the business units. These new institutions included a bankruptcy law, a competitive banking system, personal and value added tax systems, and a bond and stock market. In addition, a two-tier banking system was implemented, which restricted the central bank to those functions normally associated with central banks in the West (credit policy, exchange controls, issuance of bank notes, etc.). The lending function was transferred to newly established commercial banks that could, within limits, compete with one another for business.

In 1988, a bankruptcy law facilitated the dimunition of governmental interventions by allowing for the liquidation of loss-making enterprises, although the government was still extremely reluctant to close down inefficient factories. The same year, new tax reform was adopted, creating three new tax systems: a general turnover (value added) tax, a personal income tax, and a company tax. The major purpose of introducing value added tax was to reduce direct governmental subsidies of certain firms and activities. Principally, the value added tax has created a neutral situation for all business entities. Moreover, the bond and stock market was created and the stock exchange started to operate in the summer of 1990. Thus, Hungary's economists and policy-makers accepted the fact that, to build the market economy, a capital market is essential and this is not viable without a stock exchange. The liberalization of the labor market was supported by eliminating discrete wage regulation. Thus, the regulation of wages was stopped.

The transition suddenly confronted individual managers and their organizations with the responsibility to survive by utilizing the resources available and managing them effectively. The external security net was removed, and suddenly responsibility was delegated to the individual manager, although it was not always accompanied by the appropriate degree of authority or discretion in decision making. The government retained control in certain areas, including wages and regulations, but required formerly inefficient state enterprises to be competitive, effective, and efficient. The socialist system provided a great deal of protection for the individual. The move away from this system has created a great deal of anxiety. Obviously part of the anxiety is due to the massive changes that are occurring. However, part of it also stems from a loss of the individual employee's expertise and recognition under the former socialist system.

In Hungary, as in other former socialist countries, employment was traditionally provided by the state or cooperative institutions. In 1982, more than 96 percent of the workforce was employed in the state-owned sector. By 1988, the proportion had declined to 94 percent. In some sectors, such as construction and trade, private sector employment had increased by as much as 15 percent over that period.

Economic performance and business values

What the Hungarians have been able to do in such a short time is impressive. Real GDP has grown and inflation is predicted to continue to slow down as domestic and external deficits are further reduced. The IMF is pleased with Hungary's performance: the stabilization program ended in 1997. Unemployment has stabilized. Hungary has attracted 37 percent of all direct foreign capital investment into central and eastern Europe since 1989. The biggest investors are the US and Germany, followed by Austria, France, and the UK. Only seven years after emerging from four decades of communism, Hungary has succeeded in transforming its economy. A key factor is that, unlike many of its Comecon neighbors, Hungary had had some experience in dealing with western business people in the 1980s. During the early phases of the transition, company managers were allowed to experiment with western management techniques and introduce some western technology. Hungary became the Soviet Union's conduit for pharmaceuticals and high-tech goods, such as computers.

The Hungarian challenge

The question of the fate of Hungary is open. What are the challenges faced by a country with a European heritage, shackled by a controlled economy, now facing a global business environment? The basic domestic political challenge is to retain the stability of the multiparty system. Following the third parliamentary election, there is still no sign of democracy's failing.

The membership of Hungary in NATO and potentially in the European Union (EU) creates a somewhat different perspective on domestic and international politics. An interesting article in the June 29, 1996 issue of *The Economist* deals with the impending extension of the North Atlantic alliance to the Hungarians, Czechs, and Poles. The article also carries the results of opinion polls on what these three nations think about NATO. Some 58 percent of Hungarians are strongly for or somewhat support joining NATO, while 27 percent are strongly against or somewhat oppose it. A year later, after the invitation from NATO leaders to join NATO, the opinion of Hungarians had not changed very much. The majority of Hungarians supported NATO membership in the public vote during fall 1997. People recognized that it is very important for Hungary to join NATO because without NATO's and the US's security guarantee, the dithering European Union leaders would never accept the risk and allow Hungary into the EU. That, in the long run, would be economic suicide for Hungary.

On April 8, 1994, Hungary and Poland applied to join the European Union and were the first eastern European countries to sign the Europe Agreements. Since Hungary's political system is comparable to those of EU member states, and the advanced state of the economy was confirmed by the country's accession to the OECD, the chances of its being accepted by the EU are high. But it depends partly on Hungary and also on the internal issues of the EU itself.

Hungary, nevertheless, still faces a number of problems: namely, low economic growth, which will have to be significantly higher than the EU average over a long period in order to raise living standards to the EU level, continued high inflation, and high public debt. Also, the need to reform the social security system, whose deficit is financed from the budget, is concomitant with the problem of public debt. Improvements must likewise be made in infrastructure, industry, and technology to raise Hungary's competitiveness, and a further reform of the banking system is required. Priority should be given to the reform of agriculture, as Hungary has a surplus in agricultural trade with the EU.

Based on the ongoing support received from the EU through the PHARE aid program, Hungarians expect continuous and increasing financial support to implement the necessary reforms. Financial support is one attraction for Hungarians in membership of the EU. People in depressed areas such as Borsod county, which contains most of the old-fashioned, traditional heavy industries, would welcome any support. Unemployed workers in the north-eastern counties would appreciate EU subsidies to develop their agricultural activities. Small businesses would be happy to have at least the same financial aid program that was provided within the framework of PHARE. The list of wishes is almost endless. Financing the projects for the road system, the bridge on the Danube between Hungary and Slovakia at Esztergom, the restructuring of the health care system – these are just a few of them.

However, most ordinary Hungarians are not particularly interested in joining the EU. They consider it a natural continuation of the political and economic progress made since the end of communism. In this regard, most of them believe that it should be arranged by the Hungarian government and parliament. What they are more concerned about is their survival in the ever-changing work environment.

The rapid evolution of the Hungarian economy into a market economy has forced the country's organizations to meet the challenge of global competition and economic interdependence. Hungarian economic policy, aimed at establishing a market economy, initiated a fundamental restructuring of enterprise ownership through laws and through the various privatization programs. In the past seven years, the importance of the private sector relative to the public sector has increased dramatically. For example, between December 31, 1989 and December 31, 1992, the number of Hungarian companies held by individuals or in mixed ownership increased tenfold, and the number of individual entrepreneurs nearly doubled. The share of organizations employing only a few people has increased dramatically. By the end of 1992, 80 percent of the total number of business organizations in Hungary operated with a staff of fewer than 20; 41 percent with 10 or fewer. The share of economic entities employing more than 300 workers declined from 5 to 3 percent.

The availability and distribution of skilled workers is a potential source of considerable competitive advantage for Hungary. Although machine engineering has historically employed the most skilled apprentices, other sectors, including communications, have been gaining skilled workers at an ever-increasing pace. There is a tight labor market in some segments, which serves as a driving force for the implementation of modern business practices in Hungary. Other driving forces include changing attitudes, convertible expertise, and the increasing availability and use of consultants familiar with a market-economy business environment. Hungary has a large number of well-trained, skilled workers with wages still below west European rates. Economic reform programs are as advanced as in any other east European country. On the negative side, however, bureaucracy remains entrenched, resistant, and reactive to change. Government agencies particularly are very slow in responding to the needs of government, and the telecommunications infrastructure remains underdeveloped.

Hungary is facing a period of fundamental transformation. At the same time, never before has it been so critical to recognize the importance of human resources, and the need to make massive investments in development and training, especially at the managerial level. Hungary's internationally recognized skilled workforce must be managed more effectively and efficiently in order to maintain a long-term competitive advantage. Also, Hungarian management has been criticized for its lack of market-oriented skills, its reliance on antiquated management practices, and its lack of commitment to performance management. Western managers typically characterize Hungarian managers as slow in decision making, unwilling to take risks, too inflexible, and lacking a "spirit of adventure." Eastern managers consider western colleagues responsible for difficulties and obstacles in communication, due to a lack of respect for local ways and customs, and a lack of detailed knowledge of the regional market. An employee service/customer orientation is still the exception in most former state enterprises, and even joint ventures are finding it very difficult to change work practices developed under the former socialist system. Part of the problem is that, under the previous socialist system, the Hungarian higher education system was reluctant to recognize business and management studies as respectable and discrete academic disciplines. Business administration was considered a sophisticated type of vocational training. If they were considered at all, management/business subjects were associated with traditional university disciplines, such as economics, law, and engineering.

Hungarian workers are skilled, but their skills are not being adequately utilized. This has been a product partly of inadequately trained managers, but partly of organizational systems that exploited their workers rather than energizing and empowering them. Long-time sojourners in Hungary often remark that the former Eastern Bloc countries' failure in business and management was compensated for by the quality of Hungarian elementary and secondary education. The fact that high-school students learn college-level science and mathematics is a potential future competitive advantage. But it can be an advantage only if the students' energy and talent are channeled and managed properly.

The establishing or re-establishing of relationships with trade unions will be a critical emerging factor. The impact of the first legal strike in the former East Germany is an indicator of this trend. The unions' cooperation with governments is critical to any long-term market restructuring. The alienation and exclusion of trade unions would provide an organized institutional focus for worker alienation. Thus, the reality of business life in Hungary is the increasing degree of change and the uncertainty that such change produces. This change can only increase, requiring organizations and their employees to be much more flexible.

Conclusion

A fundamental shift is under way in how and where the world's work gets done, with potentially ominous consequences for wealthy, industrialized nations. At the same time, this shift provides potential opportunities for Hungary and other countries developing market-oriented economies. The key to this change is the emergence of a truly global labor force. New technology and the continuing drive for higher productivity have pushed companies that wish to survive to seek their competitive advantage through a more effective, cost-efficient use of their human assets. Technology and capital move easily around the world as organizations seek to obtain competitive advantage. Unless it can be proved that labor is uniquely suited to a company, there is every possibility that the entire process, or at least those parts of it not directly related to service delivery, will be moved to more labor-efficient world locations. Even formerly protected service components within organizations have been relocated to more labor-efficient countries (the processing of insurance claims in the US has been moved to Ireland, hotel reservations to Jamaica, etc.).

While the Hungarians were central and eastern Europe's pioneers in adopting democratic and pro-market reforms, unless the Hungarian government and companies learn to utilize the educational system and workforce more effectively, there is no guarantee that this second Hungarian renaissance will continue. However, with the new economic development in the country, and the prospect of joining both NATO and the EU, the potential is there.

Bibliography

Balogh, S. and Jakab, S. (1986) *The History of Hungary after the Second World War*, Budapest: Corvina.

Csath, M. (1988) "The Hungarian economic reform: problems of human resource management and corporate culture," *International Journal of Manpower*, 9.

Hoch, P. (1991) "Changing formation and privatization," *Acta Oeconomica*, vol. 43, nos. 3–4, pp. 263–80.

Kornai, J (1980) *Economics of Shortage*, Amsterdam: North Holland.

Kornai, J. (1992) *The Socialist System: The Political Economy of Communism*, Princeton, NJ: Princeton University Press.

Montias, J.M. (1989) "National values and economic reforms in socialist economies," *World Development*, 17.

Vecsenyi, J. and Kovach, R. (1993) "Surviving or dying? Organizations and strategies in CEE," Proceedings of Research Conference, International Management Center, Budapest.

Outcome of the May 1998 general election, Hungary

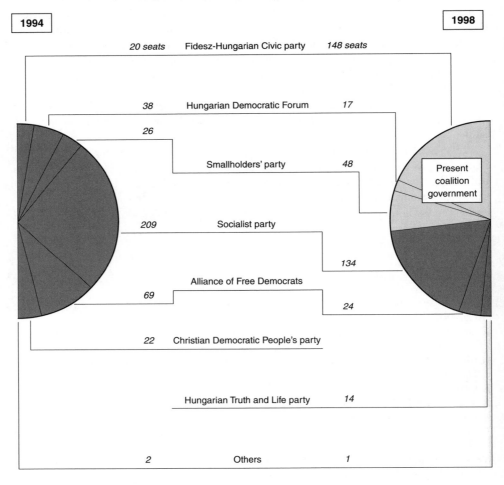

1994

1998

| 20 seats | Fidesz-Hungarian Civic party | 148 seats |

| 38 | Hungarian Democratic Forum | 17 |

| 26 |

| Smallholders' party | 48 |

Present coalition government

| 209 | Socialist party |

| 134 |

| Alliance of Free Democrats |

| 69 |

| 24 |

| 22 | Christian Democratic People's party |

| Hungarian Truth and Life party | 14 |

| 2 | Others | 1 |

Total: 386 seats

PART IV

Europe seen from abroad:
An emerging or stumbling giant?

Editor's introduction: the United States

The attitude of the United States toward Europe has always been ambivalent – when indeed the US has even thought of Europe. Nonetheless, it is widely accepted that the Marshall Plan at the end of World War II not only relaunched the European economies, but also sowed the seed of a potential pan-European organization. It is perhaps ironic that the original impetus for European cohesion came from the US, yet there is more than a grain of truth to this viewpoint.

Now, more than 40 years after the founding act of European unity, the Treaty of Rome (1957), what are the relations between the US and the European Union? Certainly they represent, alongside Japan, two of the three pillars of the world economy. Moreover, the EU and US are acknowledged bastions of democracy in the world. Furthermore, North America and Europe remain tightly bound by close cultural links, despite the occasional soul searching and subsequent repudiation of such links by the US. Naturally, as two of the three main trading blocs in the world, the EU and US must and will confront each other over certain issues. However, the cultural bases exist to help resolve these issues amicably.

What, then, are the aspects of the EU–US relations meriting further investigation?

- With nearly a dozen European nations adopting the new European currency, the euro, what will be its impact on world financial markets? On the global role of the dollar?
- With the increasing economic strength of the European Union, will there be a new deal politically and militarily between the EU and the US? If so, what are the implications for NATO?
- Given the dramatic financial crises in several Asian countries (Indonesia, Malaysia, Thailand, South Korea) in 1997–8, will the US and the EU be brought closer together as trading partners and financial underwriters of the world economy?

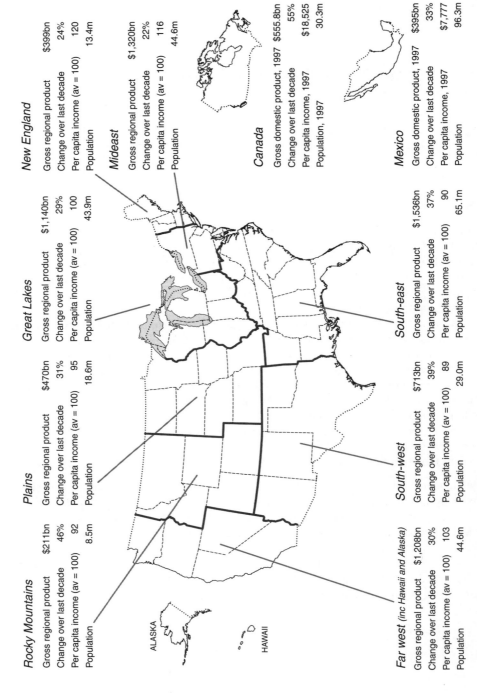

Rocky Mountains

Gross regional product	$211bn
Change over last decade	46%
Per capita income (av = 100)	92
Population	8.5m

Plains

Gross regional product	$470bn
Change over last decade	31%
Per capita income (av = 100)	95
Population	18.6m

New England

Gross regional product	$399bn
Change over last decade	24%
Per capita income (av = 100)	120
Population	13.4m

Great Lakes

Gross regional product	$1,140bn
Change over last decade	29%
Per capita income (av = 100)	100
Population	43.9m

Mideast

Gross regional product	$1,320bn
Change over last decade	22%
Per capita income (av = 100)	116
Population	44.6m

Canada

Gross domestic product, 1997	$555.8bn
Change over last decade	55%
Per capita income, 1997	$18,525
Population, 1997	30.3m

Mexico

Gross domestic product, 1997	$395bn
Change over last decade	33%
Per capita income, 1997	$7,777
Population	96.3m

South-east

Gross regional product	$1,536bn
Change over last decade	37%
Per capita income (av = 100)	90
Population	65.1m

South-west

Gross regional product	$713bn
Change over last decade	39%
Per capita income (av = 100)	89
Population	29.0m

Far west (inc Hawaii and Alaska)

Gross regional product	$1,208bn
Change over last decade	30%
Per capita income (av = 100)	103
Population	44.6m

ALASKA

HAWAII

Sources: Bureau of Economic Analysis; Statistics Canada

11

◆◆◆

US/EU relations in the last decade:
Fortress Europe to the transatlantic business dialogue

Irene Finel-Honigman
US Department of Commerce

Introduction

> Germany's biggest bank yesterday delivered a damning verdict on US indifference towards
> European Monetary Union, saying most Americans thought of Emu as a big Australian bird
> rather than an attempt to link currencies and economies in a way that could change history.
> Deutsche Bank said that such neglect could damage US interests. It blamed US politicians, busi-
> nessmen and economists for this lack of interest. ("US indifference to EMU deplored,"
> *Financial Times*, August 7, 1996)

Although there is renewed interest in the upcoming EMU by American financial markets and transnational corporations, American attitudes toward the creation and development of European Union institutions and policies have vacillated between
complacent indifference and wary defensiveness since the signing of the Maastricht
Treaty in December 1991. Former President Bush and Secretary of State Baker initiated
the Transatlantic Declaration signed in Paris in November, 1990. This official statement
affirmed policies of cooperation and support, including determination to help "consolidate the new Europe, undivided and democratic; ... promote market principles, reject
protectionism and expand, strengthen and further open the multilateral trading system."

Trade conflicts, diplomatic tensions, and profound cultural misperceptions have
marked the post-Maastricht US/EU relationship. The European Union has not helped to
clarify this situation by constantly redefining its identity and political persona. The ongoing debate between Europe *à la carte*, Europe according to strict adherence to Maastricht
criteria, and Europe in concentric circles, elegantly phrased in French as *Europe à
géométrie variable*, has often confused the American media, academics, and Washington
pundits. Decision-makers in the US are bewildered and annoyed at what they view as
indecisiveness and theoretical nit-picking.

Between 1989 and 1992 American journalists, like Alex Krause of the *International
Herald Tribune* in his book *Inside the New Europe*, Daniel Burstein in *Euroquake*, Jane
Kramer in the *New Yorker* and in *Europeans*, and Steven Greenhouse and Flora Lewis in
the *New York Times*, wrote individual country studies and analyzed the unification of

157

Europe. American business leaders such as Robert Hormats of Goldman Sachs, James Robinson of American Express, and Robert Allen at AT&T actively promoted the importance of EU unification and growth for American companies. Despite these efforts, disproportionately greater coverage of American cultural, foreign and economic policy, and political events appears in the major European press than EU coverage and media interest in the US.

Even in the age of CNN, there continues to be very little reciprocal exchange of information. Translations of American works from romance novels to political treatises are readily available in bookstores across the EU. American translations of widely read or acclaimed French, German, and Italian texts often take two to five years to be translated and are available only in university or select bookshops. Scandinavian, Dutch, and Spanish literature remains almost unknown. Therefore the American public has very limited knowledge not only of the status and issues of the European Union, but of the concerns and attitudes of its citizens.

The political agenda

Since 1988, the US/EU relationship can be divided into three periods. Euro-optimism of 1988–92 was greeted in the US as fear of a "fortress Europe." Euro-skepticism was interpreted in the US as a return to the 1970s Euro-scelerosis, meriting only detached indifference by the first Clinton administration from 1993 to early 1995. Since mid-1995 a new attitude has begun to emerge, which can be termed Euro-pragmatism. In the face of international terrorism, new post-Soviet geopolitical threats, a momentarily weakened Japan, and an unstable China, the US is again turning to Europe, acknowledging its role as America's most stable trading and political partner.

More than a half-dozen years after Maastricht, the US has slowly begun to view the EU as a geo-economic entity rather than a theoretical concept among a group of rival and separate nations. Economically, the US is beginning to realize that since 1995 decisions taken by EU officials represent the interests of 15 nations with nearly 400 million persons and a potential $7 trillion market. The US ignored or dismissed the intermediate stages in the development of European institutions, policies, and alliances. In the second Clinton administration, the US needed to dismantle its old attitudes in order to reach a comprehensive and productive partnership.

In February 1996, President Chirac in his first official visit to the US spoke to the US Congress and to an official luncheon at the State Department about a 26 to 30 nation "Eurobloc" for the next century. He emphasized that the EU is the US's most powerful and stable commercial and political ally. Within the realm of the GATT negotiations, the Dayton Accords, the redefinition of the EU's role in NATO, and the EU's negative response to the Helms Burton Act on Cuba, the US has had to accept France's position as spokesperson for a cohesive EU position.

On July 4, 1962, in his historic address in Philadelphia, President Kennedy validated General de Gaulle's Bonn declaration of July 18, 1961, in which de Gaulle called for a Europe of economic, military, political, and cultural cooperation:

We do not regard a strong and united Europe as a rival, but a partner ... capable of playing a greater role in the common defence, responding more generously to the need of poorer nations, of joining with the US and others in lowering trade barriers, resolving problems of commerce and commodities and currency and developing co-ordinated policies in all economic and diplomatic areas.

But by 1973, in a Vietnam war-torn US, when Henry Kissinger spoke of a Year of Europe there was no resonance or interest. The next most synchronous period in US/EU relations occurred in the prosperous mid-1980s. During the Reagan years both the American and European economies benefited from inflated stock markets, strong currencies, and steady growth. President Reagan cultivated relations with Mrs Thatcher, President Mitterrand, and Chancellor Kohl. The Reagan–Bush foreign policy focused on cooperation with Europe throughout the Soviet Union's period of *glasnost* and eventual dismantling.

As the US fell into a recession following the 1989 Wall Street crash, Euro-optimism reached its peak under the first Delors European Community presidency. As the European Community prepared to become the European Union, a weakened American economy rightly began to fear that a highly regulated intra-border isolationist Europe would limit access to American goods and capital investment. EU banks, often government owned or subsidized, as well as EU corporations, took the competitive lead from American companies. As American banks suffered from poor profits and restructuring led by the Citibank crisis, Europe, especially France, Germany, and the UK, became powerful rivals to the US in international trade.

Yet for the American public and media, stereotypes and traditional images of individual European countries continued. American subsidiaries of French and Italian companies in all sectors struggled to change the image of their countries and products from quaint to efficient, from picturesque to high tech. It was difficult for the American consumer to accept that EU companies were competitive equals in industrial, manufacturing, financial, and technological standards and expertise. Between 1990 and 1992, German, British, and Dutch investment in the US increased substantially, yet the American public was only obsessively aware of Japanese takeovers and capital investment. The US never went through a stage of Euro-bashing, merely Euro-indifference.

The economic agenda

When the Clinton administration came to power in January 1993 on a domestic rather than foreign policy platform, the EU was beginning to feel the impact of the global recession. The EU suffered from faltering currencies dependent on Bundesbank interest rate policies, poor showings in the Danish and French Maastricht ratification referendums, and the gradual dismantling of the Exchange Rate Mechanism, which in August 1993 led to the dissolution of the European Monetary System that had been in place since 1979. These events gave an impression of weakness, lack of initiative and cohesive unification policies. By August 1993, both the American and EU economic media assumed that the projected EMU would not and could not succeed. The goal of the young dynamic American president was to aggressively enhance and expand American exports, revitalize the

American economy and impose American objectives on global trade negotiations in NAFTA and GATT. He saw in Europe a demoralized group of nations, maintained only by a French–German coalition. The European Union appeared bogged down in details of harmonizing standards for marmalade, yet was unable to pull together a diplomatic or military solution for the worsening crisis in the former Yugoslavia.

Europe's period of loss of momentum, despite a strong showing of unity and diplomatic finessing in the GATT negotiations, was seen in the US as an inability to achieve the goals of 1992. The American press and public virtually ignored the slow but steady recovery in EU economies and the greater discipline on inflation and deficit reduction. Focus on corruption scandals in Italy, the confusing French elections, and the internal political and financial crisis between 1993 and 1995 gave the Clinton administration the impression that Europe was again a minor rather than an equal economic player. In November 1993, in symposia at the State Department and in speeches, Secretary of State Warren Christopher and Ambassador Mickey Kantor barely mentioned Europe, dismissing its role as outside the center of economic issues. This attitude shocked the Europeans and revealed a lack of historical foresight. Kantor's brusque confrontational style in the GATT negotiations alienated his European colleagues. Long term, it provoked French-led EU challenges to American decisions on WTO leadership, UN mandates, and economic security issues in Iran, Iraq, and Cuba.

In January 1994, when President Clinton left for his first European foreign policy trip, France, as spokesperson for the EU, and the US were at a political and economic impasse. France and the member states of the newly ratified EU felt insecure and wary of American intentions in the political and defense sectors. The US, stung by the concessions it granted under French and EU pressure in the last days of the GATT negotiations, remained aloof and unwilling to clarify its response to European geopolitical concerns.

Moving away from the previous administration's pro-Europe "Euro-centric" foreign policy, the Clinton administration turned to new geopolitical allegiances and markets. At the first meeting between Clinton and Delors on May 7, 1993, at the White House, the president reiterated the principles of the Transatlantic Declaration by stating:

> The European Community is our largest single trade and investment partner. Our relationships with Europe are directly responsible for an inordinate number of American jobs, and if we cultivate that relationship properly and grow our trade and investment, it will mean more economic opportunities for the American people ... We fully support Europe's efforts toward further integration and we will work with the European Community to achieve our common good.

However, in reality the US practiced "conspicuous detachment" in its approach to European concerns and issues. The focus of the first Clinton administration was to revitalize and strengthen its trade policies in 1993. The Department of Commerce under the guidance of Secretary Brown developed its Big Emerging Markets strategy. The policy targeted ten countries outside of the European Community and Japan as top potential export markets within the next decade: India, the Chinese Economic Area, Indonesia, Korea, Argentina, Brazil, Mexico, Turkey, Poland, and South Africa. After the passage of NAFTA in 1993 and the APEC summit in 1994, the attitude was that mature stable European markets did not need nurturing or assurance.

In January 1995, two major events occurred that demanded a reappraisal of US/EU trade. The devaluation of the Mexican peso and the subsequent impact on Mexico's political and economic status created wariness about investment in emerging markets. The Mexican crisis brought into question the potential gains promised under NAFTA. It also damaged the culturally fragile US/Mexican relationship. The second Clinton administration also has to deal with the impact on EU/Mexican and EU/Latin American trade and export strategies. The peso crisis also revived in the US a backlash of isolationist trade sentiment. A Republican Congress with little or no experience of international commercial issues is unlikely to encourage new trade and investment initiatives.

In January 1995, the European Union, on schedule, integrated three of the four European Free Trade Area (EFTA) countries, Sweden, Finland, and Austria, increasing the EU to 15 countries. These EFTA countries are long-time military and political allies of the US in sensitive strategic areas.

After the integration of the EFTA countries, "Showcase Europe" and "Showcase Germany" were the new buzzwords on the cover of *Business America*, the official publication of the US Department of Commerce. Alan Tonelson wrote in *International Economy* in May–June 1995, "unlike America's trade with either the BEMS, Japan, China or other rapidly growing Asian economies, its trade with Europe is balanced, mutually beneficial and responsive to market forces and exchange rate shifts." There was renewed sentiment that in international relations it is wise to cultivate old friends and allies before seeking new untested allegiances. In March 1995, discussions took place between Ambassador Kantor, Secretary Brown, and EU trade commissioners and ministers Sir Leon Brittan and Dr Martin Bangeman, concerning a Transatlantic Free Trade Agreement. The purpose of this ambitious and perhaps even utopian project was to bring about a breakdown of trade barriers between the EU and NAFTA signatories.

On April 25, 1995, Jeffrey Garten, former Under Secretary of International Trade, launched the Transatlantic Business Dialogue (TABD) in a speech in Brussels. He spoke of a New Economic Architecture. He emphasized that American firms should refocus their strategy to increase their exports to Europe in aerospace, information technology, and services. In cooperation with the new EU Commission President, Jacques Santer, he acknowledged the EU as a "formidable global competitor" and a partnership that should not be taken for granted: "It would be a tragedy if we slipped into adversarial stances, concentrating on irritants and differences, losing trust and confidence as well as the spirit of cooperation that we developed over the last half-century in what has been one of history's most successful partnerships." The follow-up meetings in Seville in November 1995 brought together business and government leaders from the EU and the US. It included Alex Trotman of Ford, heads of Alcatel, Renault, and Siemens, joined by EU ministers and Secretary Brown. The agenda was to initiate a dialogue on trade, regulatory, and commercial policy issues.

In the annual report by the EU Commission on *US Barriers to Trade and Investment*, the list of EU concerns includes the complexity of American standards and state-by-state regulations, the use of Section 301 and Super 301, procurement issues, and the fear that the US is reverting to unilateralism in its trade negotiations. The US, in its *US Trade Global Outlook* of 1995, mentions among its main concerns the EU's continued lack of transparency, agricultural subsidies, audio-visual quotas, and rules concerning country of origin. In 1996 tensions caused by the EU Broadcast Directive, which would have strictly limited access to American cultural products, were reduced when EU culture ministers agreed not to impose binding broadcasting quotas for European television.

The TABD was viewed as an important step toward cooperation in the US/EU Summit on June 12, 1996. The US and the 15-nation EU remain each other's largest trade partners. Two-way flow in trade exceeded $400 billion in 1996 and investment reached nearly $800 billion. Stuart Eizenstat, the new Under Secretary of International Trade, at a Conference on Euro Services in June, 1996, emphasized the need for closer linkages with the European Union. He was seeking to pursue the issues he espoused during his tenure as US Ambassador to the EU: review of the US/EU regulations in the former EFTA countries, the extension of the European Atomic Energy Community Treaty (Euratom) on civilian nuclear trade, increasing access for American agricultural products, and improving US/EU telecommunication cooperation. He emphasized ties with European nations: "We must continue to stress our Big Emerging Markets initiative while at the same time continuing our strong relations with mature markets that have historically been the foundation of our trade and export growth."

Economic performance and business values

Jacques Attali, Mitterrand's economic advisor, wrote in *Europe(s)* in 1994: "L'Amérique se pense comme une utopie d'Europe." The United States was created in response to Europe. The US has always sought a separate identity that would encompass European culture but could rewrite historical destiny. Since *Democracy in America* (1838), when Alexis de Toqueville first analyzed the American initiative and propensity to gain power through business and commerce, Americans have viewed themselves as dynamic and futuristic in contrast to a romanticized and historic Europe. The US in the post-World War II era became a global power with little or no knowledge of the three subjects that are at the core of the European education and cultural heritage: history, geography, and foreign languages. These subjects, from the primary through the MBA level, are the most ignored and berated subjects in the US curriculum. Yet they are the focus of European educational, political, and economic policies.

The focus in individual European nations and in the EU on legal, social, and political institutions is far greater than in the US. The American constitution mandates the role of each branch of government. European nations as well as the EU apparatus in Brussels make economic decisions with long-term goals. The US continues to enact economic and commercial decisions for the short term, based on profit and results.

The complex, often incestuous, financial and legal partnership between public and private sectors in the EU is misunderstood in the US. Yet in the financial sector, European banks have never had restrictions between their banking, investment, and insurance activities such as have been imposed by the Glass Steagal Act in the US since 1934. Attitudes toward banking, individual participation in the stock market, and the role and responsibility of corporate shareholders are totally different in both cultures.

Neither the American public and politicians nor future American business leaders are familiar with the Gaullist and Mitterrand vision of a Europe of nations. There is often a confusion and merger in the American perception between the EU, a political institutional process, and the financial principles laid out in the Maastricht Treaty for European Monetary Union (EMU). The EU challenge for the next decade will be to maintain historic and cultural integrity and diversity within unity. This will also be an issue for an increasingly minority- and ethnically-sensitive US.

It is new and difficult for the US to accept the EU as a strong competitor in multilateral negotiations. Europe as a whole by the early 1980s had taken up Servan-Schreiber's call to arms in *Le Défi americain* (1967), often to the total amazement of American industries, especially in the aviation, aeronautics, optics, and chemicals sectors. EU companies are also active rivals for third country markets in traditional luxury food, clothing, and cosmetic markets.

Alain Peyrefitte wrote in his memoirs of working with General de Gaulle, *C'etait de Gaulle*, that the mistrust of the US toward a united Europe was based on a sense that American hegemony was at stake. On May 24, 1962, de Gaulle said, "They are reacting to the idea that their predominance could be challenged" (p. 150). The Clinton administration's high-level advocacy for American exports again "sometimes raised the hackles of other governments, notably French government and business leaders who saw in it a new source of US hegemony" (*Journal of Commerce*, April 11, 1996).

At the heart of the GATT debate on how to define US cinema and media is the synergistic relationship between culture and economics in the EU. The Maastricht Treaty's economic and political agenda incorporates linguistic directives and subsidizes cross-border educational initiatives. NAFTA, dealing with a bilingual Canada and a hispanophone Mexico, totally ignored these issues. The assumption is that corporations would deal with negotiations and communications on an *ad hoc* basis. The work ethic and the definition of what constitutes full employment, employee rights, and benefits differ radically between the cultures.

Attitude to the future of Europe

At a time when the EU is working through the Intergovernmental Conference, when EU financial markets are establishing the structures and mechanisms for the euro and EMU, when the EU is taking on a larger and more proactive role in NATO, and when CEE (Central and Eastern Europe) countries' ascension to the EU is coming closer, the American public and media will have to rediscover the EU not as recipient of aid, fledgling rival, or tense and adversarial competitor, but as "a partnership of equals."

Echoing the concerns voiced by Kissinger in *Diplomacy*, Dominique Moisi wrote in the *Financial Times* on July 24, 1996:

> The US could be the guarantor of stability in today's multipolar world. But instead it appears as a psychologically self-sufficient – and at times even provincial – actor, a great power endowed in part against its will with global responsibilities and means. It often gives the impression that it wants to be the global leader – but only in behaviour and style. If the US really wants Europe to act as a diplomatic and strategic power on the world stage, it must begin to treat it as an equal, and not only in words. To do so, Washington needs to move from leadership to partnership with Europe.

Dealing with fragile re-established nations in the former Soviet Union which are transitioning from demand to market global economy, the US/EU relationship remains a cornerstone of political and financial stability. The US must become knowledgeable and respectful of the EU. The EU must re-evaluate its responsibilities. Environmental issues, aid to the poorest regions, and social problems will beset both continents. The American decision to revert to unilateral trade sanctions imposed on EU companies in the D'Amato bill on Iran and Libya and the Helms Burton Act on Cuba has aggravated US/EU relations.

At the onset of the second Clinton administration, the US and the EU share a fear of increased international terrorism, a delicate and unstable balance in Asia, and the rise of Islamic extremism. These global risks have increased the need to enhance cooperation in security, intelligence, and counter-terrorism measures. The US will have to take into account the opinions of its European allies. As already proven in the official protest to the D'Amato bill, dialogue will have to replace unilateral trade sanctions or dominance. In order to dispel EU fears of new American isolationism, the US administration and Congress will have to continue a tradition of internationalism, promoting open markets and democratic governments. The EU in turn will have to show far greater willingness to bear responsibility for its military security and internal conflicts.

Bibliography

Aron, R. (1990) *Memoirs: Fifty Years of Political Reflection*, New York: Holmes and Meier.

Ash, T. G. (1993) *In Europe's Name: Germany and the Divided Continent*, New York: Random House.

Attali, J. (1994) *Europe(s)*, Paris: Fayard.

Burstein, D. (1991) *Euroquake*, New York: Simon and Schuster.

Cogan, C. (1995) *Oldest Allies – Guarded Friends*, Westport, CN: Greenwood Publishing.

European Commission (1993–5) *Report on US Barriers to Trade and Investment*, Brussels: Services of the European Commission.

Finel-Honigman, I. (1996) ''French–GATT impasse: negotiations à la française,'' in Kreinin, M. (ed.), *Current Issues in Commercial Policy*, Oxford: Elsevier Science.

Finel-Honigman, I. (1996) "US/EU: competitive partners or strategic competitors?", Occasional Paper no 77, Center for International Business and Research, University of Maryland, May.

Galbraith, J. K. (1994) *A Journey Through Economic Time*, Boston, MA: Houghton Mifflin.

Heilbroner, R. (1993) *21st Century Capitalism*, New York: W. W. Norton.

Kennedy, P. (1993) *Preparing for the Twenty-First Century*, New York: Random House.

Kissinger, H. (1994) *Diplomacy*, New York: Simon and Schuster.

Kramer, J. (1988) *Europeans*, New York: Farrar, Strauss and Groux.

Krause, A. (1991) *Inside the New Europe*, New York: HarperCollins.

Lewis, F. (1987) *Europe, a tapestry of Nations*, New York: Simon and Schuster.

Peyrefitte, A. (1994) *C'etait de Gaulle*, Paris: Editions De Fallois, Fayard.

Price Waterhouse (1994) *Doing Business in the European Community*.

Rosenberg, N. and Birdzell, L.E. (1986) *How the West Grew Rich: The Economic Transformation of the Industrial World*, New York: Basic Books.

Servan-Schreiber, J.-J. (1968) *The American Challenge*, New York: Athenaeum Press.

Tocqueville, A. de: (1845) *Democracy in America*, vol. 2, New York: H.G. Langley.

US Congress (1995) *National Export Strategy: Meeting Foreign Competition, Third Annual Report to the United States Congress*, October.

US Department of Commerce (1995) *US Global Trade Outlook 1995–2000: Toward the 21st Century*, March.

US Department of Commerce (1995) *The Big Emerging Markets: Outlook and Source Book*, Berman Press.

US International Trade Commission (1989) *The Effects of Greater Economic Integration within the European Community on the United States*, July.

Editor's introduction: India

A glance at newspaper headlines in the late 1990s reveals an old but recurring story: religious and political strife between Hindus, Muslims, and Christians in India, and nuclear competition between Hindu India and Muslim Pakistan. Moreover, the Hindu fundamentalist party draws increasing strength from these events and indeed captured the leadership of the nation. At the same time, the Gandhi family – even through adopted family members – has relaunched the political fortunes of the Congress Party.

India's turmoil, with its largely religious roots, continues to surprise European observers. However, a nation of profound religious conviction and of so many different faiths can scarcely be imagined without conflict. Prabhu Guptara has stressed the influence of Christianity in his country of origin, but he might have chosen Hinduism or even Islam for his perspective on this infinitely diverse land.

Given this diversity, accompanied by enormous economic potential, which questions should be dealt with further?

- India faces two regional enemies – China and Pakistan. Can an enduring peace be made with either? If so, how, in light of India and Pakistan's entry into the nuclear club?
- In the world's largest democracy, is there a solution to the recurrent religiously inspired bloodletting?
- Will India continue its movement toward a more open economy with links to the outside world, or again retreat behind trade and monetary barriers?
- What can Europe learn from India?

India

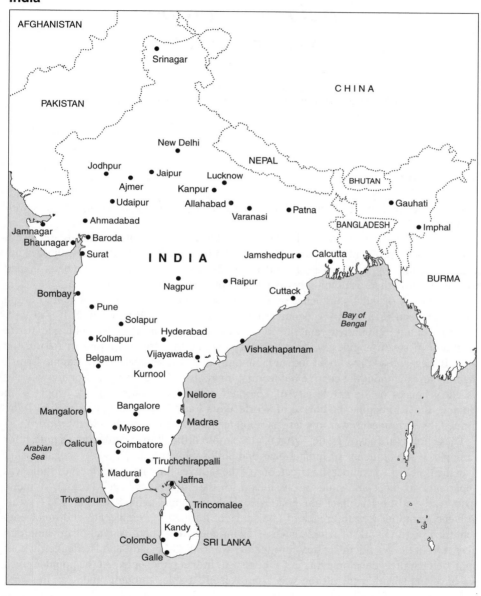

12

India and Europe:
A distant embrace

Prabhu Guptara
UBS Executive Management Centre, Wolfsberg, Switzerland

Introduction

That Europe made India is a well-known story; that India made Europe is less well known.

For the former, turn to Mangalwadi (1996, 1997) and Mangalwadi and Mangalwadi (1993), which document the extent of what India owes to Europe. Mangalwadi does not argue what follows, but the very boundaries and constitution of India have been shaped by Europe. And there is nothing between these that has escaped its influence.

For the story of India's influence on Europe, I am afraid there is no book at all. Europe has never been interested in documenting its debt to India. But imagine, if you will, Europe without trigonometry and the concept of zero; imagine British shipping up to the invention of steam engines without Lascars; imagine the British Empire in Africa, the West Indies, and so on without Indian labor and, later, Indian enterprise; imagine British manufactures without the captive but teeming markets of India; imagine London without its curry houses or the whole city of Leicester without Gujaratis (that is, people from Gujarat, India); imagine the course of World Wars I and II without Indian soldiers (who formed, by turn in each war, the largest volunteer army seen until then in the world).

These points are easily made. What is much more difficult to even begin to suggest, for example, is the influence of Indian ideas and philosophy on Europe, which began earlier than the times of Alexander the Great, one of the motives for whose conquest of India was apparently to meet and hold discussions with the "gymnosophists" (yogis) of India, specifically at the Buddhist universities of Nalanda and Taxila (Basham, 1954). This influence continued, with breaks of course, right through the eighteenth and nineteenth centuries via the work of people such as Heinrich Heine when Romanticism came into play, and in the twentieth century through the work of Kirkegaard and Heidegger, whose approach parallels developments in the history of Indian philosophy. At the popular level, we have Indian influence all the way from Aesop's Fables through "Indo-Jaz Fusions" and the Beatles to "Indie music" and the band Kula Shaker's recent chart-topping success "Govinda-Jaiya." In brief, India has had a continuing influence and in many cases a form-ative influence: for example; on "alternative" lifestyles and New Age attitudes.

That the mutual impact of Europe and India has been so substantial should be no surprise. After all, there are no impassable rivers or mountain ranges dividing what is called Europe from what is called India; what divides these two areas of the main land mass of the world is nothing more solid than traditional nomenclature. Most Europeans and Indians speak, to this day, one family of languages and have influenced each other's literatures profoundly.[1]

However, those millennia of influence and interaction are in the forefront of no one's mind nowadays. India used to look up to Europe and the US (which is Europe's spiritual heir), but now looks much more to eastern Asia. Europe too looks instead to eastern Asia and the US. Mammon prevails over spirit; things prevail rather than ideas. For the present, the embrace has grown distant. Why it is so is another story, not for this occasion. What is for this occasion is an attempt to reflect on the present situation of Europe from an Indian perspective, to see what light if any is thrown on the current intra-European embrace from the perspective of a product (myself) of that earlier interaction between Europe and India.

Unity in diversity

From an outsider's point of view, there is at least one theme where Europe and India are often said to reflect each other, and that is "unity in diversity." However, India has such enormous variety that, had the British not conquered all of India and created the present political framework of the subcontinent, it is doubtful if what is India today would have been a country at all.

Briefly, let me recount something of that diversity. Linguistically, the last Indian census documented over 1,000 spoken languages (languages, not dialects), of which 15 are recognized for official purposes. This means that speeches in the Indian Parliament need translation into 14 languages, while speeches in the European Parliament need translation into only five. Of course, that is not surprising, if one considers that India's population is roughly three times that of Europe, even if India's population is crammed into a surface area which is roughly equal to that of Europe (from London to Moscow is almost exactly the same distance as from Trivandrum in the south to Srinagar in the north). Racially, if one distinguishes between three basic racial types in the world (European, African, and Chinese), each of these types is found in India. Religiously, India is the largest Hindu country in the world, and the third largest Muslim country (after Indonesia and Bangladesh), but India also has over 20 million Christians, which is more than the entire population of many European countries. Sikhs, Buddhists, Jains, Jews ... we have them all; I can think of no religious group that is unrepresented in India.

This has resulted in an unusual situation, where at least in my generation it was common to celebrate the festivals of all the religious communities even though one might belong to none; the usual saying was "any excuse is good enough for a celebration." Unfortunately, that tradition of tolerance has come under threat, principally as a result of the rise of Hindu fundamentalism, as was illustrated by the early 1999 attacks on Christian communities by Hindu fundamentalists. In any case, highly religious as India is, it is still one of the more corrupt countries in the world, mainly because the majority religions see no necessary relationship between religiosity and morality (Mangalwadi, 1992; see also Guptara, 1984).

Every conceivable variety of cuisine, dress, and value-system is to be found in this peculiar country, which has some of the poorest people in the world as well as some of the richest. A member of the nuclear and space "clubs" and more or less the world-center for computer programming, it still finds 70 percent of its population getting about by ox-cart. A signatory to every worldwide treaty except that on Nuclear Non-Proliferation, it is not perhaps the most enthusiastic implementer of the requirements of any of these treaties, most strikingly in environmental matters: Bombay and Delhi are considered among the most polluted cities in the world. Many of these paradoxes are, of course, not unique to India among developing countries.

Democracy and Christianity

One thing that is unique in India among developing countries is democracy. Of all the ex-colonies of the nineteenth-century European powers, India is the only one still to be a democracy; other countries have valiantly attempted to establish democracy for a while before collapsing into chaos or dictatorship, or both. India is in fact one of the few non-Christian countries to have been able to make democracy (of some recognizable sort) work for as long as 50 years. Why this should be so is interesting and I suggest may have something to do both with the phlegmatic temperament of the peoples who inhabit the country (a direct consequence of the caste system) and with the balance of powers astutely worked out by the founding fathers of the country. There is a balance not only between the states and the center, of course, and between the government, legislature, and judiciary (the "three pillars of democracy"); but also between the different aspects of the national security system, some of which are responsible to the Home Ministry, some to the Defence Ministry, some to the prime minister and some directly to the president, not to mention the security wings of each state, which have a similar deliberate lack of focus. This makes a military coup extremely unlikely, since no one person or group can command the allegiance or even coordinate all the possible centers of military power.

India also has a rather advanced system of intelligence agencies. Certainly at one stage, there were 16 different national agencies involved, again with a similar deliberate lack of focus, so that a plot from any quarter was likely to be discovered by one or other of these agencies. Though I do not necessarily approve of all the methods that some of these agencies have been alleged to use, I might mention that as a result of an incidental experience with one such agency, of which I had fallen foul for the duration of a lunch hour while still at school, and as a result of another incidental experience with another such agency while involved in some social work in one of India's border regions, I have the highest possible respect for the caliber of these agencies.

However, the astute balance of powers is only one factor in India's democracy, and perhaps not the most important one. A more important factor may be that the generation of people who led India to independence were immensely influenced by the message and values of the Bible: India was the principal target for the efforts of British evangelism, which systematically penetrated the British colonial enterprise and used it (one could say, subverted it) for Christian purposes. The role of the culture thus created in India by the joint efforts of Christian individuals, schools, colleges, and other institutions has had a crucial role in the survival of democracy in India. This becomes clear when one considers the experience of countries in the former Eastern bloc: democratic constitutions and institutions by themselves do not produce democracy; it is the culture that enables institutions, constitutions, and democracy to survive (Storrar, 1997). What is it about Christian cultures that has nourished democracy? Protestantism particularly brought to a high point of development certain values and institutions, which originate in Judaism.

Democracy is popularly imagined to originate in the Greek city states, but the Greeks were never able to make the democratic idea function for any length of time. Democracy probably has no single point of origination, but versions of democratic practice exist in various tribes throughout the world, and all the foundation stones of democracy are present in the Jewish scriptures (which Christians call the Old Testament). Most importantly, the concept of truth itself and of morality as belonging to the character of God and therefore as being intrinsic to the universe; that gender and racial or family origin or even social position (such as that of king or priest) make no difference before God; that the king's law is subordinate to God's law (the basis for the separation of powers between government and judiciary in modern societies); that power brings responsibility; that there are prophets with a special sanction and indeed a particular responsibility to speak the truth, even about and to the most powerful people (which has developed into today's "fourth column" of the press and the media); that the existence of special roles such as that of priest or king or prophet does not detract from the fact that everyone is responsible (why otherwise go to the bother of participating in the forums, discussions, and actions which are the lifeblood of democracy?); that everyone has a responsibility not only for their own family but for the community as a whole (or why willingly pay taxes or be involved in community activities outside the family?); that it is essential to know God for oneself and love God with all one's heart and mind and strength through a study of the Word of God (the Bible), which was the foundation of literacy and of intellectual life for the vast mass of people in Judaism as well as in Protestantism; and that, for everyone, duty and morality are more important even than life itself.

Such ideas and values are fundamental to the creation and survival of democracy, and though such ideas exist in attenuated form outside Protestantism, they are not essential to non-Protestant traditions, whereas they are essential to Protestantism. Modern media and institutions (such as the United Nations through the Declaration of Human Rights, drafted by a Lebanese Christian, Charles Malik) have popularized and made almost universal ideas that were revolutionary in their day and that have no substantial basis outside the Jewish–Christian framework. This important fact is often obscured by the equally important fact that democratic ideas and values naturally find an echo in every human heart because we are all made by the same God and reflect God's character. However, democratic ideas and values that exist in spoken or written form have been more difficult to embed and root in Catholic, Orthodox, Muslim, and other cultures (in that order) because such ideas and values find themselves opposed to the dominant institutions and informal ways of life of such societies. Now that the generation of Indians educated in Christian schools has been overtaken by a much larger generation of people educated in secular institutions (even the Christian institutions have been largely secularized), and Hindu revivalism has become dominant politically, the key question for the future of India is: can the center hold?

The answer, as in Europe, depends in part on economic progress. It could be argued that the success so far of the European idea is due to a situation of increasing economic prosperity since World War II; all the evidence indicates that, whenever the economy progresses more or less satisfactorily, the acceptance and implementation of the idea of Europe proceeds apace; but that, whenever the economy slows down, the popular acceptance and the official implementation of the idea of Europe slows down too. It is a bit like that with the idea of India. Whenever the country makes reasonable economic progress, the "fissiparous tendencies" (as Indians usually call them) tend to fizzle out; whenever the economy is in the doldrums, the infighting multiplies.

Clearly, the possibility of progress in India is bound up with the success of the attempt to liberalize the country. It is not easy, and it will not be easy, rapidly to loosen the hold of the Indian Establishment, which has, since independence, come to consist not only of the hereditary overlords who traditionally ruled the country, but also of the professional meritocracy of the civil authorities, the unprofessional opportunism of the political class, and the crassness of the *nouveau riche*. Popular attention, however, focuses on the considerable complications caused by an entrenched trade union movement. The speed, consistency, and effect of economic reform will undoubtedly play a part in stabilizing or destabilizing democracy, as it has in European history.

Science and technology

It is worth reflecting on the fact that when Europe had nothing worth talking about, India already had a high civilization, witness Mohenjodaro and the Indus Valley civilization, roughly 2500 BC. What most people do not realize is that this continued to be the situation for over 4,000 years, even as late as the seventeenth century AD; India was rich while Europe was poor. Yet in a short while the situation began to be reversed, and today India is ranked only as a "developing country," while Europe has some of the highest living standards in the world.

The reversal of fortunes was, in my view, due mainly to the birth of science and technology (combined with increasing democratization). Pre-scientific ideas and speculations existed in Greece, Egypt, Mesopotamia, Persia, China, India, and other countries, but one key fact prevented these ideas from becoming science: people from these societies who indulged in such speculations belonged to a class of people and a system of thought which regarded this world as being less important than the next world and regarded real work ("getting your hands dirty") as something for the lower classes. Biblical thought is, in a sense, other-worldly too; but it emphasizes the importance of this world (this is a real world, made by a real God). The Bible also emphasizes the significance of human actions in this world (the disobedience of Adam and Eve changed all subsequent human history for the worse, just as the obedience of Abraham and Moses changed all subsequent human history for the better).

It was the Protestant thinkers who emphasized this element of biblical teaching, and certainly all the early scientists (Protestants or Catholics) were people who believed that they, as God's metaphysical creation, were exploring (as they were intended to explore) God's physical creation – even if they and it are now "fallen" and therefore not perfect, as they and it once were. Bacon fathered the experimental method in a Christian society and could not have fathered it in a non-Christian society. This becomes difficult for post-modern westerners to see, brought up as they are on mythologies of the conflict of science and faith centered on Galileo and Darwin, but from a non-western point of view, it is fascinating to see how essential the biblical framework was to the possibility of science.[2]

Of course, science by itself would never have enabled Europe to rise so quickly. Another ingredient was essential. This was the rise of technology. Let me suggest that the process which converts science into technology, whatever else it may require, certainly requires the application of capital. And here we run into a most interesting story.

The rate of capital accumulation was incredibly enhanced by the lifting of the ban on usury in twelfth-century Europe. It is important to understand that the ban on usury was not invented by modern Islam. All ancient societies forbade usury, from the Chinese to the Indian, to the Jewish, to the Greek, to the Native American. And the effect of forbidding usury is to make capital accumulation a rather slow process, possible at a rapid rate only by rather violent means, legal or criminal, or related to war and other such extraordinary events. Moreover, the rate of capital accumulation was naturally reduced by the human tendency to indulgence and profligacy. So, even after the Roman Catholic Church lifted the ban on usury, capital accumulation (though it took place more rapidly than it had ever done earlier in human history and led, for example, to the invention of modern banking in Italy and Switzerland) did not take place as rapidly as it did after the Protestant emphasis on living a sober and modest life had become dominant in certain European societies. It was this rapidly accumulating capital in Europe, which could not be applied in Protestant parts of the world to the usual dissoluteness of rich people, which was applied to the new possibilities created by science to convert them into technology. In turn, this made possible the enormous expansion of these European economies through trade and commerce and (later) empires, so that in a mere 100 years European societies started outclassing non-European ones and began to drive history.

Postmodernity and the future

We now live in a period of history that is beginning to be called the postmodern age. We feel that we have come to the end of a phase of history and do not know what, if anything, is next. Individual liberty has become total self-absorption. Wealth has deteriorated into mere materialism. Loosened from its moorings in moral and social considerations (Ellul, 1964), technology has reached an apogee and we are surrounded by more than we know what to do with; we do not even have enough space in our houses and perhaps on our planet for all the clutter that we have created. Technology makes it foreseeable for a single robot-controlled and robot-repaired set of machines to produce all the manufactures that are needed, if not desired, by everyone on this earth. In such a world, what employment can we offer the masses, even if they are all well educated as a result of the multimedia revolution? What future can we envisage for humankind?

On the way to a genuinely global society, even if the idea of Europe is only a temporary halt at the level of regionalization (along with other such regions in North America and eastern Asia), the issues with which Europe is wrestling today are the great issues of our age: the redefinition of work, the distribution of wealth, and the political organization of society. It was European thinkers such as Luther and Calvin who, following the Bible, first defined work as something worth doing in itself; it is European thinkers such as Charles Handy who are leading the thinking about what it means to "work" in today's automated world. It was in Europe that the influence of Christian democracy produced a balance between wealth generation and wealth distribution; if there is to be any chance of continuing social stability, this balance needs to be striven for anew, though not necessarily or only through parties affiliated to the Christian Democracy movement.

As the automation of production leads to mass unemployment in the West for the first time, and we struggle with the creation and indeed the possibility of a service economy, the key debate will center around the validity of democracy. Parliamentary or representative democracy will be called into question for the first time in "advanced" societies by the possibility of direct democracy (a form of democracy that has been practiced more or less successfully by small countries such as Switzerland). On the other hand, democracy itself will be called into question by the desire of the super-rich to control the resistance of the mass of the population to the blandishments of "mega-commerce" and the "logic of economics," which will tend to impoverish and enfeeble the masses. The important question, once again in history, will become: who has a right to vote and does the vote of an independently wealthy person have equal value to that of an employee or that of an unemployed person?

It will be interesting to see whether democracy survives the emergence of post-Christian societies for longer than three or four generations. In India, there is a saying that the first generation establishes a particular way of thinking and acting (*karam*), by the second generation that way of doing things begins to be internalized in the consciences of the people or group concerned (*sharam*), and by the third generation that set of values and actions becomes so firmly established in the lifestyle as to be accepted without thinking (*dharam*). Conversely, when a group of people formally abandons a particular set of values (*dharam*), the following generation still feels in their consciences and acts almost unconsciously according to the old and now formally abandoned value-system (*sharam*); it is only in the third generation that the habit of operating on the basis of the old values and mindset (*karam*) finally begins to die out. Perhaps that is what the Bible means too when it talks about spiritual and moral choices having consequences down to "the third and fourth generation."

Conclusion

In the past, countries traveled down the two separate roads of coming together or coming apart; today, countries are traveling down the single road of coming together in certain areas of socio-econo-political life while coming apart in others; tomorrow, centralization will win because centralization has its own dynamic and technology speeds that dynamic. Centralization, however, is not to be confused with progress, and progress itself is not unidirectional or inevitable: the rapid modernization of Iran led to the Mullahic reaction which still holds that country in thrall. Nor can one guarantee that progressive movements will remain progressive: the Muslim movement, so progressive when first initiated through the Prophet Muhammad (peace be upon him), soon became reactionary. This can be seen in centuries of Muslim influence that turned North Africa from a center of intellectual ferment into the desert it has been for the centuries since then.

The fact that industrialization in Britain produced the reaction of the Luddites (and that globalization produced the "fortress America" attitudes of Pat Buchanan) shows only that, as in the world of physics, "every action produces an equal and opposite reaction." The advantage of democracy is that open dialogue and debate between the opposing forces can result in a relatively harmonious resolution of the conflict, as in the existence of lifestyle choices and the building of at least some minimal environmental considerations into all industrial and commercial activity. The disadvantage of the absence of an open society is that the ruling cliques (relatively open, as in most traditional societies; or relatively hidden, as in the case of China today) merely arrange things for their own aggrandizement with minimal concessions to everyone else and to all other points of view.

If Europe is simultaneously coming together and coming apart, this is no different from what has happened every other time in history and at every other such historic moment in other parts of the world. At every moment in history and in every place, one movement becomes dominant, but if it becomes too strong, it creates a reaction. India and the US offer some parallels for what is happening and what is going to happen politically and economically: for example, as the euro is created. There will be questions regarding what is the right balance between centralization and regionalization, and pressures at particular moments in one direction or the other. At times of prosperity, no one will doubt that Europeanization is the right way to go; at times of lack of perceived growth (such as the present), there will be popular disillusionment with the idea. But what really matters is whether the spiritual, intellectual, economic, technological, and political forces that create, nurture, and maintain an open society are encouraged and flourish. These are what create the music within which any embrace (distant or close) was, is, and will be worthwhile, productive, enjoyable, and humane.

Notes

1. For India's influence on the UK, see Guptara (1986), which attempted to draw together for the first time a list of all the books written originally in English by people of non-European backgrounds who acquired British citizenship and settled in the UK.
2. The father of the scientific method, Francis Bacon (1561–1626) argued that a scientist was intended to be "the priest of God's Book of Nature."

Bibliography

Basham, A.L. (1954) *The Wonder That Was India*, London: Sidgwick and Jackson.
Ellul, J. (1964) *The Technological Society*, New York: Knopf.
Guptara, P. (1984) *Indian Spirituality*, Nottingham: Grove.

Guptara, P. (1986) *Black British Literature: An Annotated Bibliography*, Aarhus, Denmark and Warwick, UK: Dangaroo Press.

Mangalwadi, V.K. (1992) *The World of Gurus* (2nd edn), Chicago, IL: Cornerstone.

Mangalwadi, V.K. (1996) *The Missionary Conspiracy*, Mussoorie, UP, India: Nivedit Good Books.

Mangalwadi, V.K. (1997) *India: The Grand Experiment*, Farnham, Surrey: Pippa Rann.

Mangalwadi, R. and Mangalwadi, V.K. (1993) *William Carey*, Mussoorie, UP, India: Nivedit Good Books.

Storrar, W. (1997) *Christianity and Democracy*, Handsell.

Editor's introduction: Japan

Finally, we come to Japan. It is fitting that we deal with Japan last, since it is an island kingdom with a civilization limited only to its archipelago. Moreover, throughout its long history, Japan has remained largely protected from, if not closed to, the outside. It is this last factor that distinguishes Japan from another island nation on the other side of the globe, the United Kingdom.

Were we to prolong the comparison, we might note that insularity has spawned xenophobia in Japan, while the UK is more rarely accused of this particular flaw. Indeed, Japan is such a closed shop culturally that even after three or more generations in that country, Korean immigrants' descendants have still not successfully integrated into Japanese society and are perceived as foreign.

Hierarchy and respect for it used to typify both Japan and the UK, although class barriers and respect for the royal family continue to fall in the latter country. In Japan, only the disastrous end of World War II could lower the status of the emperor from that of demi-god to revered leader. Within the firm, clear hierarchical lines persist in Japan, as well as an emphasis on age as a criterion for respect. One does not transgress these lines with impunity. The foreign firm which wishes to promote a younger, dynamic employee over the head of an older one may well regret that decision later.

Such an act would break the *wa* or harmony of the enterprise. The *wa* is the cultural key to the functioning of the firm in Japan. If this harmony, based on mutual recognition and respect among employees, is upset, the functioning of the firm suffers. Expatriate managers ignore this critical factor at their peril.

Moreover, the recognition of "place" and "face" within the firm and in society is the outward manifestation of the mechanism of shame. Thus, any action that might be perceived as shameful to an employee will be rejected by that employee, but also by all his or her fellows. The extreme case of this phenomenon is *hara-kiri*, which still exists today. The example of the death of the president of Japan Airlines following a tragic crash clearly illustrates shame and its consequences.

Questions for further study on Japan and Europe:

♦ In a trilateral economic world of Europe, the US, and the Far East – especially Japan – can the first and the last be brought together without the consent of the US? What forum is appropriate for such *rapprochement*?

♦ As one of the few Asian countries not to have been colonized, does Japan serve as a model? If so, for whom?
♦ What impact will Japanese financial restructuring have on Japan politically? As a business center and trading nation? On Europe?

Japan

Area: 377,819 sq km

Language: Japanese

Currency: Yen (Y)

Population: 125.8 million (October 1 1996)

Main cities and population: (1996)

Tokyo (capital)	7,962,000
Yokohama	3,320,000
Osaka	2,600,000
Nagoya	2,151,000

Constitution

National government
The ruling Liberal Democratic Party (LDP) holds 261 seats in the 500-seat House of Representatives. The new Minshuto (Democratic Party of Japan – an amalgamation of four parties of which the original Minshuto is the largest) holds 92 seats. The second largest opposition group, the Peace and Reform Network, holds 47 seats. A new cabinet was installed in September 1997

National legislature
Bicameral Diet; comprising the 500-member House of Representatives, elected every four years, and 252-member House of Councillors, elected for six-year terms, with half of its number elected every three years. Under 1994 legislation, there are 300 single-seat constituencies and 200 seats filled by proportional representation in the House of Representatives

Main trading partners
(share of total trade to world 1997)

EXPORTS

China	South Korea	Hong Kong	Taiwan	US
5.2%	6.2%	6.5%	6.5%	27.8%

IMPORTS

Australia	South Korea	Indonesia	Taiwan	US
4.3%	4.3%	4.3%	12.4%	22.4%

Economic summary	1999*	2000*
Total GDP ($bn)	4,169	4,652
Real GDP growth (annual % change)	1.8	2.3
GDP per head ($)	32,830	36,520
Inflation (annual % change in CPI)	0.4	0.8
Unit wage costs (annual % change)	0.5	1.0
Industrial production (annual % change)	1.4	1.2
Unemployment rate (% of workforce)	3.7	3.6
Broad money supply (annual % change)	3.43	3.50
Foreign exchange reserves ($bn)	221	230
Government expenditure (annual % change)	0.0	−0.1
Government debt (% of GDP)	106.3	110.2
Current account balance ($bn)	109	123
Merchandise exports ($bn)	383	422
Merchandise imports ($bn)	269	294
Trade balance ($bn)	114	128

* Forecast

Sources: EIU; ING Barings

13

♦♦♦

Europe through Japanese eyes

Robert Orr
Nippon Motorola
Stephen Anderson
US Department of Commerce

The origins of the Japanese nation are like a Japanese painting of a misty mountainous skyline – shrouded in mythology and mysticism, of a variety that has often been used to rationalize the political objectives of the Japanese state.

In each of Japan's major revolutionary changes, it has been foreigners that have provoked that change: the Chinese with the introduction of Buddhism in the eighth century; the Europeans with the infusion of technology and efforts to introduce Christianity in the sixteenth century; the Europeans along with the Americans in the 1850s with a commercial and military challenge; and – in the aftermath of war – American attempts to remake Japan in the occupation, which at best only partly succeeded.

Early encounters: 1500–1900

The first European visitors to Japan set in motion a dynamic that inexorably led to change and to the first tentative steps by Japan to enter the global stage. We say "tentative" because it would face many reversals over the next 400 years – reversals that still occur from time to time to this day.

The first Portuguese visitors to Japan were referred to as "Nanbanjin" or southern barbarians, since they probably came from Macao, the Portuguese trading port off China. With brightly colored European garb and an appearance that the Japanese had never seen before, they were an oddity. But in addition they brought with them a technology that the Japanese learned to copy with surprising alacrity: the arquebuse or musket.

Soon other Europeans were making their way toward Japan from their Asiatic outposts. The Portuguese were followed by the Spanish and then the Dutch. One Dutch trading vessel was captained by the first Englishman to visit Japan, Will Adams, whose story was loosely adopted by James Clavell for his worldwide bestseller *Shogun*.

The Europeans quickly found themselves in the midst of a civil war that had already lasted almost 100 years when the first landings took place in 1542. As a consequence, as time went on and in order to secure their interests, the various European powers sided with whichever clan they thought would help them. Each European power tried to foment suspicion among the Japanese toward the other. The Jesuits, in particular, had a large presence. Their mission of religious conversion provoked misgivings toward the Jesuits by some clan leaders, which the Dutch traders were quick to exploit.

All the major warring clans were intrigued by the technology that the Europeans introduced, particularly the weaponry. One major warring clan, that of the Lord Oda Nobunaga in the last years of his life, insisted on wearing European armor and drank grape as opposed to traditional Japanese rice wine (sake).

With the death of Oda in Kyoto in the late fourteenth century, there remained two possible Lords who could unite the country: Hideyoshi Toyotomi and Tokugawa Ieyasu. Hideyoshi came close to unity and might have achieved it had he not gotten sidetracked with Japan's first overseas war, an invasion of the Korean peninsula. The invasion became a protracted guerilla conflict and eventual débâcle. He died before his last troops were able to withdraw. Tokugawa, employing Dutch advisors, was able to finally unify the country, thus closing what is known in Japanese as *sengoku jidai*, or the period of the country at war, with a decisive victory at the battle of Sekigahara in 1616. The result was the creation of a Shogunate that ushered in relative peace and domestic tranquility for about 250 years, at the price of maintaining a hermitic kingdom for the whole period. The extent to which Japan would fall behind the western nations technologically would become painfully obvious when the country was reopened by US Commodore Matthew C. Perry.

The immediate effect of the creation of the Tokugawa Shogunate was a gradual movement against the Jesuits by the new government, which moved from Kyoto to Edo (present-day Tokyo). The inroads that Christianity, and particularly Catholicism, had made alarmed the Shogunate. The state initiated an oppressive policy toward the Jesuits and those Japanese who had converted, resulting in the expulsion of the Jesuits and the slaughter of many Japanese Christians.

The Dutch, on the other hand, had convinced the Shogunate officials that their primary interest was trade and commerce rather than introducing their own brand of Christianity. As a consequence, the Dutch and Chinese traders would be more or less the only foreigners allowed into Japan until the mid-nineteenth century. But even the Dutch would be limited in their access to Dejima island in Nagasaki Bay. Throughout that period, the Dutch would be allowed once or twice a year to travel up to the main island of Honshu to brief the Shogun and his charges on the affairs of the outside world. While the Japanese retained a great deal of interest in Europe, they chose not to engage the continent. Likewise, Europeans showed little interest in engaging Japan.

Given their position within Japan, the Dutch became the prism through which European civilization was viewed, and not surprisingly they made sure that the Japanese received the Dutch version of developments. One side of this slant is that the only foreign language accepted in Japan, and then only by an elite group of scholars, was Dutch. In some circles in Japan, the Tokugawa era is also known as the *Rangaku jidai*, or the period of Dutch learning. It even inspired some haiku, such as a verse that went "Geese flying south for winter, that is Dutch writing," thus reflecting the exoticism and peculiarity which most Japanese attached to the westerners, including their writing system which did not contain Chinese characters.

This cozy little world would begin to wear thin as the Europeans began to encroach further into Asia, on the heels of the age of discovery, with a more virulent brand of imperialism. British traders, followed by the Royal Navy, as well as American and Russian ships, would increasingly challenge Japan's shores.

In 1852, the Dutch warned the bureaucrats in Edo that a large American flotilla was on its way to the capital, but the Japanese refused to give credence to the reports. When the Perry mission was spotted off the Ryukyu Islands, the Shogun's forces feverishly moved to shore up their coastal defenses. But by the time Perry's *kurofune* or black ships arrived at Edo Bay on July 8, 1853 and exposed their guns for all to see, the Tokugawa regime knew it would be no match for such fire power. A new day was at hand for Japan.

Engaging the West

Japan's next course correction was brought about primarily by fear. Britain's Opium War against China (1839–42) sent a chill through the whole region and suggested that all were potential targets of European aggrandizement. Japan watched the British actions closely. It reinforced their predilection to keep westerners at arm's length while simultaneously learning as much as they could from them. This approach became the foundation of Japan's approach to the West throughout the Meiji period.

Perry's visit to Japan was not the first in the nineteenth century. The Dutch had maintained their trading relationship. Indeed, several American traders had arrived flying the Dutch flag in order to soothe Japanese sensibilities. However, Perry's visit was by far the most traumatic and not only led to the establishment of an American mission but also opened the door for European powers to make similar claims to concessions. The immediate result was the use of gun boat diplomacy by Russia and Great Britain at Shimonaseki, a development that further undermined Japanese confidence in their Tokugawa institutions. The longer-term result was the recognition that Japan was weak. The imposition of unequal treaties on Japan by all the European powers plus the US sapped Japanese sovereignty through provisions that allowed such things as extraterritoriality. The latter would remain a thorn in Japan's side for the rest of the century. These treaties, which so glaringly pointed to Japan's inferiority, became a driving force for the revision of national entities. In fact, the encroachment from the West was the incendiary act that led directly to the downfall of the old Shogunate regime and the restoration of imperial political power, previously dormant for centuries.

With the inception of Emperor Meiji's reign in 1868, Japan embarked on a full-blown course to catch the West in everything from military organizations to political bodies to industry. To commemorate the symbolism of the changing of the guard, the former imperial capital recognized the seat of Japan's *de facto* power in Edo and renamed it Tokyo or "eastern capital."

In spite of the appeal of the superior western models, there were forces in Japan that were not willing to concede the failure of the old institutions. This led in 1877 to the Saigo Uprising, the second domestic rebellion within the old samurai class. With its subjugation, the crystallization of Meiji power was complete, not necessarily through the emperor himself, but rather via an elite clique of senior samurai called the genro, who handled the affairs of state. With the promulagation of the Meiji constitution in 1890, the genro would constitute the real power in government at least until the election of Hara Kei as prime minister in 1918. In actuality, their control lasted until the military's drive for power in the 1930s.

Many Japanese advocated combining western technology with Japanese spirit (*Wakon Yosai*). Many Japanese have traditionally viewed their spirit and tenacity as a defining superiority toward the West, irrespective of any temporary technological inferiority. Others wanted to get rid of foreign influence altogether and cried "sonno Joi" – expel the barbarians, revere the emperor. In the end, while the barbarians were not expelled, the emperor was increasingly revered. Furthermore, the Japanese did seek out western achievements in the social and scientific realms that best served their interests.

Some of their initiatives worked well. Some were naive and some were just simply ridiculous. Perhaps the grandest manifestation of the latter, and one that reaped European scorn, was the Rokumeikan in Yokohama. This was a dance hall in which Japanese put on elaborate balls for themselves and European residents. The direct aim was to help convince the Europeans that Japan was indeed "civilized" and could have the same kinds of social activity as London, Paris, or Berlin. It failed because negotiations on revising the treaties were broken off a few weeks after the fanciest of the dress balls sponsored by the Japanese government. However, other efforts were more astute. The genro sent out the "best and the brightest" of the samurai class to scour the world, seeking the best models for Japan. They did not always choose the best, but the end goal was maintained: build a society that would be strong, end the unequal treaties, and put Japan on an equal footing with Europe. The lessons they learned based on the colonial impulses of the Europeans reinforced Japan's instincts that a "rich country, strong army" was the best route. Nineteenth-century European colonialism provided a road map for twentieth-century Japan.

But some remarkable cultural synergy did come into play, in a mutual fascination with the arts. Europeans, particularly French and Japanese artists, began to draw much from each other's artistic cultural legacies. Toward the end of the century, Impressionist painters such as Monet, Manet, and Van Gogh were influenced by Japanese art. Many Japanese artists studied in Paris.

In order to lay the framework for Japan's future and finally dispose of the hated unequal treaties, the Japanese adopted the aspects of western civilization that they viewed best suited to them: the Royal Navy became the model for the Imperial Navy. Certain aspects of American education and civil life also became a model. Unfortunately, so also did the Prussian constitution of 1850 – itself a reaction to the European upheavals of 1848. This document embodied strong imperial institutions and enshrined militarism. The Prussian – later German – army also became a model.

The primary purpose, as with the Rokumeikan, was to show the West that Japan was also a western nation, since Japan was adopting western structures. It was irrelevant whether or not the core structures were among the most reactionary. The primary goal was to rid the nation of the unequal treaties imposed by the European powers and to move Japan to the center stage of regional colonial competition.

Imperial baptism

With the adoption of the 1890 Meiji constitution, Japan could show to the European powers political structures that seemed to be European and thus "civilized." Japanese leaders felt that this was essential to their efforts to relieve themselves of the shame of the unequal treaties. The first treaty ridding Japan of unequal clauses was signed in London in 1894. Other countries followed suit.

As Japan modernized in the late nineteenth century, Tokyo's imperial appetite also developed. In 1894–5 Japan fought China for control of the Korean peninsula and came away victorious. While some of the European powers were pleased with Japan's victory, others viewed the rise of Japan with a great deal of wariness. Russia in particular had Far Eastern designs and was alarmed at the conditions that Japan had placed on China to end the war. When Japan demanded territorial concessions on the Liaotung peninsula, Russia along with France and Germany "advised" Tokyo against acquiring this possession. Japan relented, stirring considerable domestic resentment toward the European powers. To the Japanese, the demands being made were in the same pattern as those that the European powers had made of China. Thus the "Triple Intervention" became one more landmark on the road to the virulent Japanese nationalism of the 1930s and 1940s. This animosity was further fueled when three years later Russia laid its own claims to the peninsula that St Petersburg had forced Japan to renounce.

But the Triple Intervention débâcle, along with Britain's positive response to eliminate the unequal treaties, moved the two countries closer together. For Britain, the attractiveness of a Japanese ally was to enlarge the projection of the Royal Navy without having to actually dispatch ships. For Japan, an alliance with London could be used as a hedge against growing Russian power in the East. In January 1902, the alliance was signed. The pride of the Japanese, having as an ally one of the most powerful states in the world, was palpable. These events would prove vital in Japan's coming war with Russia.

Competition between Russia and Japan over both the Korean peninsula and Manchuria had not abated after the Triple Intervention. It had, if anything, intensified. Relations had reached a boiling point when Tokyo decided on a pre-emptive strike without warning on the night of February 8–9, 1904 on Port Arthur. This successful military action would resonate 37 years later in the Hawaiian islands against the US. Japanese forces not only defeated the Russian armies on the Korean peninsula and in Manchuria, but also routed the exhausted Russian Baltic fleet, which had been consistently denied calls at ports under the British Empire on its long, wearing voyage from Europe.

A peace treaty was brokered by the US president, Theodore Roosevelt, at Portsmouth, New Hampshire, in August 1905. The initial reaction by the average Japanese was one of elation at being the first Asian nation to defeat a European power. However, many came to believe that in the ultimate settlement Japan had been short-changed once again. This sentiment further inflamed nationalist passions.

Tokyo's outright annexation of Korea in 1910 made Japan the undisputed regional power in east Asia, particularly since China's Manchu dynasty was in its death throes. In Europe, two Balkan conflicts ignited, moving toward continental conflagration by the summer of 1914. An ally of Great Britain, Japan became the fourth country to declare war on the central powers after Britain, France, and Russia. Japan entered the war with relish due to domestic economic troubles. Japan also saw the chance to destroy German power in east Asia. Britain initially asked Tokyo to fight only a limited war, destroying German naval vessels, but taking no action against German holdings in China. Tokyo ignored this plea and moved on Berlin's interests throughout the region, including the South Pacific.

Japan also took advantage of the situation to move toward its longer-term goal of greater power in China. In issuing its 21 demands, Japan hoped to render China a vassal state. The US objected to the demands as a threat to the "open door" policy for China. Both Washington and Tokyo had held each other in mutual suspicion at least since the competition over the Hawaiian Islands in the 1890s. This suspicion was exacerbated by immigration issues on the west coast of the US. America finally entered World War I in 1917, ostensibly because of the renewal of Germany's unrestricted submarine warfare. Tokyo felt this a flimsy excuse and believed the real goal to be the expansion of the American naval presence in the Pacific.

American suspicion of Japan was further stimulated by plans for intervention in Siberia. With the collapse of first the czarist and then the Provisional government in Russia and the ensuing Bolshevik takeover, the country erupted in civil war. British forces intervened though Murmansk. Japan sent 75,000 troops into the heart of Siberia. Americans countered with 7,000 troops landing in Vladivostok. All of these contingents were there supposedly to protect immediate national interests, but the American move was clearly due to concern over real Japanese intentions and ambitions. These occupations would last until after the war's end.

With the armistice in November 1918, Japan expected to be a full and equal player in the peace process at Versailles. One of Tokyo's principal objectives was to have added to President Woodrow Wilson's 14 principles a clause recognizing the equality of all races. Since the European powers represented at Versailles continued to possess colonial holdings, this was not a welcome proposal. Racism in the US was rampant. Many Japanese naively thought Wilson's idealistic rhetoric would lead naturally to the acceptance of this clause. They were stunned to see that it went nowhere. Once again nationalism was inadvertently encouraged by the reaction of the US and the European powers.

But by this time, Japan was increasingly recognized as a great power. A principal at the Washington naval disarmament conference in 1921–2, Japan agreed to substantial reductions in ship tonnage, which once again triggered a nationalist response in Japan. But the most significant impact of the conference was the subsequent British termination of the Anglo-Japanese alliance. This action caused considerable shock among the Japanese people as they had come to see the alliance as a stabilizer in regional affairs. For Britain, the Russian threat had simply abated with the Japanese victory in 1905, followed by the Russian revolution and civil war.

All of these events moved Japan toward a more nationalistic stance. In the 1920s, there was a brief flowering of democracy. However, the global economic crisis and the rise of militant rightists led Japan's relationship with the European powers and the US to a fork in the road in the 1930s.

The road toward global war

By the end of the 1920s, the Japanese military was beginning to stake out a path toward regional supremacy. The western powers had long held sway over the Japanese military. Top naval officers had been trained in either Great Britain or the US. The army elite had been educated in Germany or by Germans. This led to a fractionalization of the military, with the navy generally believing in closer ties with the Anglo-Americans and the army having confidence in the rise of Germany.

The consolidation of a Chinese republic, after years of conflict among the warlords, led to Japanese intrusion first in 1928 and then more conclusively in 1931. The Mukden incident represented a full-scale military action, culminating in the creation of the Manchukuo puppet government under Tokyo's auspices. This action resulted in western condemnation, notably the Stimson doctrine, and led to Japan's withdrawal from the League of Nations in 1933. The western powers had become impotent to curb Japanese aims in north-east Asia.

The emergence of European fascism was to create a further outlet for Japanese nationalist sentiment. For many Japanese, the government's actions were consonant with what the western powers had been doing for years in China. What they did not realize was that the age of imperialism was over and thus no longer an acceptable form of international behavior – particularly for a non-western power. Moreover, Japanese actions in China were sometimes based not upon government, but rather upon military decisions. In effect, Japanese regional decision making had become a runaway train.

The 1930s was a period of political turmoil of a sort that Japan had not witnessed since the Meiji Restoration in 1868 – and just as bloody. Political and industrial assassination became a regular feature of Japanese national life. The ultimate manifestation of this violence was the dramatic coup attempt on February 26, 1936, known in Japanese as the *ni-ni-roku jiken*. The attempt failed, but nonetheless irrevocably set Japan on the road to a fully fledged militarist state. At one point during this episode, Japanese naval guns from Tokyo Bay were trained on the Diet Building, the seat of Parliament.

The result of the attempted coup was a shift in government further to the right. The Japanese military elite had been inching toward the Italian and German totalitarians, but this incident helped to confirm the movement. In an effort to ward off a perceived potential Sino-Soviet encirclement, Tokyo signed the Anti-Comintern Pact with Rome and Berlin in 1936, even though China would not have a communist government for another 13 years.

The outbreak of war in China in July 1937 was the beginning of a quagmire from which Japan, despite a terror campaign that in Nanking would horrify even the Nazis, would never be able to extricate itself. It was a "Vietnam War"-style débâcle that led directly to national destruction.

Germany was the European country most directly affected by Japan's war in China. On the one hand, Japan was an Anti-Comintern partner. On the other, Japan's actions in China clearly threatened substantial German commercial interests. This situation tended to temper German enthusiasm for Japanese operations in China, irrespective of diplomatic alignments. In Nanking, Japan came close to blows not only with the Americans over the sinking of the USS *Panay*, but with the UK as well over the attack on HMS *Ladybird*.

Germany's primary aim was to retain Japan as an ally in the event of war with the Soviet Union, thereby doing for Moscow what had been done for Berlin in World War I: namely, provide a war on two opposite fronts. Japanese and Soviet forces did engage twice, the more significant action being at Nomonhan. This engagement was essentially an indecisive war of several weeks' duration that featured the deployment of hundreds of bombers and artillery in a massive display of firepower on both sides. It was a useful lesson for the Japanese, who came to the decision that a strategic movement against the Soviet Union would be costly. Hence, a southern assault against south-east Asia and the US Pacific fleet appeared more logical.

The signing of the Tripartite Pact, in essence an alliance among Germany, Italy, and Japan, was the defining moment in establishing the Axis in 1940. This pact created the indelible image of unity, however false it might have turned out, of the three wartime belligerents. As later became apparent, the real level of cooperation among these powers would be insignificant compared to the Anglo-American-Russian alliance with the underpinning of the Lend-Lease allocations.

Despite all the rhetoric of cooperation, the Nazi leadership still viewed the Japanese through the lenses of racial superiority. Many Japanese came to regard the Germans as arrogant. Indeed, the Japanese had developed their own notions of racial superiority. So much for steadfast friendship.

Germany's early wartime successes against Poland, the Low Countries, France, Denmark, and Norway deepened the admiration of Japanese rightists for the Nazi regime and emboldened them to take more aggressive actions in Asia. Following the freezing of Tokyo's assets and the placing of an oil embargo on Japan by Washington in the summer of 1941, Japan decided to strike. With a swiftness and deliberateness reminiscent of their attack on the Russian fleet at Port Arthur, Japanese naval planes raided the huge US naval facility at Pearl Harbor, thus bringing the US into the Pacific War.

In addition to the US, Japan's European adversaries in Asia were the Dutch in Indonesia and the British colonial outposts in the region. French Indochina was also occupied by Japan, although the Vichy French government was technically an ally. It was Japan's occupation of all these European holdings that made it difficult for them to return to colonial status once the Imperial Empire had been vanquished in 1945. The motion toward independence was irrevocably unleashed.

Europe and Japan were devastated by the war, thus ensuring a lengthy period before economic recovery could take place. The experience would have a lasting effect upon the protagonists and upon their international behavior. The lesson drawn from the war by the UK and the US was never to give a totalitarian regime the opportunity to be an aggressor. Punish aggression early, they concluded. There must be no more appeasement like British prime minister Neville Chamberlain's appeasement of Hitler in Munich in 1938. However, for Germany and Japan the lesson learned was never to give their own military the chance to perpetuate aggression. Thus was born an emphasis on a smaller defense force and a reluctance to dispatch troops overseas – even in support of United Nations activities. This world-view would sometimes conflict with those of the UK and the US in places like the Middle East in the 1990s.

Out of the ashes and into the sunlight

The havoc of the war essentially terminated Japan's relations with Europe, with the exception of the UK. However, even the latter was limited due to the dominance of the US in the postwar occupation. From 1945 until 1952, Tokyo's foreign policy was conducted in Washington.

The occupations that occurred in Europe and Japan were also profoundly different. In Germany, the Third Reich ceased to exist. In Japan, there was continuity from the wartime regime to the peacetime regime. The German occupation was a multilateral affair with France, the UK, and the Soviet Union dividing the country into zones. The Supreme Command of the Allied Powers (SCAP) was a multilateral affair only in name. In reality, it was an American show from start to finish. Washington believed that it had borne the lion's share of the war in the Pacific. In addition, the lessons of Soviet–American competition over German policy moved the US to exclude Moscow from Japan as much as it could. The other European powers were casualties of this preoccupation.

These preoccupations created very different Cold War dynamics. In Europe, a multilateral defense regime emerged from the multilateral occupation: namely, the North Atlantic Treaty Organization (NATO). In Japan, a bilateral framework was born from a unilateral occupation: namely, the US–Japan Security Treaty. Thus Europe, in much of the postwar period, would be seen from the perspective of Washington. This influence would gradually recede as Japan emerged as an economic power and as European economic recovery got under way. In both cases, Washington supplied massive amounts of aid through the Marshall Plan in support of American goals and to thwart any Soviet ambitions in both regions.

European fears throughout much of the 1950s and 1960s focused on cheap Japanese goods flooding European markets and destroying local manufacturers. This attitude often resulted in arcane restrictive policies undertaken by one or more of the major European countries and directed specifically at Japanese imports. There were also broader policy actions, such as the European resistance to admitting Japan to the General Agreement on Tariffs and Trade (GATT) on a most favored nation basis in 1955, or later opposition to Tokyo's membership in the Organization for Economic Cooperation and Development (OECD) in 1964. The latter was finally achieved through strong American backing. In fact, Japanese protectionism was essentially sanctioned by the US. This is ironic in view of the trade conflicts of the 1970s, 1980s, and 1990s. However, Washington believed that a strong Japan was the best insurance against regional instability and communism.

Despite European fears, Euro-Japanese trade was fairly balanced during much of the postwar period. The Japanese export drive was primarily focused on the more open American market. The signing of the Treaty of Rome in 1957 was treated with interest by the Japanese press, but there was also a sense of distance. With Japan in the midst of its economic miracle, much greater attention was focused upon the US and Asia.

Japanese sensitivities toward Europe were mainly aroused by the often condescending comments of European leaders. In the early 1960s, Charles de Gaulle referred to Japan's prime minister, Hayato Ikeda, as a "transistor salesman." In 1979, a classified European Commission report leaked to the press referred to Japanese homes as being "rabbit hutches" – a phrase that many Japanese did not necessarily dispute, but did resent hearing about publicly. After Edith Cresson became the French premier, a report circulated that she had called the Japanese "ants." In any case, she was very critical of Tokyo's economic policy. Many in the West had come to see the Japanese as economic animals.

For the Japanese, Europe in the 1960s and 1970s looked increasingly like a large cultural museum. Yes, the Old Continent had been great once. However, due to their labor strife, the Europeans had lost their edge and had slipped into the dustbin of history. The UK's economic problems were called the *Igurisubyo* or English disease. Increasingly, Japanese responses to the market access problems faced by European business executives in Japan mirrored what they said to Washington: you must try harder.

While trade problems arose between Europe and Tokyo, one of the most stunning experiences that Japan had with Europe was the violent demonstrations that greeted Emperor Hirohito during his trip to Europe in the 1970s. Many Japanese were surprised to see the vehemence of the bitterness – particularly in the Netherlands, where many people retained dark memories of their colonies' treatment at the hands of the Imperial Army during World War II.

On the eve of the 1980s, with economic troubles looming on the horizon for Japan – with both the US and Europe – all parties had to recognize that Japan had emerged as the second largest economic power in the world. Neither Europe nor the US could afford to be dismissive of that reality.

Japan and Europe in the 1980s

During the 1980s, Japan coordinated its security and trade concerns with Europe. Japan's Ministry of Foreign Affairs maintained a Cold War footing based on the Yoshida Doctrine of close ties to the US, and acted with restraint in security relations under the American-led alliance. Japan's security planners were concerned about Soviet transfers of advanced weaponry from their European borders. While American and European agreements for arms control reduced tensions on one side of the globe, Soviet forces were being upgraded in the East. Japan also had never signed a peace treaty with the Soviets. The disputed Northern Territories in the Kurile Island chain meant that Soviet fighter planes were based just north of Japan. Despite such worries and concerns about coordination with NATO, Japan trusted the American security umbrella and focused attention mainly on its trade with Europe.

In the 1980s, Japanese leaders reacted to ongoing preparations for economic integration in Europe. Integration that began in the coal and steel industries had moved to a broader economic community that attracted Japanese firms. This integration process could now provide Japan with the opportunity to trade with a single market, but only if means were found to assure access. "Fortress Europe" evoked deep fears in Japan because it hit at the truths about stereotypes of Japan as a "small island trading nation," whose trade surpluses might no longer be acceptable to Europe. These fears involved complex politics.

Japanese conservative politicians responded positively to Margaret Thatcher in the UK. Neo-conservatism was apparent in the US under Ronald Reagan, and resonated with a similar neo-liberalism under Thatcher. Such political sentiments meant that political ties were improved through a common conservative reform movement under the then prime minister, Yasuhiro Nakasone.

At home, Nakasone encouraged Japanese liberalization through administrative reforms. Nakasone also urged Japan to take a leadership role in Asia. His efforts at G7 economic summits were especially successful in improving relations with Europe. As a concrete result, Japanese business interests made a pronounced increase in investment particularly in the UK, with automobile, electronics, and other manufacturing ventures.

American observers speculate about Japan's contribution in global affairs during this era. Senator Daniel Moynihan said wryly, "We will look back at the 1980s as a time when we [Americans] borrowed a trillion dollars from the Japanese – and threw a party." Japanese purchased as much as 40 percent of US Treasury bonds at auction. This situation led to criticisms of America's overdependence and of the engineered transfer of Japanese consumers' savings. Taggart Murphy has noted that this "real price of Japanese money" hurts both Japanese savers and future generations. But the emergence of Japanese economic power was certain.

From the end of the Cold War to the Gulf War

By the end of the 1980s, events had overtaken the planners. October 1987 saw a drop in New York stock prices, and two years later Japan experienced a rapid decline in real estate values. Yet at the same time, the speculative bubble of the late 1980s had also led to plans for a 600-ship American navy and the aborted efforts of Mikhail Gorbachev to reform the Soviet Union. When the Soviet Union's collapse began, a set of revisionists in the US looked back at the spendthrift period as disruptive in the world and at home. Revisionist critics such as Clyde Prestowitz noted: "The Cold War is over and Japan won."

The end of the Cold War certainly marked a turning point for Japan. The reunification of Germany and the euphoria of the opening of eastern Europe meant that Japan the trading nation faced new challenges in the global economy, including a new Europe. In addition, the Japanese had developed a certain arrogance about their success. For a time, Europe had been seen as a museum whose economies did not produce high technology and remained slow to change. The short-lived euphoria was replaced by confusion about the collapse of the Soviet Union and the war in Bosnia; Japanese leaders were not eager to be involved in either, but were displeased when not included in security discussions.

By the 1990s, a new level of cooperation led to annual Japan–Europe summits. From 1991, the Japan/EC Joint Declaration (with what was then the EC) reconfirmed a common commitment to freedom and democracy, free trade, human rights, and other common values, and charted a course for joint contributions to the solution of global issues and strengthening of the Japan–Europe partnership. Since the joint declaration, Japan and the EU have held annual summits, as well as engaging in dialogue and cooperation in a wide variety of fields on a broad range of levels. In the field of economic relations in particular, while the trade imbalance hit record high levels in 1992 and became a major subject of concern, great efforts on both sides have helped to steadily reduce the gap.

The aftermath of the 1990 Gulf War was a setback for Japan. In the global alliance arranged by President George Bush, Japan was perceived as slow and reluctant to respond. A belated dispatch of minesweepers and a huge monetary contribution of $16 billion met Japanese commitments, but did not satisfy the alliance members' expectations and volatile public opinion. Japanese leaders felt the criticisms of Europe and elsewhere for their reluctance to revise or reinterpret the "Peace Constitution" of Japan. Article 9 of the constitution limits the offensive powers of Japan and keeps Japan from commitments of troops overseas. Although wartime foes of the Japanese military are reassured by this limitation, the efforts of Japan to be a normal country with global roles were hampered by debates about constitutional limits.

Slow efforts continue to rebuild post-Cold War institutions. Japan has committed itself to joint defense of a 2,000-mile perimeter surrounding its islands. This perimeter led to Chinese protests about an aggressive, rearmed Japan. The key concern is the Taiwan Straits, which fall within the perimeter. However, the security concerns of Japan in its region do not directly affect Europe, except perhaps for relations with Russia. In November 1997, Prime Minister Hashimoto met with President Boris Yeltsin. The two leaders committed their countries to a deadline for a peace treaty by the year 2000. Security appears to be improving and opening the way for further economic developments.

Economic relations revisited

The Maastricht Treaty again sparked Japanese fears of a "fortress Europe." The treaty took effect in 1993, thus strengthening the political unity of the EU itself.

In addition to problems of a specifically Japan–EU nature, there is active cooperation on more global issues, including the environment and development assistance. Ties between Japan and Europe have been relatively weak compared to those between Japan and the US, or the US and Europe. However, the policy initiatives arising from the joint declaration are helping to improve the balance of relations among these three partners.

Recent summits illustrate the efforts to rebalance. Mr Ryutaro Hashimoto, prime minister of Japan, Mr Wim Kok, president of the European Council, and Mr Jacques Santer, former president of the European Commission, met in The Hague on June 25, 1997, for the sixth summit between Japan and the European Union. They underlined the important role of EU–Japan relations in world affairs and expressed the view that these should be further developed and deepened. In this context, they noted the broad convergence of macroeconomic policies and emphasized that current internal developments and structural economic reforms in the EU and Japan will have an impact on international politics.

Diplomatic developments will also contribute to shaping other forces of global integration. The three summit participants reviewed key developments in Europe, including the establishment of Economic and Monetary Union and the international implications of the introduction of the euro as a currency. The European side outlined the new institutional reforms of the EU following completion of the Intergovernmental Conference and the prospects for enlargement of the EU. Both sides acknowledged that these developments would enlarge the role and weight of the EU in world affairs and would have important implications for the Union's external political and economic relations, including with Japan. In the meantime, the Japanese side stressed the importance of its structural reforms at home, including fiscal and economic structural reforms and financial system reform. Japanese planners suggested that the reforms were designed to ensure strong domestic demand-led growth in the medium to long term and, thus, to create a socioeconomic system in line with the trend of today's increasingly integrated world economy. In November 1997, with the collapse of a regional bank and one of the four leading securities firms, Japan also showed resolve in avoiding direct government manipulation of financial markets. The continuing reform process entails costs.

The overall state of trade relations is positive and improving. The persistently high Japanese current account surplus with the rest of the world has fallen significantly over the last few years. Nevertheless, the EU continues to see this surplus as a reflection of market access difficulties in Japan for foreign firms. In contrast, Japanese exporters may face fewer structural barriers in the EU. EU policies aim to deal with the problem of the current account surplus in Japan through increased trade generated by the removal of market access obstacles, thus promoting the dynamism of European exporters and investors, industrial cooperation, and a better understanding of the Japanese system. Though Japanese reform continues slowly, the likelihood of rapid change in Japan will depend on the finance industry's restructuring. The latter will fall short of the hoped for "big bang" that led to London's success earlier.

Key Japanese policies toward Europe address the trade imbalances. Following peaks in the Japanese current account surplus of 4.2 percent of GDP in 1986 and 3.2 percent in 1992, the surplus fell to 2.2 percent of GDP in 1995. Furthermore, the EU surplus on trade in services (including investment income) is steadily rising, and the EU deficit on trade in goods is steadily decreasing. Overall, the trend means that the EU has been going through a period of dynamic growth in exports to Japan, with a positive impact on overall growth and employment rates in Europe. However, improvements are not evident in all fields of economic activity: for example, the latest figures show no change in the very large imbalance between EU investment in Japan and Japanese investment in Europe. For 1998, these figures suggest that market access restrictions are still significant. Moreover, the pressures in Japan to export are rising due to sluggish growth of domestic demand.

Institution building and regional politics

Japan is also active in regional leadership and institution building as regards Europe. Bilateral talks for summit participants addressed the specific political and security situations in their regions. The participants considered that maintenance of a stable and secure political environment was essential for their continuing economic development. They shared the view that institutions for multilateral dialogue can play a significant role in reducing tensions and misunderstandings, and they confirmed their intent to work together to this end as appropriate.

Asian-Europe summits (ASEM) should lead to wide-ranging, balanced, and deepened links between Asia and Europe. Starting in 1997, ASEM re-emphasized and stressed the significance of the long-standing EU–Japan partnership, and diplomats attached particular importance to the successful second ASEM summit in London in April 1998. Both sides also stressed the significance of the Post Ministerial Conference of the Association of South East Asian Nations (ASEAN). The common views expressed the hope that enlargement of ASEAN will contribute to the enhancement of peace, stability, and prosperity in the region and will promote respect for human rights and democratic principles in the new member states – a hope partially belied by the regional economic débâcle of 1998. Both Japan and Europe also expressed satisfaction with the increasingly important role played by the ASEAN Regional Forum. Japan emphasized that the active participation of the European Union in these various groups is a welcome expression of its keen interest and involvement in Asia.

A specific example of shared concern is Korea. Both Europe and Japan expressed their continued support for the Four Party meeting proposal aimed at achieving permanent peace on the Korean peninsula and called upon North Korea to accept the proposal without delay, as well as to engage seriously in South–North dialogue. The diplomats expressed satisfaction with the activities of the Korean Energy Development Organization (KEDO), which will facilitate compliance by North Korea with its non-proliferation obligations. They shared the view that continued support for KEDO would be valuable. Both sides welcomed the conclusion of negotiations for Euratom to participate in KEDO. Building upon the high degree of cooperation between the EU and Japan engendered in this process, both sides acknowledged the usefulness of an *ad hoc* exchange of views in the field of non-proliferation on the Korean peninsula.

Japan shares European views on the need to encourage China to take further steps to integrate into the world community. The countries share a strong interest in the future peace and stability of Hong Kong and its maintenance as an economic and financial center in the region. In addition, they expressed their common desire to contribute to its smooth transition to the status of a Special Administrative Region (SAR) of China. Both sides looked forward to dealing directly with the Hong Kong government in all areas of policy reserved for the SAR, and to the effective implementation of the 1984 UK–PRC Joint Declaration and the 1990 Basic Law. These imply ensuring Hong Kong's continued stability and prosperity as well as preserving its way of life, its high degree of autonomy – including an independent monetary and economic system – its fundamental freedoms, and the rule of law. Yet on human rights and trade disputes, Japan has not replaced the US as a leader.

Japan attempted diplomatic leadership at the Kyoto Conference on the environment. At what was known as the "COP III" or the Third Conference of the Parties to the UN Convention on Climate Change, Japan saw that the EU took an aggressive lead with its proposal. As the host country, Japan was sensitive to its responsibility. Prime Minister Hashimoto made a promise to seek successful conclusions. Japan needed to broker agreements between an aggressive European position championed by leaders such as Helmut Kohl in the midst of election campaigns and a more cautious American position protecting domestic interests.

Diplomatic and economic leaders have already built a comprehensive partnership, and both Japan and the EU appear to wish to deepen this relationship further. At the same time, the asymmetries of the Japanese economy make for tensions. Whether the reforms of Japan can keep pace with the integration of Europe remains to be seen. If the reaction is to build a "fortress Asia" in response, the promise of global economies and world peace is in danger. This reaction seems improbable following the 1998 plunge in several Asian economies. Nonetheless, the worries persist.

Bibliography

Borton, H. (1970) *Japan's Modern Century*, New York: Ronald Press.

Maul, H.W. (ed) (1993) *Japan Und Europa: Getrennte Welten?* Bonn: Forschungsinstitut der Deutsche Gesellschaft fuer Auswaertige Politik.

Mendl, W. (1984) *Western Europe and Japan Between the Super Powers*, New York: St. Martin's Press.

Daniels, G. and Drifte, R. (eds) (1986) *Europe & Japan: Changing Relations Since 1945*, Paul Norbury Publications, 1986.

Neumann, W.L. (1963) *America Encounters Japan: From Perry to MacArthur*, Baltimore: Johns Hopkins University Press.

Seitz, K. (1991) *Die Japanisch-Amerikanisch Herausforderung (The Japanese-American Challenge)*, Bonn: Aktuell.

Schoppa, L.J. (1997) *Bargaining with Japan*, New York: Columbia University Press.

Tamarin, A. (1970) *Japan and The United States: Early Encounters 1791–1860*, London: MacMillan Press.

Tsuchiya, R. (ed) (1993) *EC Sogo to Nihon*, Tokyo: Chuo Keizaisha.

Wilkinson, E. (1981) *Misunderstanding: Europe vs. Japan*, Tokyo: Chuokorosha.

Japan

Retail sales
Annual percentage change

Source: Datastream/ICV

Real growth and inflation
Annual percentage change

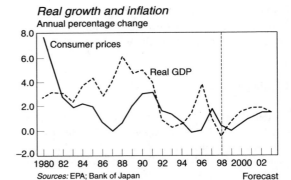

Sources: EPA; Bank of Japan   Forecast

Capital productivity
An international comparison
Per cent

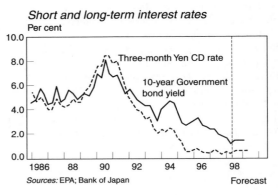

Sources: OECD; Economic Planning Agency

Short and long-term interest rates
Per cent

Sources: EPA; Bank of Japan   Forecast

Japan: composition of manufacturing
Yen '000 bn

	1995	1994
TOTAL MANUFACTURING	119.29	117.25
Food	13.53	13.67
Textiles	1.92	2.10
Pulp and paper	3.47	3.30
Chemicals	9.96	9.64
Oil and coal	5.32	5.47
Ceramics and cement	4.24	4.35
Primary metals	8.58	8.18
Metals	7.00	6.91
General machinery	14.11	13.31
Electrical machinery	18.73	18.06
Transportation equipment	12.07	11.65
Precision instruments	1.75	1.76
Others	18.59	18.84

Sources: OECD; Economic Planning Agency

Appendix

The Three Pillars of the Global Economy: The European Union, the United States, and Japan

Although the EU, the US, and Japan are clearly the pillars upon which the global economy is based, the three are not equal. As can be seen from the following graphs and charts, there are discrepancies not only in relative size of the economies, but also in geographical area, population, and so forth. It is also clear that economically, the EU and the US are at near parity. Finally, the development of trading areas is a strong trend as we enter the twenty-first century. However, the trading areas are of very unequal size and strength.

Statistics:

How do the European Union, the United States, and Japan match up?

	EU15	USA	Japan
Area[1] (thousands, km^2)	3236	9373	378
Population[2] (millions, 1996)	373	265	126
Density[1] (per km^2)	115	29	329
Labor Force[2] (total, millions, 1996)	168	134	67
Unemployment[3] (based on ILO guidelines)			
1995	11.1%	5.5%	3.1%
1996	11.2%	5.4%	3.5%
1997 2Q	11.2%	5.0%	3.2%
GDP[3] (1996, US $trillions at current prices and exchange rates)	8.58	7.26	5
Inflation Rate[3] (1996)	2.4%	2.0%	0.0%
Imports[4] (1996 all products, US $billions)	725 (extra-EU)	817	349.7
Exports[4] (1996 all products, US $billions)	800 (extra-EU)	624.8	411.4
Share of World Imports[4] (1996)	17.8%	19.9%	8.5%
Share of World Exports[4] (1996)	20.5%	16.2%	10.7%

Sources:
1. Eurostat, 1996
2. OECD, Quarterly Labour Force Statistics, 1/97
3. OECD, Main Economic Indicators, August 1997
4. Eurostat – External and Intra-European Union Trade, 8–9/97
Conversion rate 1996: 1 ECU = $1.26975

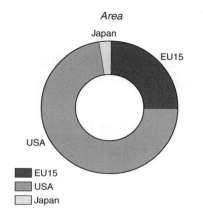

Area

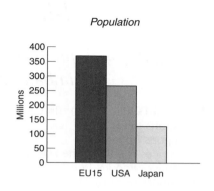

Population

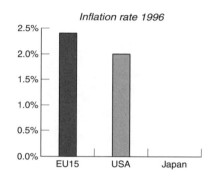

Inflation rate 1996

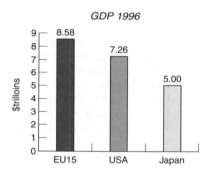

GDP 1996

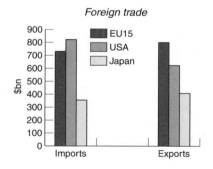

Foreign trade

Share of world trade

Bilateral trade:

Relative equality between the EU and the US but imbalance with Japan

1. US–EU15 TRADE (1996)[1] (In US $billions)

US Exports to the EU	127.5 (up 4.49% from 1995)
US Imports from the EU	142.7 (up 14.9% from 1995)
US Services Exports to the EU[2]	72.3
US Services Imports from the EU[2]	54.6

Top Imports/Exports (1996)[3]

Top 5 US Goods Exports to EU (in US $billions)

Office machines/computers	14.9
Aircraft/parts	12.7
Electronic components	7.0
Motor vehicles/parts	5.5
Medical instruments and supplies	7.1

Top 5 US Goods Imports from EU (in US $billions)

Motor vehicles/parts	16.0
Aircraft/parts	7.5
Office machines/computers	5.2
General industrial machines	5.1
Blast furnace, steel, mill products	4.6

2. US–JAPAN TRADE (1996)[1] (in US $billions)

US Exports to Japan	67.5
US Imports from Japan	115.2
US Services Exports to Japan	35.9
US Services Imports from Japan	14.4

Top Imports/Exports (1996)[3]

Top 5 US Goods Exports to Japan (in US $billions)

Office machines/computers	5.6
Electronic components	5.5
Cash grains/other crops	4.6
Motor vehicles/parts	3.8
Aircraft/parts	3.4

Top 5 US Goods Imports from Japan (in US $billions)

Motor vehicles/parts	31.3
Office machines/computers	14.5
Electronic components	7.8
Photographic equipment/supplies	4.7
Metalworking machinery/equipment	3.4

3. EU15–JAPAN TRADE (1996)[4] (in US $billions)

EU Exports to Japan	35.6
EU Imports from Japan	52.5

---

1. US Department of Commerce, ITA 1997 (Census basis)
2. Services figures calculated on a Balance of Payments basis
3. US Department of Commerce, ITA 1997 (Census basis): 3-digit SIC product group
4. Eurostat – External and Intra-European Union Trade, 8–9/97. Conversion rate 1996: 1 ECU = $1.27

Foreign direct investment/mergers & acquisitions:

Who invests in the US and where does the US invest?

1996 Foreign Direct Investment in the US[1] (historical cost basis):
   Total Amount in the US: ($US billions)   630.1
         EU: 372.2   59% of US total
         Japan: 118.1   19% of US total
   Top Investors in the US by country: ($US billions)
         UK   142.6   23% of US total
         Japan   118.1   19% of US total
         The Netherlands   73.8   12% of US total
         Canada   53.8   9% of US total
   Effects of European (EU + EFTA) Investment in the US:
        Nearly 6 million US jobs are supported by European (EU + EFTA)
        investment[3] (12.5% of all US jobs)

US Foreign Direct Investment Abroad[1] (historical cost basis) (1996):
   US 1996 Total Amount: 796.5
         EU   348.4   44% of US total
         Japan   39.6   5% of US total
   Top Destinations for US Direct Investment: ($US billions)
         UK   142.5   18% of US total
         Canada   91.6   12% of US total
         Germany   44.3   6% of US total

Mergers and Acquisitions 1996[2]
   Foreign Acquisitions of US Companies in the US
   Number of deals: 628; value: $69.9 billion

        Most active countries: (values in $US billions)
        Canada: 153 deals   6.10
        UK: 145 deals   16.20
        France: 39 deals   8.80
        Germany: 36 deals   11.60
   Foreign Acquisitions in Europe
   1996 Crossborder Deals in Europe at large: 1,836 deals, value $114 billion
   US acquisitions in Europe: 501 deals, value $35.7 billion (largest acquirer)

Sources:
1. Survey of Current Business, July & September, 1997
2. Mergers & Acquisitions Magazine, March/April, 1997
3. European-American Business Council, Washington DC, 9/97

Regional trading areas:

There are more world trading areas but of differing size, strength, and structure. What are the implications for global trade and politics?

	EU15 (Customs Union)	EEA (FTA)	NAFTA (FTA)	MERCOSUR (Customs Union)	APEC	ASEAN
Area (thousands km^2)	3236	3661	21,300	11,800	44,000	3386
Population (millions)	372	376.7	384.5	204	2,166	481
GDP (US$ trillions)	8.6	8.75	8.25	1.2	15.6 (1995)	0.63
EU15 Exports to Area (Goods; US$ billions)			165.1	23.5	221.9	51.7
EU15 Imports from Area (Goods; US$ billions)			161.2	18.9	237.5	48.9
US Exports to Area (Goods; US$ billions)	127.5	129.3	189.3	18.6	388.6	43.49
US Imports from Area (Goods; US$ billions)	142.7	146.9	229.5	12	532.2	66.24
Total Exports (Goods; US$ billions)	800 (extra)	791.2 (extra)	1041.257	84.6	2332.9	349.5
Total Imports (Goods; US$ billions)	725 (extra)	740.4 (extra)	1001.73	78.6	2455.7	336.0

Sources:

EU: Area, Population (Eurostat – Facts through Figures 1996); GDP (OECD, Main Economic Indicators, August 1997); US exports/imports (US Department of Commerce, ITA); Total exports/imports (Eurostat – External and Intra-European Union Trade 8–9/97)

EEA: Area (Eurostat, 1995); Population (Eurostat, 1996); GDP (OECD, Main Economic Indicators, August 1997 (EU + Iceland + Liechtenstein + Norway]); US exports/imports (US National Trade Database 1997); Total exports/imports (Not incl. Liechtenstein) (IMF Direction of Trade 1997)

NAFTA: Area (US Department of Commerce, ITA); Population (OECD); GDP (OECD – Main Economic Indicators, August 1997) [t]; EU exports/imports; (Eurostat – External and Intra-European Union Trade 8–9/97) US exports/imports, Total exports/imports (IMF, Direction of Trade 1997)

MERCOSUR: Area, Population, GDP (US Department of Commerce, ITA), EU exports/imports (Eurostat – External and Intra-European Union Trade 8–9/97); US exports/imports, Total exports/imports (IMF Direction of Trade 1997)

APEC: Area, population, GDP (The World Bank Atlas, 1997) [t]
EU exports/imports (Comext2, September 1997)
US exports/imports (US Department of Commerce, ITA); Total exports/imports (IMF, Direction of Trade, 1997) [t]

ASEAN: Area, population, GDP (ASEAN Secretariat: Selected Indicators 1997); EU exports/imports (Eurostat – External and Intra-European Union Trade 8–9/97); US exports/imports (US Department of Commerce, ITA); Total exports/imports (IMF Direction of Trade 1997) [t]

t = total, figures for member countries added together

Index